SUPER
SEARCHERS
MAKE IT
ON THEIR OWN

SUPER
SEARCHERS
MAKE IT
ON THEIR OWN

Top Independent Information Professionals Share Their Secrets for Starting and Running a Research Business

Suzanne Sabroski
Edited by Reva Basch

CyberAge Books

Information Today, Inc.
Medford, New Jersey

Second Printing, 2004

*Super Searchers Make It On Their Own: Top Independent
Information Professionals Share Their Secrets for Starting
and Running a Research Business*

Copyright © 2002 by Suzanne Sabroski

Super Searchers, Volume X
A series edited by Reva Basch

Library of Congress Cataloging-in-Publication Data

Sabroski, Suzanne, 1963–
   Super searchers make it on their own : top independent information
professionals share their secrets for starting and running a research busi-
ness / Suzanne Sabroski ; edited by Reva Basch.
      p. cm. -- (Super searchers ; v. 10)
Includes bibliographical references and index.
   ISBN 0-910965-59-5
 1. Information services industry. 2. Information services. 3.
Information scientists. I. Basch, Reva. II. Title. III. Series.
   HD9999.I492 S23 2002
   025.5'2'068--dc21

                                                                2002001495

Printed and bound in the United States of America

Publisher: Thomas H. Hogan, Sr.
Editor-in-Chief: John B. Bryans
Managing Editor: Deborah R. Poulson
Copy Editor: Dorothy Pike
Production Manager: M. Heide Dengler
Cover Designer: Jacqueline Walter
Book Designer: Kara Mia Jalkowski
Indexer: Enid Zafran

Dedication

For Alan
My husband, my best friend, and a true entrepreneur

About The Super Searchers Web Page

At the Information Today Web site, you will find *The Super Searchers Web Page*, featuring links to sites mentioned in this book. We will periodically update the page, removing dead links and adding additional sites that may be useful to readers.

The Super Searchers Web Page is being made available as a bonus to readers of *Super Searchers Make It On Their Own* and other books in the Super Searchers series. To access the page, an Internet connection and Web browser are required. Go to:

www.infotoday.com/supersearchers

Table of Contents

Foreword

With this book, the Super Searcher series clicks over into double digits. *Super Searchers Make It On Their Own* is the tenth in this growing collection of titles, yet only the third to which I've contributed an editor's preface or a foreword. I asked Suzanne for permission to do this because, of all the Super Searcher titles I've edited so far—on business research, on legal, medical and healthcare, journalism, primary research, and so on—this particular book is one in which I have considerable background as well as a strong personal interest.

I worked as an independent information professional, a freelance online searcher (I personally am averse to the term "information broker," which Suzanne will tell you more about), from 1986 on, going out "on my own" full-time in 1988, until writing, editing, and other interests eclipsed the research aspects of my business a couple of years ago. I know from experience what it takes to be a Super Searcher. I was lucky enough to have worked, first as a research associate and later as Director of Research, for Sue Rugge's Information on Demand, a pioneering independent research business based in Berkeley, California. Several of Suzanne's interviewees pay tribute to Sue as a formative influence, whether they knew her well or not. Sue was my friend as well as my professional mentor; I'll always be grateful for her presence in my life, and I miss her to this day.

I think of my time at IOD as the golden age of the independent research profession. We described ourselves as a general research firm, tackling everything from canine hip dysplasia to heads-up avionics displays to the market for designer sunglasses. Many of my colleagues, including some whom Suzanne interviews in this book, maintain that the era of what I used to describe as "We do everything but chemical substructure searching" is long past, that you need a niche, a specialty that enables you to build on past experience and contacts, in order to succeed today. That may be true. But the knowledge that we might be asked to research just about anything, that none of us in the research department could predict, when we picked up the phone (requests via email were rare in those days), what someone would ask us to find, was scary, exhilarating, and ultimately empowering. We had the expertise, and we had access—thanks to our close proximity to UC Berkeley—to the necessary resources to research almost every topic. We didn't know the answers, but we knew where to look them up, what databases to search, how to find the experts we had to contact.

Super Searchers exist in every research-intensive field. But Super Searchers who also possess the entrepreneurial spirit—who are willing to take the risks associated with starting and marketing a small business instead of just hiding in a back room doing research—are an elite within an elite. They are well worth listening to, because they not only know how to search well, but how to search efficiently and cost-effectively. They also know—even while pulling all-nighters out in the office—the importance of balancing the demands of work and home. They have learned, the hard way, what it takes to succeed in business and in life.

Two books I wrote after leaving IOD, *Secrets of the Super Searchers* (1993) and *Secrets of the Super Net Searchers* (1996), established the pattern for the current series—informal conversations with expert researchers in which they willingly share not only their favorite search tools and techniques, but also their thought processes. In the words of my colleague Barbara Quint, one of the Super Searchers I interviewed in my 1993 book, these conversations take you "inside a searcher's mind." Search engines come and go, but the ability to analyze a research project, to break it down into its component parts, to plan an approach, select the appropriate resources, refine results, regroup, and try again—deftly, gracefully, knowledgeably, doggedly—is a timeless set of skills, and one that Suzanne captures and conveys wonderfully in this book.

Reva Basch

Past President, Association of Independent Information Professionals

Executive Editor, Super Searchers series

Acknowledgments

Although writing a book can be a lonely task at times, a project of this size only comes together with the collaboration of many people. Without a supportive environment and proven publishing system, the stories of the Super Searchers could not be told. For that, I am appreciative of Information Today, Inc.

Thank you to Mary Ellen Bates, Tom Culbert, Jodi Gregory, Marty Goffman, Lynn Peterson, Mark Goldstein, Chris Sherman, Crystal Sharp, Chris Dobson, Peggy Carr, and Amelia Kassel for sharing their experience, expertise, and insight into what it takes to Make It On Their Own. Each of these individuals has mastered a unique combination of business and research skills, and it was my pleasure to get to know each of them a little better through the interviewing and editing process.

A special thank you to Reva Basch for her wisdom, support, open-door policy, and calming presence in the background of this adventure. Early on, when this book existed only as an idea, Super Searcher author T. R. Halvorson shared with me that I could not possibly be in a better position as an author than to have the chance to work with Reva as my editor. Somehow I knew everything would be okay then.

Thank you to Dorothy Pike, fellow Minnesotan and email friend, for her accuracy, care, and commitment to transcribing the first half of my interviews. As well, thank you to Patty Shannon of The Workstation for jumping in when we needed her and quickly and skillfully completing the process. Thank you to Deborah Poulson for reeling in all the details of production. And an extra special thank you to John Bryans for his encouragement and enthusiasm, and for taking a chance on a first-time author.

One name you'll hear often in the pages of this book is Sue Rugge. I am grateful to her, in memory, for making the independent information profession an attainable goal through her practical and personal style. She was a tremendous influence in my life simply by being herself, and in a measure she helped raise my kids. Many times, as I was feeding a baby or sitting in a park or attending a music lesson, her books were nearby, inspiring me. Sentiments of appreciation as well to the memory of Myra T. Grenier, another early pioneer of this industry, in whose name I received an award that allowed me to attend my first Association of Independent Information Professionals (AIIP) conference.

Thank you to the movers and shakers of AIIP who have become my colleagues, my friends, and my co-workers. This is an amazing group of people who, by their collective wit and wisdom, I am convinced, could not only answer any question in the world but also have fun and make money doing it. Beyond that, AIIP is a community of real people who care about and support each other in a day and age when this is hard to find. Going to AIIP conferences each year is like going to summer camp. Whatever obstacles exist to functioning as an independent, AIIP has provided the seeds to a solution, and whatever is accomplished is accomplished through volunteer hours.

Closer to home, I have been richly blessed with family and friends. Thank you to my parents, Bob and Lois, and my brother Bob Jr., for providing a loving and supportive home that was my foundation. To Karin, for true friendship over the many years and miles. To my children, each a precious gift of God, for the joy and meaning you've brought to my life. And to my husband, Alan, the man of my dreams and the love of my life, for absolutely everything.

Finally, yet foremost, my personal acknowledgment to the simplicity and the truth of Job 19:25 and John 3:16, and the inspiration of Philippians 4:13.

Introduction

In the spring of 1991 I had stayed late at the library in the College of St. Scholastica with a group of other grad students. We were supposed to be studying for a final in online research, but the conversation drifted to real life and the practicality of what we were learning. "Well, I heard you can make money finding stuff for people in these databases," one person at the table remarked. "The yellow-pages advertising deadline is next week, so I'm going to throw an ad together and see what happens."

I never saw the ad in the local phone book, and to my knowledge not much happened with this individual by way of a business, but the concept was fascinating. Since I absolutely *loved* online research and the Boolean logic on which it was based, and the thought of working professionally from home was so appealing, my investigation began. Was it true? Was this legitimate? Would people actually pay me to do research for them, and was there in fact an entire industry developing around this concept?

As it goes with most aspiring independent information professionals, this investigation led to two things—the late Sue Rugge's book, *The Information Broker's Handbook* [230, see Appendix], and the Association of Independent Information Professionals (AIIP) [172]. Both were encouraging sources of practical advice and personal stories that affirmed, yes, this business was legitimate and in fact quite exciting.

Over the years I have spent researching and eventually entering this field, what I have enjoyed most is getting to know some very interesting people and learning how they combine their business and research skills to succeed as entrepreneurs. How they know where to look for answers. How

1

they are able to function alone and yet be highly effective with clients. How they run a business and make money. How their work increases their clients' bottom line. How they balance everything in their lives. How they are able to see connections between the marketplace and their clients' information needs. And how they explain the value of their services.

These are the stories of eleven Super Searchers who did Make It On Their Own, and who exemplify two major trends in today's society—the explosion of the Information Age and the rise of the independent professional.

It's widely noted that some time after World War II, knowledge began to drive the world's major economies, and today we find ourselves overwhelmed. We see more information in a month than people in the nineteenth century saw in their entire lives. Think about it—books, videos, TV, radio, CD-ROMs, DVDs, newspapers, magazines, databases, microfilm, billboards, people's heads, and now the Internet. So much of our time is spent filtering and searching for relevance. It's a far cry from simply reading the bulletin board at the town hall once a month or hearing the latest from the neighbors. We need professional help to keep track of it all.

Combine the concept of information overload with the acceptance of outsourcing work to independent professionals in today's marketplace, and you begin to see part of a much bigger picture. The home-based worker, the micropreneur, the consultant, or, as author Daniel Pink has identified them in his recent book, members of the "Free Agent Nation" [226]—whatever term is used, conservative estimates come in at around 30 million independent workers in the United States alone. Some call it nothing less than an economic revolution, as people reclaim their freedom and take control of their professional and personal lives. It's exciting to know we are not alone.

In the spirit of the Super Searcher series, you will learn about research tips, techniques, and sources. We'll cover the same ground that some of the information industry's leading experts cover each day: How Mary Ellen Bates knows when to go to the commercial online services and when to go to a Dear Abby column. Why Marty Goffman does an exhaustive patent search and how this goes far beyond a quick check of the Internet. How Tom Culbert uses a combination of dusty archive collections and talking to the right people. Why Amelia Kassel sticks to online and tailors her specialization around that. How Chris Sherman identifies and tracks the newest search engine technologies and analyzes their usefulness for searchers. How Peggy Carr collaborates with other independents and why she still believes in brick-and-mortar libraries. What kind of information is public record, how it is useful to Lynn Peterson's clients, and why this brand of research is not for the novice. How Jodi Gregory serves her niche markets and has the client satisfaction measurements to prove her effectiveness. How Chris Dobson helps companies develop their own information tools. How Crystal Sharp operates in Canada, doing both secondary and primary research. How Mark Goldstein absorbs between 200 print and 300 electronic information subscriptions each month and shares this knowledge with his clients.

But we're going to go two steps beyond following these Super Searchers through databases, libraries, print media, and the Internet. The first step is into the marketplace where the validity and value of information research is put to the test. Searchers know good information when they see it, but there is a whole new level of skill involved in finding clients, cultivating relationships, and delivering a product that satisfies a need. There is the matter of a business to run, with bills to pay and daily tasks to be done. There is knowing how much work to take on, and when to outsource. There are issues such as copyright and licensing and how they affect the information retrieval and delivery process. And perhaps most importantly, there is the issue of marketing—or, as small business experts Paul and Sarah Edwards [96] put it, getting business to come to you.

The second step we'll take beyond searching is into the personal realm. Who are these people? What combination of education and experience do they have? How do they balance work and play? Do they work 24/7 or do they have a life? What do they particularly like about what they do? Is it the thrill of the hunt? What opportunities do they see for the future? While I promise we won't talk about kids and dogs (okay—we'll give equal time to cats) too much, this is an important piece to include, because not only was getting to know these people so much fun, but it takes a well-rounded individual to keep everything together and run an independent research business at the same time. Running a business and being a searcher can swallow up a person's life unless deliberate choices to maintain balance are made. And one more point: As you read each person's story, it is interesting to see the common threads emerge: how they discovered information research, the emergence of personal computer technology, the downsizing of corporations, the desire for a flexible lifestyle, the appearance of the

Internet, and the realization that they were not alone in finding and pursuing the opportunity of independence.

You've heard the phrases, "Information is power," "To stay ahead of the competition you've got to stay informed," and "Smart decisions are based on the right information at the right time." The independent information profession is all about identifying that critical information and getting it into the hands of clients. You could think of the work product of an independent information professional as a tailored evening newscast—as if a broadcast journalist had spent his or her day searching the world on your behalf, so you have the precise information you need at the end of yours. It's about a basic formula for business success—define a need, meet that need, and deliver results. And never stop learning, evaluating, and improving.

One of the challenges in creating this book was ending it. If not for a deadline and the reality of other time constraints, it would have been easy to keep going and interview many more information business owners. The people I interviewed reflect a mix of generalists and niche researchers, including many who have adapted to change and found new opportunities in those changes. Ten years ago there was no need for search engine analysts, but today searchers depend on the information they provide. Ten years ago independent information professionals would be called upon to locate basic company information, but today this kind of information is just a few keystrokes away from everyone's desktop.

Although many people do more of their own research nowadays, we battle the perception that everything is on the Internet and it's free for the taking, like picking cherries off a tree in July—as if quality, timeliness, validity, and relevance have all been preapproved by "computers." So, educating clients about information itself has emerged as a valuable service.

You'll also meet people in different stages of business development. Some have reached a level where they are established in the industry, with a stable of repeat clients. Others are looking ahead, still developing their products, services, and techniques. Describing who we are and what we do is a moving target, and it's worth taking a look at different levels of development and different stages in the entrepreneurial thought process, as well as different types of research businesses.

Finally, it needs to be said that independent-minded people tend to speak their minds; that's an integral part of their personalities. They are not afraid to disagree and often have strong opinions. You'll hear some of those opinions in the pages that follow. You'll find common ground as well as individual expression.

One issue on which the interviewees differ is what we should call ourselves as a profession. The debate arises repeatedly. While some like the term "information broker" and often link it to the high ethical standards held by industry pioneer Sue Rugge, others feel the media has compromised the term in the public's mind. Quite unfortunately, "information broker" has become the term of choice in sensationalized stories featuring hackers, identity thieves, and dumpster divers. Its misuse has created a dilemma for the small information business owner, who lacks the clout to stand up and say, "Hey, you just really insulted me!" to the Federal Trade Commission or major media outlets.

"Shady information broker" stories are a great source of frustration for those of us in the field, because even cursory research on the part of federal investigators and journalists would reveal AIIP as the leading professional organization, along with the Web sites of top practitioners in the industry. One thing that has characterized AIIP from the beginning has been the establishment and promotion of a code of ethical business practice, and this has encouraged high standards among members of the profession. You don't survive in this industry if you break the rules, and word does get around. Those rules include not misrepresenting yourself to obtain information and not obtaining any information through illegal means. Perhaps the profession itself has fallen victim to a larger case of identity theft. The best way to take it back is by successfully serving one client at a time, because word gets around when something good is happening, too. For our purposes here, and in line with AIIP, we'll just go with the term independent information professional, or IIP.

That said, here are some observations from my experience of spending time with the pros. By no means is this an exhaustive list of industry trends, as much more could be said about searching, marketing, business management, and deliverables.

The Business

- Working from home has gained acceptance in the marketplace. Most professionals are now quite comfortable with the concept, and no longer feel they need to act like they have a "real" office. While routines and schedules still must be adhered to, it's no big deal if the dog barks in the background. That said, some IIPs do lease commercial office space, whether for increased visibility, room for growth and expansion, or just a clearer separation of work and personal life.

- A field once dominated by library science professionals has grown and evolved to include those with business, marketing, legal, scientific, and particular industry focuses. The researcher develops industry expertise, or the industry expert learns to do research.

- While business cards, brochures, newsletters, and advertising have their place, the most effective marketing technique for IIPs is networking. To build a business, it is necessary to get out of the office and shake hands with people.

- IIPs need to generate their own visibility and establish their own credibility. Writing for publications and speaking at conferences are effective tools, as is participation on email lists and volunteering for professional association duties.

- As in any business, there is a need to define a target market and go where clients and potential clients hang out—niche industry conferences, professional or trade association meetings, or local business functions.

- Most IIPs draw upon the professional services of accountants, attorneys, and Web designers unless they themselves have specific expertise in these areas. Sue Rugge's time-honored advice, "Do what you do best and hire out the rest," is a recurring theme.

- In long-term relationships, both the client and the IIP are well served. The IIP can stay in touch with the client's internal issues and information needs, yet offer a fresh perspective from the outside. The client develops an understanding of the IIP's capabilities and resources, which often leads to more work.

- Most IIPs consider a Web page a necessity. They use it to establish a presence and educate potential clients about their services. It is not usually intended as a way to obtain clients, although, as search engine technology and Internet user sophistication improves, some IIPs feel this is changing. Sample projects or particular skill sets described on their sites have, in fact, sometimes been picked up by Web surfers, resulting in large projects.

- While not working for one organization affords a certain freedom and independence, it increases personal accountability and potential liability. A careful eye toward contracts, claims, and confidentiality agreements is needed.

The Work

- While most projects are delivered to clients electronically these days, a hard copy can sometimes tell a better story and serve as an effective marketing tool. Nice-looking reports often get passed around and into the hands of potential clients.

- There is less demand now for traditional information delivery, or "rip and ship," as it was commonly known. Most projects involve at least a degree of analysis and value-added work. Clients can easily retrieve basic information from the Internet.

- One of the most common reasons to go online is to locate experts—authors, academics, industry analysts, and executives. Finding an on-target article is often just the beginning of the research process.

- The growth of the Internet and the resulting information glut has increased appreciation for the skills of an information professional. Clients will often call for help when they have spent hours trying to find something on their own and are frustrated with their inability to do so.

- Finding an industry niche and offering specialized services is almost essential these days. Specialization is necessary for clear communication in marketing. On a practical level, too, you can't be an expert in everything. Nor can you simply say, "I am a researcher."

- Whether it is referred to as the reference interview or "determining client needs," it is an integral part of the research process. Understanding how the information will be used also aids in project development.

- End-user adoption of information services has not erased the need for IIPs. What is emerging is more of a consulting role in the client's organization. While developments like natural language searching and ask-a-question services might appear threatening on a competitive level, a computer cannot step back and see the big picture. A computer cannot form a relationship.

The People

- To make it on your own, you have to be your own driving force. There is nobody telling you what to do. You have to want to succeed, and you have to be committed. Taking the risk makes you halfway successful already, because you have to believe in the concept of your own success. The fact that you're willing to shed your dependence on a single organization speaks for itself.

- You need a combination of skills and the ability to switch gears. You need to be able to work alone as well as interact effectively with clients, potential clients, and colleagues.

- Nothing is ever simple. If anything characterizes this group of people in terms of personality, it is an insatiable thirst for information. No stone is left unturned in the search for an answer, even when making personal decisions.

- Time management and organization are big issues, and people take different approaches. While some love gadgets and have every possible electronic device networked and wired together, others keep life simple, refusing to get even a cell phone.

- Networking, referrals, and cooperation tend to characterize these individuals, as opposed to a competitive spirit. To a large extent, individual success contributes to the growth and recognition of the profession.

In line with the format of the other books in the Super Searcher series, we did not include Web site URLs within the interviews. As you might imagine, this group of people had a lot to say about the sites and sources they rely on, so I have compiled a resource list as an appendix; I note such references in the text where appropriate. Although such a list becomes a moving target as well, it is still extremely valuable, running the gamut from niche sources to general business sites. This list will be periodically updated at the Information Today page, www.supersearchers.com. We did not include a glossary, since it no longer seems necessary to define terms such as modem, bookmark, or ISP. We speak the same language nowadays as our clients—and the general public.

Once again I am grateful to each of the individuals you will meet in the following pages. What they have to say will enlighten, educate, and inspire you. They will inspire you not by sharing stories of their glamorous jet-set lifestyles, but by providing a reality check on starting and running your own business. Hard work, intelligence, and a measure of calculated risk are what you will see, and a future with wide-open opportunities. I hope you enjoy reading this book as much as I enjoyed creating it, and that those considering a career as an independent information professional will be inspired to take the plunge.

Mary Ellen Bates

Business Research for Business Professionals

Mary Ellen Bates is the owner of Bates Information Services, providing business research to business professionals and consulting services to the online industry. An internationally known speaker and writer based in Washington, DC, she is the author of five books, including two Super Searchers titles, *Super Searchers Do Business* and *Super Searchers Cover the World.*

mbates@BatesInfo.com
www.BatesInfo.com

Let's begin with your background. Tell me how you came to be an independent information business owner.

I started out as a special librarian and worked for a number of years in law libraries, in both private law firms and for the federal court system, and then went on to manage the library at MCI. After a while, I realized my career path as a corporate or special librarian would require that I manage more people and get more into administration, which I really didn't want to do. I have an independent streak a mile wide in my makeup, and somewhere around the mid-1980s I heard of information brokering. I remember thinking that it sounded like an interesting thing to do. I thought about it for several years, started saving business cards and—more importantly—my money, and imagined what it would be like to be working from home and running my own business. And then I just did it. I quit my job and my first client was my last employer, MCI.

Thinking about your work as a special librarian, what experience did you gain that was important or valuable to your work as an independent?

Mainly it was my experience at MCI. At the time that I worked there, it was a small, entrepreneurial kind of wild-and-crazy place where you could make any mistake as long as you didn't make the same mistake twice. And you could try anything as long as it didn't cost anything, which was a great experience. It encouraged creativity and risk taking, and I learned a lot about how to market myself and the information service within the organization. People didn't know about the library when I started it, so a lot of my efforts involved marketing within the company. I learned how to manage a budget and did all kinds of research. A firm background in information from my M.L.S. at Berkeley helped too, because it gave me a foundation to think about how information is organized and managed.

You prompted my next question about your formal education. Which pieces of your undergraduate and graduate degrees were relevant to your business?

Well, not much in my B.A., which is in mathematical philosophy—although, as it turns out, that was Boolean logic back in the early days before many people thought that way. When I got my bachelor's degree, I swore I would never work with computers, but then I stumbled into my first library job and took to it like a fish to water. That's what prompted me to go back and get my M.L.S. I was managing a database within a library at a law firm, having had no idea what I was getting into when I started, but finding that I loved it.

Can you think of any courses in your library training that stand out?

I took one course in special librarianship, which was the only one they had twenty years ago. I took a lot of programming and computer classes; one of the benefits of being a graduate student at Berkeley was that you could bump the undergraduates to get into the popular computer classes. You didn't have to take all your courses within the library school, so I took a good amount of information technology and information management courses as well as the regular M.L.S. coursework.

That sounds like a good foundation to understand the computer side of our business.

I wouldn't necessarily encourage people to do that today. That was back when people were using punch cards for programming. At the time it was very useful, because at my first job I was building databases, and it was a very low-level kind of programming that I had to do. These days, I would certainly encourage people to take more business classes, because you have to talk the lingo. I just didn't see myself being a corporate librarian when I was going to library school.

How did you handle the logistics of getting started, such as setting up your office space and equipment?

I was lucky in that my house has a full basement that I used to rent out. It was empty at the time that I started my business, so I took it over, which was nice because I had a little kitchen and the whole nine yards. The living room became my office. The first thing I did was contract with a graphic artist to design a corporate logo. It took a long time to get a logo that the artist and I were happy with. I'm really glad I did that, because it enabled me to start my business looking established. I wince when I see new businesses that have funky-looking stationery and business cards—it looks like they've just started out and aren't willing to spend any money on their business. The logo design cost a lot of money, but I'm really glad I made the investment.

Then I went out and bought a computer, the highest-end printer I could find, a fax machine; I got all my different phone lines in order, did the paperwork for the local Washington DC business licensing agency, and set up accounts with the online services.

What about professional advice from an attorney or accountant?

I did some brief consulting with an attorney. I didn't talk to an accountant in the beginning, as I'm pretty comfortable with that kind of thing. My attorney helped me think through my corporate structure; the best choice for me was to set up as a sole proprietorship. Then I just bought QuickBooks [104, see Appendix] and set up my business accounts to make it easy to report my income and expenses to the IRS.

I did all this planning and preparation on weekends and evenings, before I actually launched my business, and I took a few vacation days from my job. That was important because then, when I started, I didn't have any excuse. I couldn't say, "Oh well, I can't really start marketing myself yet because I have to noodle around with my computer a little while." I had all this stuff done, so that on day one, I had to get out there and start hustling.

What are the advantages of having your office in your home?

Actually, my office is outside my home now. After about five years we did a major renovation of the house, and I moved my office to a carriage house above the garage, so it's separate from the house itself. This is even better because I cannot go out there to just check my email and get sucked into two hours of work after dinner. It's ideal for me because I don't have to deal with a commute, but it's separate enough from the house itself that I can manage the time that I'm spending there.

So there's a physical separation there as well as the psychological separation.

Exactly.

Thinking back to the early days of your business, your first client was your previous employer. What about the clients that you had to go out there and find?

I had been collecting business cards for several years before I started my business, and one of the first things I did once I started working on my own was to send out letters and brochures to everyone I knew announcing that I had started my business, and to please give me a call if I could be of assistance. Then about a month later, I sent out postcards saying hello from Bates Information Services, and here are some of the projects we've worked on recently. I'm still in the habit of sending post-cards out every few months because you just have to get your name in front of clients' faces all the time. Once I did that, some of the people who had known me before started calling, but it was a slow process. I gave a talk for the local Special Libraries Association (SLA) [201] chapter about how to select an information broker and things that potential clients should ask, and got a little bit of work that way. I also contacted an association of sales managers and had an article published in their journal.

Any hard lessons or anything you might have done differently, looking back?

It's really funny. I heard from other people and read in books such as *The Information Broker's Handbook* [230] that cold calling doesn't work, mass mailing doesn't work. And I said, "Well, maybe it doesn't for you, but maybe it will for me." And I tried it—and it doesn't work. Cold calling is so painful anyway, I quit because I couldn't stand it. Then I did small mass mailings, if that isn't an oxymoron, but got no responses at all and realized that was not something that was going to work. So I don't think it was a huge mistake or a wasted effort, but I've got an independent streak and sometimes I don't learn from advice. Since then, I have learned to take other people's advice a little more to heart. When I keep hearing over and over again that something doesn't work, I recognize that it probably doesn't work.

Let's move things up to today. Tell me about your business and the services you offer, and how you describe yourself.

I generally tell people that I provide business research to business professionals and corporate librarians, and consulting services to the online industry. The majority of my work is business research for people in companies, or for consultants, and that's pretty broad. It includes everything from "Tell me about who manufactures and who buys optical amplifiers" to "What are trends in the prefabricated housing market in Japan?"

Some research is a little less straightforward. For example, I worked with a public relations firm to build a portal site on business process re-engineering, and my part was finding and annotating Web sites that they could plug into the portal. My online consulting is with professional online services as well as start-ups—dot-com type companies—where I help them understand their market and how to establish their business.

I was looking at your Web site recently to see what you've been up to, and I noticed that you have highlighted your advanced reference interview skills training. Could you tell me about that?

I do half-day training courses in advanced reference inter-viewing techniques. It's interesting, because all the talk about providing good service and meeting the needs of clients and understanding the market comes back to understanding user needs, and that all comes back to doing a good reference inter-view. It's something that librarians take for granted, especially people who have been doing it for five or ten years. They find that it's really useful to spend half a day thinking about the whole process and developing some new techniques, and learning to actually manage the process instead of just taking a request. They realize that the whole thing is a negotiation, a two-way street with a lot of interaction.

So your market for that training course is primarily librarians?

Yes. I gave a couple of talks and then all of a sudden people started calling and asking me to come and do the workshop for their organization. It's becoming quite popular.

Now, taking a look at the actual research you do, what commercial online systems do you subscribe to?

I subscribe to Dialog [35], Dow Jones [39], LexisNexis [69], Profound [100], DataStar [30], Hoover's [56], and Stat-USA [120]. I set up other accounts as needed, and of course there are aggre-gators on the Web that I use.

How do you know when to use a commercial online system? What type of information do you go there for?

It's when I need to use the power search tools, when I need authenticated information, when I need to do in-depth research, when I need to offer value-added research. Clients can do Web searches themselves. What I offer when I use a professional online service is access to information that they can't get somewhere else. I would say there are very few research projects where I don't spend at least part of the time in a professional online service. I think it's malpractice not to use them, because there is so much stuff there that you can't find just searching on the open Web.

Could you tie that into an example of a general industry research project?

One big research project that I did recently involved consumer perceptions of color ink-jet printers. Why they buy color ink-jet printers, what factors do they take into account, what don't they like about them, and what features do they look for. It was real broad. I started out going to the Web sites of the main color ink-jet printer manufacturers to look through their spec sheets to see how they describe their product, which helped me identify what they thought differentiated the products. I looked at what features they had that their competitors didn't have, to get a general sense of what to watch for. Then I went to the professional online services to search through newspapers. I needed to scan as many papers as I could find, thinking that most newspapers have an "Ask the Computer Guy" kind of column. Believe it or not, I actually looked through *Dear Abby* and *Ann Landers*, and there was a discussion in one of those two columns about that very topic. Then I went over to the industry newsletters for the digital camera/printer market and found a lot of good stuff there. I went into the general trade press and found what the photography, computer, and printing/publishing press were saying. I also purchased individual pages online from market research reports. I covered a lot of ground in maybe an hour, and never would have been able to cover those sources on the open Web, and certainly not in that amount of time. I did end the search on the Web, however, checking computer discussion forums and Usenet [128] newsgroups, and found one market research study about ink-jet printed pages. Once the searching was done, I spent a lot of time doing analysis of what people were saying—the hot buttons, the percentage of comments that were positive and negative, what people were saying about specific brands and specific issues, whether they consider particular features to be a drawback or not. It was a long project, but a lot of fun.

That leads into my next question about the Internet. Could you talk about the open Web versus the invisible Web, and what kinds of things you'd find on each?

My use of the phrase "open Web" means that it's stuff you can find using a search engine, keeping in mind that no search engine covers more than fifteen percent of the open Web, and that even searching a number of search engines together is only going to catch maybe forty or fifty percent of the Web. I'll search the open Web if I'm just looking for a needle in a haystack, or for any mention of a topic. Your gut kind of tells you that it's the sort of thing that's likely to be out there. Another category, which I call "gated sites"—these terms are from *Researching Online For Dummies* [235], which I co-wrote with Reva Basch—would be things like most newspaper archives, where the back issues of newspapers are often available online, but you can only get them by going from one paper's site to the next and doing a search in each paper's archives. Market research companies will sometimes put summaries of their market research up on their Web sites, but this means doing a search at each individual site to find the information you want, and often you have to register before you can even do that. Then there are the professional online services, which are another flavor of the gated Web—sources like Dialog or Dow Jones that require a subscription and a familiarity with advanced search techniques.

What about locating PDF files?

That's just part of the invisible, or perhaps I should call it the semi-opaque, Web. PDF files are somewhat searchable through Google [53]; in fact, there are a couple of ways to search them. Say you're looking for PDF files that discuss competitive intelligence. You would type "competitive intelligence" filetype:pdf or you could type "competitive intelligence inurl:pdf". It's not a comprehensive search of PDF files, but it beats any of the other search engines. Other types of formatted files are harder to find and generally aren't indexed by search engines. The best way to find them is to rely on portals, subject guides, and other finding tools built by experts in the field.

When you're out there on the open Web, how do you evaluate a site for reliability?

Just like librarians have always evaluated sources. You look for features such as who's maintaining it, what point of view do they have, do you recognize the brand, does the material sound right or does it sound weird? You look to see how frequently pages are updated. If you find dead links, you tend to think it's less reliable. I generally don't have time to contact the Web site owner and ask questions, although some people do that. I go by first impression. If it's something I recognize or that seems to be authoritative I'll give it more credibility than if it's Joe Blow's Web site.

Do you have any favorite Web sites for business and company research?

If I have to use a search engine, which is usually my last choice, I'll use Google. I tend to use About.com [4] because of the industry guides, portals such as the Librarians' Index to the Internet [70], and the Dow Jones Business Directory [38]. For U.S. companies, I always look through the EDGAR filings at the U.S. Securities and Exchange Commission's (SEC) site [130] or at FreeEdgar.com [49]. I also use Corporate Information [27], Wall Street Research Net [137], Business.com [17], and CEO

Express [21]—they are all well-organized directories of business-related sites.

Do you ever have projects that take you back to the books? I'm thinking about print sources, archival research. Or is that the kind of thing you might subcontract out?

I subcontract out all my library research, mainly because when you do library research you usually have to photocopy stuff at some point. I don't have an account with the Copyright Clearance Center (CCC) [177] or any other way of paying royalties for any of those photocopies, so I contract out all of my photocopying and manual library research to people who have CCC accounts.

While we're talking about subcontracting, you've said before that you sub out all your telephone research. In a typical project, do you find the sources and sub out "Please call Joe Jones at ABC company?" Or do you just tell your subcontractor "I need an expert on the XYZ industry to tell us ...?"

It depends on the project. It's not just "find an expert," but it's "Contact this company because we need to find out about X." You can't really drill down to the right person from an online directory. The other phone research that I often get is something like, "Identify the government source for X." Again, I'll give my subcontractor whatever pointers I have, but most of that's just going through government phone trees until you find the people you need to talk to. I do what I can to help, but I use phone researchers to do some of that initial research, too. I don't hire people who say, "Give me the phone number for the people to call and I'll call them." That's useless; I need someone who can help me *find* those experts.

How do you price your projects? What kind of billing works for you?

I work on an hourly rate basis, but I establish a not-to-exceed budget on all my projects. That's the only way I can work with a client to figure out how big a job is supposed to be and how much the client wants to spend on it.

Do most of your clients want to see work in hard copy or electronic form?

It's almost all electronic. I've got a few clients who accept hard copy, too, but very few. In fact I noticed recently that I haven't ordered new stationery in about two years. I used to go through it every six months. I'm just not sending out that much stuff in hard copy anymore, because most clients would rather have it in electronic format. It's easier for me that way also.

We often hear the term "value-added services" today, and I'm wondering how much of a typical project is actual information retrieval versus value-added services, compared to when you first started out.

I'm certainly doing more analysis today than I used to, partly because people have the budget for it. People are more stressed out and pressed for time, and would rather have their researchers do those extra steps of synthesizing and analyzing material rather than just give them a data dump. It varies by project, but for me the ratio is about 60:40 or 70:30 research to analysis. That includes summarizing material, sometimes pulling together a PowerPoint presentation with the key points, highlighting key information, and doing spreadsheets or tables of data I've extracted.

How do you know when to end a project? Do you feel it's directed more by the budget, or by your time? Or do you just develop a sense for this over time?

Usually I can tell when I'm finished. I'm not going to spend any more time on a project if I find the answer right away. And sometimes it's just the particular subject; you could spend three times as long and find more stuff, but they need it tomorrow and there are only so many hours in the day, and this is as much as I can do in that time.

Looking at your range of services, speaking and writing are also a big part of what you do. How do you maintain your balance of research versus writing vs. speaking?

I started out viewing my speaking and writing mainly as marketing tools, because it's a great way of establishing credibility and developing contacts. Since then, they've become revenue sources. For example, I do a talk on the future of the information profession for special librarians and offer a challenge to think differently about our profession. It's been so well received that, after every talk I do for a library group, I get two or three people asking if I can do a similar talk for all the librarians within their organization. It's the same thing with the advanced reference interview skills. That started out as a talk I gave at Online World [91] a number of years ago, and has morphed into more of a revenue source than I had originally anticipated. And I always learn; at every single speaking gig I get something back from people in the form of new ideas, and I really enjoy it. It's been a tremendous source of renewal and a way to keep me fresh.

Wow. We haven't even gotten to your writing yet.

I write for *Searcher* [223] and have a back-page column in both *EContent* [212] and *Online* [220] magazines. I'm also the contributing editor for the *Information Advisor* [215] newsletter.

In 1999–2000 I finished three books in twelve months, and that was something I'll never do again. They were all very different books, and I enjoyed each of them. The experience was fun, but it was just a huge amount of work. My most recent one was *Mining for Gold on the Internet* [233], published by McGraw-Hill. It's about how to find investment and financial information on the Internet. Before that was the second edition of *Researching Online For Dummies*, which I did with Reva Basch. That was written for a more general audience—obviously not for dummies, but for people who are serious about researching. That was a lot of fun in a completely different way, and it's always great working with Reva. The other was *Super Searchers Do Business* [237], which was the first of the Super Searchers series, and is a collection of interviews with business researchers. So, three very different books in very different formats; all focusing on online research, but with very different emphasis.

I've since completed another Super Searchers book on global research, *Super Searchers Cover the World* [236]. Like the other Super Searchers books, it's a collection of interviews with expert online researchers; this one consists of fifteen interviews with people from all over the world. It was a tremendous experience, getting such different perspectives on the research process.

Sounds like you have to manage a pretty intense schedule.

I would say I average two speaking engagements a month. Spring and fall are definitely the busy times for speaking because that's when most of the professional conferences are. It's tough in the sense that I'm a one-person business and every day that I'm out speaking somewhere is a day that I'm not in my office available to my clients. So there's always a trade-off, but that's part of running a business. The writing workload really fluctuates.

How do you keep it all together? Do you rely on any favorite time-saving devices or tricks of the trade?

I use a hard-copy Franklin Planner and I can't imagine life without it. If I ever lost my Franklin Planner I'd have to shoot myself because I would completely lose everything. It's perfect for me. I put in my schedule for what's due when, figure out when I need to start preparing for it, and then I don't worry about it in the meantime; it's fabulous. That's my biggest secret. I work very well under deadline, so it's just a matter of keeping in my mind what needs to be done when, and working back from the deadlines. I use QuickBooks for accounting and Eudora Pro [44] for email, which I like because it filters all my email subscriptions into separate files.

Now that you are so well established in the profession, is there anything else you do specifically to market your services?

I continue to do the same things that worked in the beginning. I collect business cards from people and send out a client newsletter to all my prospects and clients. I also have a free quarterly email newsletter. I post the current one on my Web site and then do updates that I send to anyone who's on my subscription list. That's what I've been doing since day one and it's always worked, so I don't mess with it.

How important do you think it is to have your own Web page?

I never expect to get any business directly from it, because people who have time to surf the Web are not the people who are willing to pay for my kind of research. But it's like a listing in the yellow pages. It shows a certain amount of credibility. It lets me have an online brochure, so if people have already heard about me they can go to the Web site and see what I've written and where I've spoken recently, to get a sense of what I'm all about before they call me. But I can't think of more than a couple of clients I've gotten directly from the Web site. I have not designed the Web page, nor do I intend it to be a way to actually attract clients from the Web itself.

Do you list yourself anywhere else? What about yellow pages or any industry or expert directories where you actually pay for a listing?

I'm a member of SLA and the Society of Competitive Intelligence Professionals (SCIP) [199], and am now an active speaker in both associations. I originally joined to have my name in their directories, so that's kind of an indirect payment for a listing. I'm also a member of AIIP (Association of Independent Information Professionals) [172].

I do not pay for a yellow-pages ad because most of my clients don't come from the local area, and I think it's foolish to pay for a yellow-pages listing in only one town if your clients are all over the country. I do have a business phone listing, as opposed to residential, because you have to sound credible to the client who is trying to find you through Directory Assistance. I've never seen the point in paying for listings in other directories because I don't think my clients would look there. I think if they did, they'd probably be calling ten of us, and I just don't have the time to bid against ten other information brokers. I would much rather spend my money and resources attracting people who come to me on a referral, or because they've read a book I've written, or heard a talk and are interested in having me do work for them.

That leads us into the importance of word-of-mouth marketing and client retention. What

kinds of things do you do to stay in touch with your core clients and keep them coming back?

Letters and postcards—that's pretty much it. When I have time and feel like doing some fun writing, I'll send out another newsletter issue. I send out postcards that show anonymized versions of a few of the recent projects I've done, and say "if you need any work done, call me at my 800 number." That always reminds a few people who haven't called me for a while to call back.

Thinking about how independent information professionals could define their success, how are you more effective working for a client as an independent rather than in-house? What can you do that you couldn't do if you were somebody's employee?

What I offer to clients is, number one, twenty years of online research experience, which they may not have in-house. I have subscriptions to a number of online services and a familiarity with them all, which a lot of in-house researchers would not. They may specialize in one online service, but not in the others outside their industry.

Some of my clients need someone outside the organization to do the research. They may not want their name associated with the project, or sometimes, even with Web searching, they don't want their email address connected with the research.

Another thing I offer is a fresh perspective. I can sometimes see the forest for the trees. Generally, the clients that I do research for either don't have a library themselves, don't have an in-house researcher at all, or it's their librarian who is calling me because he or she has a project that requires too much time and resources, and they need to outsource it. So, one of the other things I offer is simply the availability to do the work.

Now, with regard to the daily grind and the mechanics of running a business, do you handle all that yourself? Do you outsource any office tasks or have any employees?

I have no employees. Never have and don't intend to. I work really long hours and don't mind that. I keep all the work in-house, partly because I like knowing where it all is. I prefer to do the accounting myself because then I always have a handle on what's coming in, what's going out, cash flow, and profitability by quarter. I do just about all my own online research. I do my own marketing because I think I understand myself, my strengths, my value, and my clients better than someone on the outside would.

I do outsource tasks like stuffing envelopes. When I'm sending out a newsletter, there's a sheltered workshop nearby that does all the folding, labeling, and stamping, and they're great. A modest price and the work is fabulous.

We sometimes talk about the overwhelming amount of information in society today as a marketing angle for information professionals, but it's difficult even for us to stay current with everything. How do you track important industry developments?

I read all the information industry magazines. Generally, I get them read on the plane when I travel to speaking engagements. My carry-on luggage consists of five or six magazines. For the email newsletters, mailing lists, and discussion groups, I send them all to a folder in my email software and then download it to a little hand-held PC and read them on the subway. I read BUS-LIB-L [148], the private discussion forum for AIIP members [146], SLA Business & Finance [157] and Solo Librarian's lists [161], the discussion list on Free Pint [150], and the Web Search newsletter from About.com [164].

Professional associations can be a great source of information, but they also provide a way to connect with people. As the first recipient of AIIP's Sue Rugge Memorial Award in 2000, you were recognized for your contributions to nurturing the growth of new business owners. Could you reflect a bit on that?

I was very surprised and touched to have been given the award. It really meant a lot to me, as Sue had been so helpful when I started my business, and she continued to be a friend and colleague until her death in June of 1999. I've benefited a lot from my membership in AIIP, and I'm grateful for all the help and informal mentoring that more experienced members offered to me when I started my business. I've always tried to pass along the favor to newer members, and I'm immensely grateful to have been given an award in Sue's honor.

What is the most bizarre client request or funniest project you've worked on?

One of the first jobs I got was to find out the history of bungee jumping. Oddly enough, I found the perfect article in *Playboy* magazine, which was available online on Dialog—without the pictures, of course. It was the whole story about how it was started by a group of kids in England that called themselves the Dangerous Boys or something like that, and they did dangerous things for fun. Bungee jumping was the most dangerous thing they could think up, so they started doing it and it caught on from there. The article included a description by the author of his first bungee jump, which was great. I would never in my life go bungee jumping, but it was a fun request and where I found the answer is sort of an interesting story—not one of your expected sources.

Running your own business, especially when it's in your home, is something that can take over your life if you don't maintain some balance. How do you escape when you need to?

Seeking balance, that's a tough thing. It's easy for the business to take over your life if you're not careful. An important thing to keep in mind, I think, is that we're better researchers if we have a life, and I'm not always the best example for having a life. One thing that helps is that I have a dog; that makes a big difference during the course of the day. I stop, take the dog for a walk, and get a reminder that it's not all work.

Yes, mine's lying next to me and I always hope that the UPS guy doesn't come when I'm on the phone, because she goes nuts and has interrupted more than one phone call that way.

Oh, no kidding! Mine's part husky, so she just starts howling sometimes when I'm on the phone and it's really embarrassing! It's funny; when I first started my business, practically nobody worked out of their homes. I was very conscious of whenever the dog would bark, and wouldn't want the client to hear that. I'd hit the mute button immediately. Since then, people laugh and say, "Oh you've got a dog. That's great." It's much more common to be dealing with independent people who work out of their homes, so it's not a downside like it used to be.

The other thing that keeps me sane is that I'm a long-distance runner, so that forces me to get out of the house several days a week to go on a long run. I run marathons several times a year. During the week when I need a break, a nice long run clears the mind. I don't think about work. I don't think about anything but running, and it's very cleansing.

When you work on your own, you have to be your own driving force. What do you think is

necessary on a personal level to keep it all together?

I think it's important to have a good support system behind you. It's an odd balance, because to succeed as an independent, you have to be a loner in the sense that you are comfortable working by yourself all day long and are self-motivated and self-managed, but you have to be good with people, too. It all comes down to client management skills. If you aren't a person whom your clients enjoy dealing with, they're going to find someone else who's easier to deal with.

The other thing that is important, and maybe this comes from my California roots, is maintaining a feeling of personal abundance—that your life is rich. That you have friends and family and interests outside of work, and that life is good. I think that generally having a positive attitude helps a lot. Feeling that you're not desperate or anxious for work. Being relaxed about the whole thing even when the calls don't come in. Knowing that you are a successful businessperson and that people *will* call you, and that the business *will* come in. Clients are attracted to people who feel happy and successful. If you can manage to avoid feeling desperate or anxious about your business, your clients are attracted to you in a way that they're not to someone who is nervous or scared about whether this is going to work or not.

I think that's an important element. You need to be confident enough to work alone, but when the phone rings you can switch gears and interact with people. Also, I remember feeling, in the beginning, just thrilled that someone would even want me to work for him or her. You get over that.

There are a couple of parts to that. Part of it is feeling confident enough that another job will come in that you can say no to this one. It's so important to be able to turn down a job. If you don't think you can do a splendid job, if you think this is a push for you or that it goes beyond your capabilities, the worst thing you can do is take it on. At best, you'll barely manage to meet your client's expectations, and at worst you'll have a client who will tell fifteen other people how disappointed he is in your work. It's hard to turn down work in the beginning when the business isn't coming in, but you have to realize that you're better off spending that time marketing than taking on a job that you're going to tank at.

The other part is developing a sense that failure is not an option. When I started my business, I couldn't even imagine folding it. It just didn't enter my mind. From the very beginning, I was thinking about how it was going to feel to have been in business for two years. I think that makes a huge difference, because your vision almost subconsciously guides the decisions that you make. After a couple years into my business, a cousin of mine said, "Well, gee, I guess you're not looking for another job anymore, are you?" I just burst out laughing and said, "No, I'm not looking for a job at all. I always intended this to be a long-term business." In order to succeed, you can't take a "try it for awhile and see if it works" attitude. You have to be committed to doing this for at least two years.

What do you think the future holds for the independent information profession? What trends do you see that may impact us?

I think it's a wide-open opportunity for people. The Internet has been great for our profession, because it's raised awareness of the information that's out there. It eliminated some of the easy, slam-dunk projects that I had eight or ten years ago. Obviously, people can do those for themselves now. We see much harder projects, questions that people wouldn't have thought to ask five or six years ago, because they didn't think the information would be available. Now there's almost the opposite sense:

"Well, of course you can find a list of every volunteer fire department in the U.S. by tomorrow—for no money."

So there's certainly a greater demand for our services now, and I don't think that's going to go away any time soon. There's more of a demand for value-added services, which is fun, because that's a more "thinking" part of the job. I don't see that slowing any time soon, because the labor crunch is going to be around for a long time. We've got the Baby Bust generation coming up now, so businesses are desperately looking for people, and they wind up having to outsource a lot of this stuff just because they don't have enough people in-house to do the preliminary analysis of the information.

The toughest thing for people entering this profession to realize is that they have to have the research background. A week doesn't go by that I don't get an email from someone saying "I'm a stay-at-home person, and I have a computer, and I want to start making money doing research on the Internet like you do, and what do I need to do first?" It's hard to convince these people that they're not going to make a go of it without a really strong background in research. You can't charge your clients for your learning curve in this field. Right now, people who enjoy doing research can find a job in a company. But as the economy constricts, as it sometimes does, more people become interested in becoming independent information professionals, because it's harder to find jobs within organizations. The number of people who are doing this tends to fluctuate inversely with the economy, but I think it's certainly a wide-open field.

What advice would you share with somebody who is on a serious track toward the independent information profession?

I would encourage them to spend four or five years in a company doing research. Find an organization that lets you do a lot of different kinds of research, that lets you market your services so that you have experience explaining what value you can add.

Try to search a wide variety of professional online services like Dow Jones and Dialog on a daily basis, so that when you decide to go independent, you've already got that knowledge base. It's not a knowledge base that you can pick up on the job once you go independent. It's not even something that you can learn in a class. I took every online research class I could take in library school, and when I think of the kind of research I did for the first couple of years after that, I wince. It just takes time and daily use of these services to really understand what's out there and how best to use them.

I would recommend taking classes in entrepreneurship, in running a small business, and in marketing, and to plan several years ahead before you actually go out and launch your business. And I'd recommend meeting and talking with other, established independent information professionals. It really helps to find out what it's like in the trenches every day; that way, you can decide whether you think you'd really enjoy this kind of job.

Super Searcher Power Tips

➤ The first thing I did was contract with a graphic artist to design a corporate logo. I'm really glad I did that, because it enabled me to start my business looking established.

➤ There are very few research projects where I don't spend at least part of the time searching a professional online service. I think it's malpractice not to use them, because there is so much stuff in those databases that you can't find just searching on the open Web.

➤ I evaluate a Web site like librarians have always evaluated sources: Who's maintaining it? What point of view do they have? Do you recognize the brand? Does the material sound right, or does it sound weird? You look to see how frequently information is updated. If you find dead links, you tend to think it's less reliable.

➤ I started out viewing my speaking and writing mainly as marketing tools, because it's a great way of establishing credibility and developing contacts. Since then, they've become revenue sources.

➤ I never expect to get any business directly from my Web page, but it's sort of like a listing in the yellow pages. It shows a certain amount of credibility.

➤ It's important to be able to turn down a job. If you don't think you can do a splendid job, the worst thing you can do is take it on. At best, you'll barely manage to meet your client's expectations, and at worst you'll have a client who will tell fifteen other people how disappointed he is in your work.

➤ I have no employees. Never have and don't intend to. I work really long hours, and don't mind that. I keep all of the work in-house, partly because I like knowing where it all is.

➤ Clients are attracted to people who feel happy and successful. If you can avoid feeling desperate or anxious about your business, your clients are attracted to you in a way that they're not to someone who is nervous or scared about whether this is going to work or not.

Thomas M. Culbert

Aviation Expert

Thomas M. Culbert is Founder and President of Aviation Information Research Corporation (AIRC), an independent information research business based in Alexandria, Virginia. His company provides information research services to leading firms in all sectors of the aviation industry and consultant services for civilian and military aviation issues. He serves as a Director of the AIIP Corporation and is an active member of several aviation and military professional associations.

tcairc@avinforsch.com

Tom, your information business is really your second career. You have a fascinating background in aviation, so why don't we begin there.

I served twenty-one years in the U.S. Air Force, both as a pilot and as a staff officer in different squadrons and flying various types of airplanes overseas. I spent five years operating in Africa and the Middle East. When I came back here to Washington, I worked in the Pentagon for the Secretary of Defense in African international security affairs. With two young children at home and changing lifestyle requirements, I eventually decided to leave active duty. I retired as a Lieutenant Colonel, went back to school, and picked up a second master's degree in aeronautical management.

I knew that I wanted to stay in the aviation community, and what I basically tried to do was to civilianize myself. I volunteered at the Smithsonian Air and Space Museum, and that introduced me to the aviation archives in the Washington area. I started to do research for the Smithsonian on a volunteer basis and really enjoyed it, so I continued with that for a couple years. One of their staffers mentioned that she knew of people who actually did research for a profession. That led me to finding Sue Rugge's book [230, see Appendix], and that led me to the I-95ers, the DC regional Association of Independent Information Professionals (AIIP) [172] group.

Interesting. So, although your background didn't include formal training in research, you picked up a lot of those skills at the Smithsonian through volunteer work?

What volunteering did was help solidify my ideas and my concept of conducting research. My education began at the University of Wisconsin-Superior, where I majored in political science and history. The Air Force sent me to obtain a master's degree in International Security Affairs at the Naval Postgraduate School in Monterey, California, as well as numerous professional military schools.

In my two tours of embassy duty in Africa, I served in the position of military attaché. That job included working with foreign militaries and serving as advisor to U.S. ambassadors in the region. It was basically an overt information-gathering position.

You started your business, then, in 1993. Once that decision was made, how did you go about setting up shop?

One of the things I always told myself was that I would never be able to open a business because of all the clerical requirements. By the time 1990 rolled around and I was seriously contemplating retirement from the military, I became interested in computers. Back in those days, the Apple Macintosh system presented the only graphical interface for the printer, monitor, and

CPU to work together. Initially I was using an old Apple IIe while doing my thesis paper for my aeronautical management master's degree. The size of my project was becoming unmanageable using the old system, so I went out and purchased an early version of the Mac.

I saw what the newer computers could do to enhance one's capabilities to run a business, especially with the communications and accounting aspects. The Internet was not a major issue yet, but the fax machine was in use and there were some communications via the early consumer online services. I was able to look at those systems and use them to overcome some of the operational challenges in the small business arena. I didn't want to become a computer geek; I just wanted to use the computer as a tool.

With regard to the logistics of operating a home business, did you get legal and accounting advice?

Yes, through coaching soccer I met a lawyer who also became a friend. I contracted with him to set up an S corporation, and went to a recommended CPA to get things off on a solid footing. There were a million questions and I was seeking answers. At that point in time, I felt that in order to do it right I needed professional help. Their services cost some money, but the reassurance has been priceless. I've enjoyed working with both of them.

Going back to those early days, do you recall your first client and the process of getting started?

Yes, it was through contacts made in AIIP. I did a couple of subcontracts for AIIP members located in the Washington area. We have the AIIP I-95 group that meets quarterly—or every 95 days or so. Lo and behold, a couple of them had some aviation-related questions and I would help them out by tracking down information as needed. I also found my first larger piece of work this way. From there I was off and running.

So, in your case, you could see value in carving out a niche right from the beginning. How do you describe the services that you offer today?

What I normally emphasize is that I am a researcher. I stay away from the "C" word—"consultant"—as much as possible. That's more of a geographical thing, probably, than anything else. Here in Washington there are tens of thousands of "consultants," and I prefer not to be cast in that community because it's an over-exposed term in this area. I've tried to hold to the researcher aspect as I market in a couple of different communities.

One service I provide is coverage of what I call contemporary aviation issues. These are current-day aviation business questions and issues of concern to my clients. In this community, I'm using my research skills to help inventors and other business-people expand their businesses into the aviation industry.

The other side of what I do is historical aviation-related research. I help academics, authors, and in some cases attorneys look at events that happened in the past. We're searching for records and documents that exist in federal repositories and are fifty to 150 years old.

Sounds like you definitely distinguish yourself as somebody who is still doing manual research, and that not all your sources are online.

Oh, absolutely. My hands get dirty working in the archives. Those old documents are really dusty.

What collections are you searching and what kinds of things are you finding? It's interesting, and so different from what most searchers talk about today.

It's not as lucrative, I guess, but it's a helluva lot of fun. My history major is paying off. When I do archival research, I will routinely investigate and search records at the National Archives, the Smithsonian Archives, the U.S. Air Force Archives, U.S. Navy Archives, and the U.S. Army Historical Institute. Those are my principal sources for the historical material. Now, the current day, contemporary issue research is different.

Then you're online?

Well, not really. The aviation industry has been changing so drastically since 1993. My clients in the contemporary arena want information that's probably less than three days old. And that information, for the most part, is not online. I certainly will look at online press articles and things like that, which may lead to an update of a topic or issue. But, basically, what I do is go into the federal bureaucracy and knock on doors and make phone calls to people in the regulatory agencies; that would be the Department of Transportation (DOT) [203], Federal Aviation Administration (FAA) [184], and National Transportation Safety Board (NTSB) [195], as well as various congressional subcommittees.

Lots of face-to-face primary research.

Yes, I'm seeking current data, in fact the most current data. As you can imagine, in the bureaucracy there are people who sit in offices and do their jobs day in and day out. They have information that is just a small segment of the big picture. If you know those people and can contact them, they're usually willing to talk to you about their project. By talking with them you can really get a sense of where a project is. This also applies to the private sector. If somebody is interested in introducing a new product into the aviation community, I talk to the managers of the major air carriers that deal with that type of product, whether it be a particular piece of ground-support equipment, a software management tool, or whatever. I find out their likes and dislikes about whatever equipment they are using now versus what might be coming down the pike. In this way I'm providing a very specialized and personalized service. I do some online work, but I would never limit myself to just what I could find online, because that data is not always the most current.

Which of the commercial online services do you use? And what do you use them for?

Primarily Dow Jones [39] and Dialog [35]. I look online mostly to find people and to learn *about* people who are the experts, so that I can either call them myself or direct my client to people they need to talk to.

What about the popularization and the growth of the Internet these last several years? How has that impacted your business, if at all?

It's really mixed. Overall, I would say that it has universalized the concept of information retrieval. In other words, everybody now believes they can find whatever they need, any time they need it, and they are willing to spend long hours looking for it. It just amazes me how professionals in the business community will play around and spend an enormous amount of their valuable time looking for information online. Especially in this town, there seems to be a maxim: "If I can't do it, then it's not worth doing."

I've seen this concept hyped with the growth of the Internet. I was watching the Internet very closely back in the early and mid-nineties. It was a tool that no one could use because it hadn't really been opened up to the public. It was just out there. I was chomping at the bit, thinking we really need to get access to this thing. Gopher and all those early search tools had limitations, but all of a sudden there was something called the World Wide Web, and that was that. So now the belief is that anybody can go out and find what they need and want. And for their purposes, most people can. It's a wonderful tool.

Do you find that people think information has a stamp of authenticity just because it's on the Web?

Yes, it appears to me that many people do not question the validity of information they find on the Internet. By that I mean that it's never even an issue in their minds. There is a need to emphasize the issue of credibility and the importance of confirming information through other sources.

How is the Internet of use to you? What do you search for?

I like Northern Light [89], which provides a formalized gathering of information versus just what's out on the Web; it draws on both free and fee-based sources. I also use a search engine called Sherlock [116] that's built into the Macintosh operating system, which does a pretty decent job of narrowing things down. Then there are the search engines like Ask Jeeves [11] and Google [53], but it's a wild and woolly world. You can use all those different search engines and get a different result each time.

The Web is a useful tool for finding books and articles, but what's really key to me is who wrote it and where are they? How do I get to the experts?

Do you operate your business on your own? Any employees or outsourcing?

I don't have any employees, and I stay away from that mainly because of accounting issues and complicating rules and regulations. Several times I have worked with another individual, but they operate as a separate corporate entity. I have also subcontracted some work. I'll bring someone in under a contract, but we limit it to the scope of a particular project.

How do you handle pricing for your services?

It depends on the client's wishes, actually. Some clients can only deal in hourly fees, while others would rather bill on a project basis. The more I do this, the better I become at it, but it's a never-ending battle. It can be very time-consuming and extremely unprofitable if you are putting out major proposals and then lose a big project. What I try to do when I'm asked the question, "Can you do this?" is write back with a proposal and brief research plan, identifying specific sources and types of information that I might be able to find. If you're not careful, you can get too specific and actually give away all of your trade secrets about how you're going to do this research, when in fact you probably don't want to reveal all this. You want to give the prospective client just enough information so that they can make the decision whether or not to hire you, but it's a real balancing act.

Can you describe a typical project that might come across your desk?

I have one client who comes back on an annual basis and asks for industry-related forecasting data. They need to know about specific types of airframes and what the forecasts are for production over the next eight to ten years. Actually, I have several different clients that routinely ask for the latest forecast on different product lines. Some of the private industry folks, such as Boeing and Airbus, put out annual forecasts of what they think is going to happen. The FAA has a conference every spring where they specifically talk about the "in" forecast for the aviation industry. So, rather than just go online and try to track some of that information on Web sites, I'll actually attend the FAA conference. And then, rather than just walk away with an FAA publication, I will talk with the people who put the report together. Plus I learn all the details from the speakers at the conference. Thus, I'm able to give my clients not only the raw data, but also some insights into what people are thinking and talking about.

It sounds like you've built up some key industry contacts over the years. That's probably one of the most valuable assets you can offer to clients.

I belong to several different aviation-related groups and associations. Some of them include aviation businesspeople here in the Washington area where we all have regulatory and legislative concerns. Most of the major airlines, most of the major manufacturers, and almost all the aviation-related associations—it's a veritable alphabetical soup—have offices here. So I attend these conferences, meetings, and luncheons, which are great opportunities to hear fantastic speakers and learn about the industry. The speakers at these events are usually on the leading edge of issues that are affecting the aviation industry today. At the same time, I'm developing relationships and meeting with industry people, so when a question does pop up, I can easily call them and get some insight into what's happening or what's going to happen next.

Even with all this primary data gathering, I tend not to do a lot of analysis. I mainly just provide the client with the data and let them make their own business decisions. I focus on information gathering and organizing, making sure it's current and complete.

Can you tell me which airline has the best on-time record?

I don't think any of them do!

On the historical research side, I'll typically have an author come to me and ask about a particular Naval engagement or a specific event, and we can go back into the National Archives and find the detailed records of the event. Unfortunately, the U.S. Air Force wasn't formed until 1948, so when you talk about aviation, you're usually talking about Naval forces and Army forces prior to that. I look into ship diaries, ship logs, incident reports, and action reports. It's really a lot of fun.

So for somebody who's writing a novel or a nonfiction piece on say, World War II, they work with you to get their aviation history facts straight.

That's correct. Sometimes we'll find gold mines of information. That's very rewarding and makes everybody happy. But sometimes, of course, there are those black holes, when you try to find something and there just is nothing there.

I've also seen photo research listed as a service in your company description.

Yes, another sideline of historical research is photographic work. What I'll do for a client is go into the National Archives and take photos of photos, and make negative copies of black-and-white photos from, say, 1938. Part of getting my business up and running was to purchase enough photo equipment so that I could go to an archive with a light stand, a 35mm SLR camera, and macro/micro lens attachments to do very good close-up photography.

Now, I read that company description of yours in a print directory. I was beginning to get concerned about not being able to find your Web page, thinking "What am I missing?" when I realized that you don't have one.

I am not a Web-page business as of yet. I may get there someday. I've mulled that over a lot, but with everything else I've got going, I guess I've prioritized a Web page down toward the bottom of my list of important things to do.

Are there any specific things you do that you would call marketing?

Yes. First of all, I have my company listed in several directories, including a couple of aviation-related directories such as *World Aviation Directory* [239] and *Airport Business* [205], which are kind of the bibles for this industry. These do generate some calls. As I mentioned earlier, I attend aviation-related shows and events. I try to get to the Paris Air Show, and have also been to an aviation show in South Africa. For me, it's a form of marketing to just be out there.

So you're marketing on an international level, then.

Yes, and on the historical side, I'm part of a couple of informal groups of historical researchers. The members are listed at several of the archives in our area. That has generated business for me, and being involved with AIIP has been a great asset. Their referral program, which I helped set up several years ago, is one way to generate calls, but my involvement there has primarily led to word-of-mouth business. I really enjoy being referred by somebody who knows me and the types of service I can provide. I had brochures at one time, but I have let them run out. I never found them to be very useful.

I belong to several aviation groups, including the Experimental Aircraft Association (EAA) [182], the Aircraft Owners and Pilots Association (AOPA) [166], the Aero Club of Washington [165], the International Aviation Club [189], and the National Air Transportation Association (NATA) [193].

What about client retention? Do you do anything in particular to stay in touch with your clients and keep them coming back?

I've tried a couple of different things. I will almost always do a follow-up call if I've not heard from a client in a while. And that pays off, because many times they will say something like, "Oh, we've been meaning to call you." I stay abreast of what's going on in the aviation industry through reading numerous

print periodicals. If I know that a client is interested in a particular issue, or a particular piece of equipment, I'll drop them an
email or call and update them on something I've seen. That
gives me an opportunity to see if they have any additional
requirements, or just to let them know that I'm still available to
help them out.

Talking about client retention that way folds nicely into a discussion of how else you stay current yourself.

I subscribe to seven or eight aviation-related journals, starting
with *Aviation Week* [206], *African Aviation* [204], *Business &
Commercial Aviation* [208], and *Regional Airline World* [221],
monitoring everything from business aircraft sales to airport
management materials. Among other things, I pay close attention to the advertisements in this reading material.

I subscribe to The Airline List [147], which has been around
for quite some time. It focuses on airline issues and airplanes. I
also subscribe to the AIIP mailing list [146], and between those
two I get more than enough to browse through. One of the things
that the Internet has done, I think, is turn a lot of people into
email junkies. Sometimes it's easier to read email than do some
other task, so I'm very careful about not spending too much time
with it.

Are you a wireless gadget person? What kinds of devices do you use to help manage your time?

The cell phone has been a real help to me, especially since the
rates have come way down. You're now talking about long-
distance calls for around seven cents a minute, which is fantastic compared to what it used to be. I don't mind calling a client
across the country and talking to him for a few minutes. One of
the phone system arrangements I have enjoyed is hooking up
the cell phone with the land line to do call forwarding. For just a

couple of dollars a month, you can set up your office phone so that calls to the office ring through to the cell phone. It's like I'm picking up my call right in my office. It has some drawbacks, but for a single-operator-type business, the benefits outweigh them by far.

Yes, I confess I have been on a fishing boat and taken a mid-week business call. The downside is that you're never really away from your work, but the upside is that you can take the call and immediately resolve the issue or provide the information. You don't have to get into a telephone tag routine. It's becoming so difficult to contact people in their offices. Most people are using voice mail and answering machines or are stuck in meetings. It can really be time-consuming to get through to the person you want to talk to. This way, if the call rings through to your cell phone—boom—you answer it and resolve it.

And that creates a track record that you're generally available by telephone, so clients know they can call and you'll be there. How does that work in terms of dividing your time between work and home?

I tend to work a lot. But I tend to tie that work effort into non-work activities with my family. It's very hard to break away from the business routine, but I can go out for a bike ride and just take the phone along. I've tried to set up a weekly schedule for certain events and activities, and it just falls apart in a heartbeat. I'll have the best intentions, but with the kids' school, homework, and sports, it gets to be hectic. But, all in all, it's not as bad as having to sit in the commuter lane for an hour each way driving to and from an office. I can get a lot more done in a home environment, so I'm happy.

You're also a published author. Tell me about your book.

Yes, it's titled *Pan Africa: Across the Sahara in 1941 with Pan Am* [234]. It is the result of both my Air Force career and my historical and Smithsonian research experiences. It relates the true story of a 1941 episode in aviation history when Pan American Airways had a contract with the British Royal Air Force in Africa. Prior to Pearl Harbor, Pan Am sent hundreds of U.S. civilians over to Africa to open and operate an air route across the continent. Eventually, some of these fellows went all the way to China. It was a fun experience getting the book together, and the Internet was a great tool to search for information and communicate with colleagues on different aspects of the book.

Have you worked on any particularly unusual or funny projects?

One time I was asked by an academic institution to find a paper that was presented at a European conference by a Norwegian professor. This was right about the time that the Internet was coming into full swing, so I was able to track the professor down to an institute in Norway. I actually called and found out that the professor was still at that institution, but that he was out of town or something and would be back in a few days. I left a message that I would be most happy to do whatever I needed to do to obtain a copy of this particular document that he supposedly gave at this lecture. Lo and behold, he called me back, and said that he had intended to give that paper, but in fact it was never given. It made it into the proceedings directory, but had never existed. Thus, I went back to my client quite empty-handed, but was able to add the fact that the reference was bogus, right from the author's own mouth.

Another time I was helping a fellow who was building a replica of a WW II German aircraft. He needed dimensional data, and we obtained some of it here through the Smithsonian. A piece of the data was missing, so we went to one of the German museums, I believe in Munich, that supposedly had some of what was needed. To set the stage here, a little bit of history: At the end of

WW II, the U.S. government collected thousands of German scientific documents and brought them all here to the United
States where they were cataloged and microfilmed. The micro-
filming of all this information took place at Wright Patterson Air
Force Base in Ohio, and all the microfilm is annotated with that
fact. Well, I wrote a letter to the German museum, and received
a package of printed material. In this package was photocopied
material, but you could see from the pages that the documents
had been on microfilm made in the United States. But these were
original German documents. So in the end, the German
museum had a copy of the American microfilm of the German
documents, and this document had gone back and forth across
the Atlantic twice by the time I received it. You've really got to
appreciate the irony of the whole scenario.

Those are great stories, and really demonstrate the diversity and fun side of your work. Now I'd like to ask about your outside interests, Tom, but I just know you're going to say something like "experimental aircraft."

Yes, I like and enjoy aviation. So working on aviation issues
and items is a pleasure. I guess the bottom line is, do something
that you like to do, and I'm doing that. It's an arena that is
extremely broad in scope. Within the aviation community you
might be talking about anything from nuts and bolts to human
resource management to safety analysis and budgeting. We
might be involved in a project with an inventor trying to build
some new type of ground-support equipment, or we might be
working with a company that wants to sell air-traffic-control
radars to a company that wants to build an airport. All those
issues are aviation-related, but very diverse. There's never a single common type of project. They're all very different, very specific, and very interesting. I have always liked the metaphor of
looking under all the rocks to see what we can find.

Do you have any advice for the aspiring independent researcher?

On the technical side, having several computers and a couple different methods of getting online is really important, due to potential failures of one system or another. Plan for and give yourself the ability to continue to function while something is getting replaced or repaired. I have several computers, and on more than one occasion, that's been a lifesaver. For example, if my regular ISP is down, I have another computer with AOL [9] installed, so that I can still get online.

Also, I use a shell account for my email. It's part of a very fast UNIX system and it allows me to get my basic email in and out very quickly, as opposed to going through a Web browser. It also allows me to telnet into my ISP and log into the shell account from anywhere in the world. This has been a real lifesaver for me while on international travel. I can always get my email no matter where I am.

Another bit of advice is to have a secure power source for your computer systems. We all think in terms of surge protectors, but what can really damage your machine are brownouts and low voltage. I've been using battery-powered backup systems for years, and I'm a firm believer in this equipment.

As you can tell from our discussion, I feel strongly that finding a niche and then offering specialized services within that field will bring the most success. I believe that you can do a better job for your client if you are truly interested in the subject matter being researched. It is more enjoyable and more personally rewarding.

Do you have any thoughts on the future of the independent information profession as a whole?

I suspect the novelty of the Internet will wear off to some degree. My guess is that it will become easier for average people to do more of their own online research. From my perspective, I certainly believe that information professionals are going to have to become more topically oriented or niche industry specific. As the library field has changed so tremendously in the past few years, I suspect that the independent informational profession is also going to continue to change, and probably become more specialized.

One of the important issues that I try to take care of, namely keeping myself trained, is a real hard thing to accomplish. I'm always doing other projects, and going back to take a class to review how to search effectively is always low on my priority list. Staying abreast of the industry and the equipment and the software is a very time consuming process. But to work in a field like this, it has to be done.

Super Searcher Power Tips

➤ My clients often want information that's probably less than three days old. And that information, for the most part, is not online.

➤ Many people do not question the validity of information they find on the Internet. It's never even an issue in their minds. We need to emphasize the issue of credibility and the importance of confirming information through other sources.

➤ I look online mostly to find people, and to learn about people who are the experts, so that I can either call them myself or direct my client to people they need to talk to.

➤ I will almost always do a follow-up call if I've not heard from a client in a while. That pays off, because many times they will say, "Oh, we've been meaning to call you."

➤ There's never a single common type of project. They're all very different, very specific, and very interesting. I have always liked the metaphor of looking under all the rocks to see what we can find.

➤ On the technical side, having several computers and a couple of different methods for getting online is really important, due to potential failures of one system or another.

➤ You can do a better job for your client if you are truly interested in the topic matter being researched. It is more enjoyable and more personally rewarding.

Jodi Gregory

Healthcare Industry Monitoring

Jodi Gregory is President of Access Information Services, offering customized research and analysis to support clients' business decisions, as well as the Nightwatch enterprisewide alert service. Based in Dayton, Ohio, Jodi brings more than fifteen years of research experience to serve niche markets in the healthcare, consumer products, and utility industries. She is a frequent speaker at healthcare and information industry conferences.

jgregory@accessinform.com
www.accessinform.com

Jodi, can you give me an overview of your background and how you came to be an independent information business owner?

My first experience with information research came when I was employed at LexisNexis [69, see Appendix], doing sales and training medical professionals on how to use their online databases. I was traveling extensively and decided to start a family and change my working situation. I stayed in touch with a lot of customers in my job and, although we were teaching them to use the service on their own, they liked having someone available who had searching expertise on the system. So when I left LexisNexis, I already had clients asking me to provide information research services.

Did you spend a lot of time planning to go into business on your own? Or did it just happen one day?

Actually, it did just kind of happen one day. It wasn't something I necessarily planned on doing, but the situation seemed right. I had the customers and I had the time, so I decided to pursue the opportunity.

What's your educational background? Were you trained in information research?

My degree is in health information management, which gave me a strong knowledge of the healthcare industry. I taught medical terminology at the community college level and worked as a medical transcriptionist while in school. So when I decided what niche to cover, healthcare was an obvious choice because it enabled me to leverage my background along with my information research skills.

Working for a company like LexisNexis, you undoubtedly took fine-tuned online research skills into your business. Was anything else in your employment relevant or helpful to what you do today?

I started my business in 1988, but I actually took some time off from being self-employed. I was asked to set up and manage a virtual library doing business research on companies for the Air Force. Working from home, I started part-time with the library, setting it up and managing it while keeping the small number of clients I had at that time. Almost immediately, the library work became a full-time job that lasted a few years. This experience enabled me to become familiar with providing research for a fee, setting up a virtual library, and working with contract negotiation.

Let's talk about the logistics of getting started. I know you maintain a home office. How did you go about setting that up? What kind of equipment did you need to get going?

I started with what I felt I minimally needed, so there wasn't a huge investment. That included the best computer I could afford, two telephone lines, a two-line telephone, and subscriptions to online services. I set up shop in the family room of our home with computer equipment, and as it became necessary, I would add things like a fax machine. My children would often be watching TV in the room as I was working. We had an arrangement that, if the business line rang, everybody would batten down the hatches and be quiet while I was on the phone. At least I attempted to make that happen. It was difficult, but I did it that way for quite a long time because of the space in our home. That was what was required to get the job done.

You probably made great use of nap time.

Absolutely! And I worked late at night.

So even though you started without a designated office space, you made it work. What were the advantages and disadvantages of operating from home?

Flexibility was and continues to be the greatest advantage. I could attend events with my children and be with them before they were of school age. Now that they are older, I can work around their activity schedules. In the very beginning, when I didn't have as much confidence as I do now, I worried about telling people that I was working from home and did my best to minimize that appearance. It was something that I didn't necessarily want my clients to know for fear that they would discount my professionalism or my skills. But as I gained confidence, it wasn't as important. I developed a great relationship with all my clients and contacts. They valued the service I provided, so it just didn't matter where I worked—as long as I delivered for them.

That's a common answer. I hear from people that it used to be something they mostly tried to hide. And the worst things always happen when you're on the phone. I once burned a bagel in the toaster. My smoke alarm was going off, and I just tried to ignore it for as long as I could.

One time I was on a really important call with a key client. I could hear my son faintly calling "Mom. Mom!" But I'm on this call and I can't get off and I'm thinking it's a routine thing that I can handle when I hang up. Finally, my daughter came running in and said, "You have to come. You *really* have to come outside." And there he was stuck way up high in a tree. I mean *way* up. I went up after him, but got stuck myself. We eventually had to call a fireman friend to get us both down.

That's a great story. Did you get more work from that client?

Yes. In fact, it's a client I still have today. I can laugh about it now.

When you launched your business, did you consult with an attorney or an accountant, or seek any other type of professional advice?

Yes, I've always believed it is important to have an understanding of all that is involved before I make any major business decisions. In fact, I have been thinking recently about hiring someone to work for me, so I called my attorney. He said, "Jodi, you are an A-plus client," because I always ask him for advice up front before I do anything. Apparently, most of his clients call when they have a problem instead of consulting with him ahead of time. I think it's a very important investment and I have not regretted it, because it helps me make better decisions.

It sounds like you have an attorney that understands your business as well as the information business, so you can get good advice on liability issues and that kind of thing.

I've actually used three different attorneys in the years that I've been self-employed, because, as my business has changed, so have my legal needs. Right now, I have a lot of contracts. I'm creating a product that requires not only information research, but also actually licensing part of the content for redistribution, and all that requires special expertise. I've constantly updated my portfolio of professionals so that they continue to meet my changing needs.

I think it's important to find people you work well with and enjoy. My attorney has a great sense of humor, but he's serious about helping me. The same goes for my accountant. He's very flexible and shows me the range of options available, as well as both sides of a decision. He might say, for instance, "Here's what some of my clients do. But here's what I recommend." I follow his advice, but I appreciate knowing what the limitations are.

You went into business as an expert online searcher. What about the running-a-business side? Did you feel a need to take any courses or read up on management?

I read online information industry journals, and the trade journals read by my clients, but I did not attend any small business seminars or anything like that. There just wasn't time in my situation. I continue to hone my online skills and take courses in that area. I've also tried to keep my general computer expertise up to date—mostly by practicing and working on my own.

Your business began with the most important ingredient for success—clients. How did you find more of them?

When I was at the Air Force library, we were so successful in doing business research that we gained tremendous credibility and created a fee-based aspect to the library, where we would be hired for specific research projects. Nobody else in our local area was doing that, and our reputation quickly grew. So, when I decided to go back to full-time in my own business, I could build on that network of relationships. I still have some of those clients to this day.

Over the years, I've worked really hard to keep my professional relationships intact and to stay in contact with colleagues. I attend the same types of organizational meetings my clients attend, such as the Special Libraries Association (SLA) [201] and professional healthcare and marketing association conferences. My clients see me in other contexts, too. The relationships I've developed as a result of this investment have been instrumental in finding new clients.

If you're being introduced to someone for the first time, how do you describe your services? Do you have a polished 30-second spiel?

I try to tailor my response to my audience. If I'm talking to someone in the insurance industry, for instance, I find out what they do in their job and then offer an example of what I could do for them, such as tracking the activities of their competitors. That seems to work best in helping me clearly communicate what I do and how I might be able to assist a particular audience.

Your Web site for Access Information Services shows that you serve target markets in healthcare, consumer products, and utilities.

Do you feel that niche markets are the way to go, as opposed to being a generalist?

I think it's very important to specialize, rather than trying to meet all the needs of a more diverse market. For one thing, you gain so much knowledge that you can build upon every time you do new research. It takes less time to get up to speed. Occasionally I will accept a request to provide information outside my expertise, but working from my knowledge base is much more efficient and I can add much more value for my customers. When I get a request outside my niche markets these days, I'm more apt to get help from another independent information professional who specializes in that particular area. They will have the knowledge that gets the job done in an efficient way and at a reasonable cost.

Otherwise you're billing for learning curve time.

If my client wants me to do work outside my specialty, then that learning curve becomes an expected part of the billable project time. But if I know of another independent information professional who can meet their need, I will likely subcontract with them to perform the work, or will refer my client to them. I tend to collaborate much more now than I did in the beginning when I thought I had to do everything myself.

You've also been marketing a service called Nightwatch. Can you talk about that? I know there's a literal side to the name of that service, too, as you tend to be a night owl.

That's correct, and that is just how the name came to be. A friend called me one night and said, "Are you on the night watch again?" Most people who know me well know that I do stay up late.

Nightwatch started because of a client for whom I was doing a daily news briefing. This news briefing had an internal brand within the company and became extremely valuable to my client and the company. It was filtered information—very filtered and very targeted. I know a lot about the business they're in, and I'm kept informed on the company's strategic direction. This enables me to very effectively filter information for them. The news briefing became very popular. As people left that company, they would call me at their new company and say, "I'd like you to do this for me." And as I began to present the concept at conferences, it took on a life of its own.

How is it different from a standard alert service on one of the professional online systems, or the ones that anybody can get on the Web now?

Our Nightwatch briefings have a very narrow focus. Each is filtered and targeted to the specific needs and interests of a particular company. A human being with a unique knowledge of the business is doing the filtering, rather than technology. This saves time because, unlike a computer, I can make a discerning decision to ensure clients aren't reading information that may be on the same topic, but not applicable to what they are doing.

The other important element is the format. Nightwatch has a unique format that enables my clients to read the headlines quickly and follow up with the full text if they're interested. This allows the news briefing to serve the whole company, while enabling different individuals to choose only the pieces that apply to their jobs.

The third element that makes the product successful is that it comes out daily and integrates all the sources the client would normally read in print, across their desktops via an intranet or online. For each client, we do a survey of what sources of information employees rely on to stay informed. By integrating key information from each of these sources into Nightwatch news briefings, they can more quickly glean what is of value from electronic sources or the periodicals that might be sitting in their in-boxes on their desks untouched for weeks. At the same time, they also realize cost savings by eliminating duplicative subscriptions.

So you've been able to replicate what you did for one company into a product that you could offer to other companies. Interesting. Is Nightwatch taking a large chunk of your time now?

Yes. In the beginning, my business was more project-based. With Nightwatch, I'm now also developing a product that, in turn, leads to even more projects. This is a wonderful problem, but what I'm finding is that in order to grow this new business, I need professional research help for the first time since I formed my own company.

As a speaker at numerous healthcare and information industry conferences, could you share an example of a presentation you might give and how that helps your business?

Most of the time, I speak at the information industry conferences on some aspect of online research, such as searching the Web. I've done intranet development projects for clients, so I speak on that as well. I've also been called upon to speak on career alternatives for my early profession of health information management, because I have really changed the direction of my career since I started in that field. The visibility always helps my business and helps me establish credibility.

Which professional online systems do you subscribe to? And what do you look for in subscription-based services as opposed to on the Web?

It's more a question of what *don't* I subscribe to. Because I do business research and a lot of my clients are in business development and marketing, I subscribe to the tried-and-true: Dialog [35], LexisNexis, and Factiva [39], and I use those heavily. I also subscribe to some online services that provide venture capital or new technology information, such as Venture Source [132] and Knowledge Express [66]. I rely heavily on analyst reports, so I subscribe to Intelliscope [63]. Quite often, I manage online information provider contracts on behalf of my clients, so I may not have a subscription, per se, but I use their passwords to do the research. These providers are typically niche vendors in the healthcare industry, such as Medical Data International [78].

How has the rapid growth of the Internet impacted your business? Do you think it has raised people's information awareness and helped position you in the sea of information?

My client requests start at a much more knowledgeable level than they used to. They are doing some initial research on their own and, in most cases, that's helpful to me. But it's added more on the tail end, where I'm doing more analysis. The Internet has given my clients a realization of how much is out there, so the importance of filtering it and targeting it to their needs has become my emphasis. I think it's actually contributed to increasing my business. Quite often, I will get a request in which a client says, "Well, I looked for this company on the Web and I didn't find much." If they want something from the Web and I'm able to find what they couldn't, it increases their appreciation for my expertise.

What do you look for on the open Web? What is of value to you there?

The Internet is great for getting up to speed on many things— even something as simple as the correct spellings of words and how people are using specific terminology. But it doesn't eliminate my need to go to the commercial online systems. I make sure that searching on the Web doesn't take away from my efficiency just because I might get something at no cost; my time is important, too. I'm very careful to try to balance that. I have a self-imposed time limit as to how long I'll look on the Web before I'll go to a commercial source and get what I need there.

Do you have any favorite search engines or sites that you rely on?

The Association of Independent Information Professionals (AIIP) [172] has experts in this area. I follow their advice to find the most effective search engines. I continue to love Google [53] as a search engine, especially if I'm looking for a specific page. I also use Query Server [103] for broad searches, but I'm always changing to others as they are developed. Two of my favorite sites are CEO Express [21] and MD Express [77]. I like the fact that they are jam-packed with links I use all the time.

Do any of your projects raise the need for manual research in libraries or special collections? Would this be the kind of thing you would subcontract out?

I did go to the library myself in the beginning, and I think it's very important to have a book in your hands every now and then, but I tend to subcontract out manual research a lot more than I used to.

Does your work entail any telephone research? Or is this also something you would contract out?

Again, although I did my own in the beginning, I primarily sub that out now. My business has risen to the level where I cannot personally do everything. There are professionals within AIIP who do telephone research really well, so now I tend to subcontract out this and other aspects of manual research. This speeds the process along since multiple research tasks can be done at the same time. It also allows me to take on more business than my time alone would permit.

As far as your pricing is concerned, it sounds like you have long-term contracts and you've developed a system for that. If somebody were to come to you as a new client, would you work on an hourly rate or by the project?

Most of the time now when I accept new work, it is on a per-project basis. Some projects that are either long term or that I've negotiated to pay in advance might be based on an hourly rate. It depends on how long the contract is and whether it's just a simple project. But either way, I always build in flexibility.

Are you finding that most of your work goes out electronically these days? Do you have any clients that still like hard-copy reports?

Almost exclusively, my clients' preference now is for electronic reports. In most cases, if I send something out in print, it's because I want the client to have a nice copy in their hands, since I've found that is what they will show other people. And this often leads to more business. I think the hard-copy report tells a better story. Maybe that's my love of books coming out. It's surprising how many times I've received new projects because somebody said, "I saw this report you did for my colleague and I'd like you to do something like that for me."

Can you describe a typical project and what kind of information you might find?

One of my clients provides a weekly report to their board of directors that shows how they are meeting their business plan goals. They need to forecast what their revenue will be, so I provide the external information to show why they are or are not meeting their goals. They have internal information, on, for example, whether they have backorders on a product or manufacturing is lagging behind schedule, which would change their forecast. My part is providing external information. I might find out about their competitors who are releasing a competitive product earlier than anticipated, which would affect their anticipated market share. Or I might find that their competitor's product has met regulatory approval earlier than theirs.

Does that take you into the patent literature? Where do you find that kind of information most readily?

Patent literature is one component, but I also track regulatory developments since there is a heavy regulatory component to the healthcare and medical device industries, where I do the bulk of my work. It means watching Food and Drug Administration (FDA) and Healthcare Finance Administration (HCFA) approvals and regulations, for instance. It also means watching the market and knowing what their competitors are doing in terms of anything that impacts their sales. For example, changes in a rival company's sales force might indicate they have greater penetration into the market. I might pick up that information in a press release or by monitoring job recruitment efforts at a competitor's Web site.

In terms of marketing your services, what do you find most effective?

I have not chosen to market myself by going to trade shows or sending direct mail. I would recommend that people just starting out commit themselves to spending a little time each day marketing themselves. This may take the form of becoming involved in organizations where their potential clients are active, or writing a newsletter to send to potential clients. What I do is build my relationships with both existing and potential clients, which leads to word of mouth business from their contacts. I think about my customers constantly. For example, if I see something that's of interest to a particular client, even though they haven't contracted with me to do repeated updates, I go ahead and send it to them. It doesn't take too much of my time or incur much cost, but it keeps them aware that I'm out there. Very often, they'll respond with an email and say, "Hey that's great. By the way, I have something else we're going to be working on. Would you talk to us about it?" Those little things really contribute to the expansion of my business more than anything else. Networking and staying in touch with clients and with other information research providers have been important keys to success for me over the years.

How do you regard your Web page? Do you feel you've gotten any business from it, or is it just a matter of necessity?

It's primarily there to give me a presence on the Internet. In the early days, I designed and built my own site, and didn't think too much about getting clients that way. But I've found that people really do look at it, so it became important to have it look good and be professionally done. I don't know that I've gotten that many clients from it, but it enables potential clients to be knowledgeable about my services before we talk for the first time.

I like to pinpoint how independent information professionals can be most effective for clients. Looking at your Web site, I saw that for one of your projects you actually measured cost savings per employee that your work provided to the client.

Oh, I can't tell you how important that was! In fact, when I renegotiated my contract with that client, I could validate the cost of my services and show them how it was saving them money to work with me as an independent information researcher.

How did you actually do the measurement?

In this particular case, I surveyed the people who received the information and asked them how much they thought it helped, compared with trying to do it on their own by searching the Web. I asked them how much time they thought it would have taken them, quantified that, and was able to show how much money it saved to have me do the work at my rate. We were able to show such a cost savings that renewing the contract was easy. It was amazing.

Now, shifting gears a bit, how do you keep it all together? Working from your home. Parenting. I like the fact that I can get my kids on the school bus, throw in some laundry, get dinner started, make a few calls, and get to work all within an hour, but sometimes it's overwhelming.

I try to make a conscious effort to partition my time so that one life doesn't overlap the other, but sometimes I'm not too successful at managing that. While the flexibility is important and, sure, I can throw a load of laundry in while I'm waiting on a report to download, I do find that when you're self-employed, there's often little to no time left for yourself. It's very difficult to say, "Okay, I'm done for the day," and my passion for the work and my personality make it even more difficult. I enjoy it so much that sometimes I don't want to stop. I try to consciously say every day, "Okay, this is the time for my business and *this* is the time for my home life." But it's one of my biggest challenges, especially as the business has grown.

Do you have any favorite timesaving devices? Are you constantly wired?

Oh, absolutely. I'd say my three most important tools are a laptop computer, Palm Pilot, and cell phone. I take the computer along wherever I go, but my most important device has become the Palm Pilot. I absolutely love it. I meet personally with a lot of my clients and it helps me keep everything straight while I'm mobile. I use my cell phone quite a bit, too, and roll over my office line to that while I'm out. I have a headset, so if I'm driving, I'm as safe as I can be. I maximize my time—I don't have any down time during the day.

Does anything just plain funny or unusual come to mind that you've been asked to do for a project?

I did have one that was a particular challenge, and I had a great time with it. It was a request from a man who had heard about the work I do and was looking for a Christmas gift for "the person who had everything." This friend was a race car driver and the man had seen an advertisement on TV for a product that you could spray in a car and it would immediately cool down the interior. He wasn't sure where he had seen the ad, but thought it had been in Bermuda or Trinidad. He suggested it might have some applications for military, which was my only clue. So I started looking at military Web sites, thinking about cooling off the inside of an army tank, and came up with nothing. But then the passion got ignited and I was determined to find this product. And thanks to my tenacity, I kept at it. I finally found a reference to a company in the United Kingdom that made a product like the one he had described, and it turned out to be the very thing he had seen. Now it's being marketed as a product that people can use on themselves, but it was initially created to cool down the interior of a car.

What a great story. It sounds like you're one of those people who loves the thrill of the hunt.

I do and, in this case, it definitely became a personal quest to find the answer.

"Living with more information than we can absorb" is a marketing angle for us as independent researchers, but it hits us personally and professionally, too. How do you stay updated and informed at a level where you feel comfortable?

I'm finding it more and more difficult to stay up on the reading that I've always done. I do it whenever I get a chance, so when other people are reading a novel on a plane, I'm very often reading information industry publications. Attending conferences has been my biggest advantage. I make time for the travel, and keeping in touch with colleagues helps tremendously. I tend to call upon others for help quite often. So instead of trying to update myself on something, I think, "Who do I know that might have the answer to this, or might know how I should go about this?" I'd say the networking component of this industry and of AIIP has been more valuable than anything. I think reading is important and I believe it's what helped me get where I am today, but as I grow the business, I have less time to do that. So I call upon my colleagues for help more often.

As a niche researcher, you're trying to monitor the healthcare industry as well as the information industry.

Yes, I need to watch both.

What associations do you belong to? What electronic discussion lists do you subscribe to?

I think the most important is AIIP, and I subscribe to their private discussion list [146]. I belong to SLA and am on two of their discussion lists, from the Business & Finance [157] and

Pharmaceutical [160] divisions. I'm also on BUSLIB-L [148] and MEDLIB-L [152]. I belong to the Society of Competitive Intelligence Professionals (SCIP) [199], and I'm also a member of the American Health Information Management Association (AHIMA) [167].

Do you attend any local chamber of commerce or other business organization meetings?

Yes, I'm a member of the Dayton Chamber of Commerce [179] and participate in a local chapter of the Medical Marketing Association (MMA) [167].

In a typical year, which conferences do you attend?

AIIP and SCIP, for sure. I'm doing a lot of work on healthcare e-commerce, so I attend E-Healthcare World [180]. In the healthcare industry, there are several medical technology conferences I attend, including those sponsored by Medtech Insight [192] and IHS—Emerging Medical Technologies [188]. I also participate in two local Fast Company [183] meetings, which are geared toward people in start-up company situations.

Sounds like although you work at home, you mix with high-energy, idea-generating types of people.

Yes, and I need that, because I'm really not an extrovert at all. I have to make myself participate more. It would be easy for me to stay secluded in my home office, but I don't have as much success when I do that as I have when I'm networking with people. I make an effort to stay in touch not only with clients, but with people that I've worked with in the past. It is a great reason to go out to lunch!

It's that balance between working alone and not getting isolated…. What is your escape mode from databases and invoices? Surely you have one.

I'm working on that, because I've left behind a lot of my hobbies, which is not a good thing. I still love to read, so I'm trying to put aside the business publications more often and go back and read some of the classics that I've never read or want to read again. I mix that with fiction that I enjoy. And even though most of my time is spent in the electronic world, I still very much like the feel of writing with a pen on a piece of paper, so I make my own cards and write notes as much as I can. That's another way I try to stay in touch with people.

My daughter and I have taken up rubber-stamping and have gone to classes together. I like doing that because you have a finished product at the end.

That's the business owner in you talking: Look, I came home with a finished product from my leisure time!

Yes, when you're running your own business, it's not that easy to start and finish projects outside of work—whether it's painting a room or doing needlepoint!

Any advice or reflections you might have for the aspiring independent information professional?

Get into the habit of managing your time wisely. While this seems obvious, it is easy to get bogged down in your work and find out you aren't being profitable. You have to be flexible and you have to be fast. Shorter deadlines are emerging as a trend. Very rarely are people planning weeks ahead for projects.

Know when to get help. It was hard for me to have confidence that I could really sustain my business early on. I would take on more than I could handle. It took me awhile to figure out the value of collaborating with others and how this would help grow my business. Meeting your commitments to your client is more important than doing all the work yourself, even if you occasionally have to break even on a project because you are in over your head and you need to get help. What's important in sustaining the business is having your clients come back. And while it's efficient to have a broad range of clients, it's also efficient to retain clients, because there's less of a learning curve working with people you know.

Have confidence in the value you provide your customer. In the very beginning, I underestimated my worth to the customer, so I probably undervalued a lot of my work.

What do you see for the future?

I see a bright future, but one that will continue to challenge us to find new ways to utilize our skills and add value for our customers. Overall, I think our reputation is growing beyond the information industry. Other professionals are more aware of independents and of the value we can provide to their organizations.

Super Searcher Power Tips

➤ At first I worried about telling people that I was working from home and did my best to minimize that appearance. I didn't necessarily want my clients to know for fear that they would discount my professionalism or my skills. But as I gained confidence, it was not as important.

➤ If I'm talking to someone in the insurance industry, for instance, I find out what they do in their job and then offer an example of what I could do for them—such as tracking the activities of their competitors.

➤ I've constantly updated my portfolio of outside professionals so that they continue to meet my changing needs. I think it's important to find people you work well with and enjoy. My attorney has a great sense of humor, but he's serious about helping me.

➤ I collaborate with colleagues much more now than I did in the beginning, when I thought I had to do everything myself.

➤ Unlike a computer, I can make a discerning decision to filter information so that it is targeted to the specific needs and interests of a particular client.

➤ I make sure that searching on the Web doesn't take away from my efficiency just because I'm trying to get something at no cost; my time is important too.

➤ In most cases, if I send something out in print it's because I want the client to have a nice copy in their hands. That is what they will show other people, and this often leads to more business. I think the hard-copy report tells a better story.

➤ What's important in sustaining the business is having your clients come back. While it's efficient to have a broad range of clients, it's also efficient to retain clients, because there's less of a learning curve working with people you know.

Martin Goffman

Intellectual Property and Patents

Martin Goffman is Principal of Martin Goffman Associates, a full service business and technical research organization established in 1985. Based in Edison, New Jersey, MGA specializes in science, technology, engineering, market intelligence, and intellectual property issues and offers expert patent research services. Dr. Goffman is also the CEO of StockPricePredictor, LLC [122, see Appendix], which provides automated patent valuations.

mgoffman@goffman.com
www.goffman.com

Marty, let's begin with your background. Can you tell me a little about what you did before you started your business?

I have a Ph.D. in chemistry from Temple University, and worked for twenty years in the metals and mining industry as a chemist initially, later as a section head, and then with patent attorneys on the licensing of new technologies, some of them my own inventions. I learned to program computers and interface laboratory instruments. I learned online searching during the early days of Dialog [35] and Chemical Abstracts Services Online [22].

How was your experience in the corporate world valuable to your work as an independent?

I think that my science background, particularly my chemistry and physics training, helps me understand the technologies involved in my work. My laboratory research skills certainly helped me understand the analysis, synthesis, and integration of data.

What made you want to make the move into your own business?

I was with the same employer for twenty years; I wanted to be on my own. I was always treated well by my employer, but there is a point where you realize, "I've got to go with my own instincts. I don't want a boss anymore. I want to make it on my own." And I reached that point. So I said, "I'm going to leave." There's something that just comes over you, and you have to give it a shot. I gave a one-year notice to my employer so that others could be trained in the technology used in my inventions, so that the company could continue to license my inventions.

You started your business in 1985. What did you do logistically to get going? How did you set up shop?

I could do nothing to help launch my business before leaving the corporate world because of contractual obligations. Once I left, I designed and built an office in the back of my house so that it would be exactly what I wanted. I had beams holding up bookshelves because I didn't want them to sag, lots of room—which I outgrew rather quickly—storage space, file cabinets, and multiple desks. I had a place for the fax machine and the copier and all the computers. Everything was organized exactly how I wanted it. It matched the way I worked.

Do you enjoy having your office at home? Does that work well for you?

I love it. I tried having an office outside the house at one point, and found that I really resented the time that it took to get there and back home. The round trip was only thirty to forty minutes, but commuting wasn't something that I liked to do. I love having my office at home, but it's not for everybody. It takes a certain discipline.

When you were setting up, did you seek out professional advice to launch your business? Did you take any specialized training?

I used both an attorney and an accountant. I did a lot of studying on the law and accepted accounting practices. I wrote a business plan and I kept it up to date. I took all kinds of training. I took IRS courses for federal and state tax issues, I took vendor training, and I took patent law courses so I would understand the patent law even better than I did when I started. I was also very, very fortunate in having a computer scientist work with me to teach me additional computer and programming skills. We did a lot of work on computerization of the laboratory organization. I already had years of experience in the integration of laboratory instrumentation with computers, years before laboratory automation was commonplace.

What do you recall about the early days and how you got your first client?

Well, most people who start a business start the business while they are still working. The thing is this: I don't think that anyone will be a success if they try to go into this business part time. I honestly believe that, with a very, very firm conviction. I didn't do anything for my business before I actually quit my job. I had given my employer a lot of notice because of the nature of the work that I was doing for them. It was important that they knew well in advance in order to get other people lined up to replace me. And when I started my business, I started my business. That's what I devoted all of my time to. There were no other distractions.

I didn't really know how to get clients. I don't think anybody does when they start their business. And what I did, I realize now, was probably all of the wrong things, but the important thing is that it worked for me. I sent out a marketing letter to thirty-eight laboratories detailing how I thought I could help them increase their business. And in that letter, I remember clear as a bell, I said I'm really too busy to call you back and follow up. If you want to talk to me, you've got to call me. Ten of the thirty-eight people called! And out of those ten, four became my clients. I still believe to this very day that the six that did not become clients were simply trying to pick my brains without ever spending their money. The other four who became clients remained with me for a long, long time. I don't know if that was the right way to do it, but it certainly worked for me. I never had to look back.

How do you describe your business today and the services you offer? I know you generally market yourself as a patent and intellectual property researcher.

Basically I do scientific and technical searching with a specialty in patent searching. But along with that, because of the nature of this product, I do competitive intelligence. Sometimes I'm able to predict with pretty fair accuracy what's coming or likely to come down the pipeline. The arrival of certain technologies in many cases foretells the arrival of certain products or services. The main focus is still patent work and the peripheral aspects of that.

It requires a strong technology background to do a good job. You have to understand the technology in order to understand what could validate or invalidate a patent. That's one of the reasons that I took a patent law class, to learn what is prior art and the whole process of seeking a patent. Searching for prior art can be a difficult and daunting process. Sometimes there's a lot more than meets the eye. Novice searchers in many cases miss the art altogether and give their clients reports that are far from complete. Of course the client has no way to know this and accepts the search results as complete and accurate. That's a disservice to the client and can lead to litigation.

Looking at patent research as a discipline, I've heard that about eighty percent of the information in a patent document is not published anywhere else, so that's a valuable source of information.

That's true. That's a statement from a company called Derwent [34], which is one of the premier publishers of patent databases and literature. And it's correct, because—with certain exceptions—if you publish elsewhere first, you're not going to get a patent. So people won't publish that kind of information in any other medium. The other reason is that a lot of details are given in the patent itself that a journal article, for instance, would rarely include. Patents have to give what is called the enablement information. To satisfy section 112 of the 1952 Patent Act, the specification must enable a person of ordinary skill in the art to make and use the invention. When you read a patent, by law, the inventor must supply details on how to make the invention. And that's critical! Therefore, you're going to get the kind of information that you may or may not get in the scientific literature. Patents also include a lot of nuances about the experimental phase that are sometimes omitted in the journal literature. Sometimes more experimental information is included in the journal articles. You never know in advance.

I understand that there are no actual terminology guidelines for the full-text portion of a patent, so the inventor can use whatever words they want to describe their invention.

Absolutely. The law says that the applicant or the inventor is free to be their own lexicographer, which means you can make up your own terms, as long as you use them consistently throughout the patent document. That's one of the reasons why it's so difficult to search patents with free-text searching, as opposed to having to draw from a thesaurus of controlled vocabulary words. Nobody uses the same terms. You'll never—well, almost never—find a *table* described as a *table*. They'll probably say something like "a planar surface with three or four perpendicular members." Or they might talk about a stabilizer member, and it turns out it's a table. If you searched for the word "table" you'd never find that particular patent.

So that's one of the reasons that free-text searching is not a good way to go. And that's why you want someone with a technical background doing patent work. All is not lost, however. There are lots of other techniques that patent searchers use. There are class codes, subclasses, and other subtle ways to search the patent literature, to find those "hidden" patents that you need to locate.

Can you talk about patent research from a competitive intelligence point of view? Years back I did a bit of patent literature searching, looking at the products of a competitor of the company I was working for, and they were thrilled with the information I found for them. They could see the actual ingredients in a competitive lubricant product that they had always wondered about.

It's always a good source of competitive intelligence information because valuable intellectual property will be patented, for sure—although, as usual, there are exceptions; some valuable technology is kept as a trade secret. Because of the patent literature, you can also define areas that companies are working on currently. Companies change their focus, and one of the best ways to find out how they're changing their focus is, in fact, by examining the patent literature and looking at the patent applications coming out of a company.

By doing that, you can also look for other companies doing research in the same area. In some cases you will find good merger and acquisition information. They may not be direct competitors, and you may find that they seek what you seek, and that an alliance with them would make a lot of sense.

Sometimes you'll see where some of the work that a company is doing is very different from what they normally do. It's not their main line of business, and the executives of the company may in fact have already made the decision to spin it off and form a separate company. We all know that this is what happened at AT&T; it spun off Lucent. And it made sense for them to do that.

So it's that kind of thing—through the patent literature, you see a company's action plan, and it just doesn't make business sense. You wonder what they are doing with this, whether they are headed in that direction as a company, or are they in fact planning a merger or spinoff of that part of the company.

Do you think that a significant number of small or even medium-sized companies don't even know that this kind of information is out there, that this intelligence is available to them?

No, I think they do, actually. People are very intellectual-property savvy today. The small and medium-size technology companies put a terrific amount of money into intellectual property because it's the main asset that they have. And they really know what they're doing.

So you do not need to educate potential clients. It sounds like they are saying, "Let's just get this done."

Yes, I don't find that it makes a lot of sense anymore to tell people "you could do this, that, or the other." These people know. It's condescending to say, "Did you know...?" "Well," they think, "of course I know. Do you think I'm an idiot?"

Tell me more about the reasons to look in the patent literature. You mentioned infringement, validating or invalidating a patent, and so on.

Patents themselves are very, very valuable texts, describing inventions whose value runs into the tens and hundreds of millions of dollars. It's this intellectual property that people want to protect. Because of the steps involved in getting a patent, it's not an insignificant cost, especially for small and medium-sized companies. They can't afford to patent every idea that comes down the pike or that they are doing research on. But for those inventions that they do want to protect, they need to know that what they have invented is truly novel, so they need a novelty search or a patentability search. What happens if you don't do a preliminary novelty search, and five to seven years later you're wildly successful, making a lot of money, but you find that you are, in fact, infringing upon another company's patent? That's pretty disturbing news. The first thing that people will do at that point is say "I'm not infringing on your patent, and even if I am, your patent's not valid." That starts the next phase of the investigation, and that's a very costly stage. So what people try to do is avoid getting into that situation by doing a very, very intensive patentability search early on. One of the problems is that a lot of start-up companies don't have the money to do an exhaustive patentability search on the technology, so they take the risk and say, "We'll worry about that later, when we're making money."

We should mention that the patent literature is international in scope, so you're also looking at what products are being developed in other countries.

Without a doubt. You don't just search U.S. patents. Foreign patent documents used to be one of the early warning signs, because the rest of the world has always published eighteen months from the time of application. That used to be the fastest way to find out what was coming along, as they were laid open for public inspection sooner than patents in the United States. In the U.S., the patent application was kept secret, and opposition to the patent could only come up after it was issued. It was a much more difficult task. But now the U.S. publishes in eighteen months, like everyone else, with certain exceptions. So foreign patent searching is something that always needs to be done. I can't think of a case where foreign patents are not checked.

What kind of changes have you seen as a result of the Internet providing access to patent literature, particularly at the U.S. Patent and Trademark Office (USPTO)? Are you finding that people come along with more intelligent questions, perhaps having done a bit of the preliminary searching themselves?

I send a lot of people to the USPTO site [129] to do their own patent searches, especially when it's an individual inventor who doesn't have the means available to hire a professional searcher. In many cases those people aren't even aware that they can do that on their own. People who call me and simply want a copy of a patent, I will gladly send to those sites. It's a wonderful way to help people help themselves. And, in fact, I send them there quite deliberately. It's not that I don't want work from them, but

I wouldn't be doing them a service. Let's say an attorney calls and just needs a copy of patent number such-and-such. It's not worth my time to go and do it and bill the attorney, when I can tell him how to locate and download it himself in the same amount of time, which is about five minutes. They're generally very appreciative of that information and find that they can do it themselves very quickly and it's essentially free, and the good part from their point of view is they can bill that time to their clients. For me to download a patent document and send it to them is just not worthwhile. I don't think it's worthwhile for any searcher.

Another important aspect of letting people help themselves is that you're able to show inventors and others the kind of work that they *can't* do on the free databases on the Web. Most notable is the lack of indexing; this is why we pay human beings to look at patents and find out what a patent really says. We talked earlier about the inventor being his or her own lexicographer. Well, because of that, you'll look at the title of an invention and you'll have no idea what it is. A typical title might be simply "Surgical Instrument" or "Blood Pressure Instrument." In the abstract, the inventor still may not talk about what it is. The rule of thumb I like to use is that journal articles always want to be found. That is why the authors publish in the journal. Patents generally do *not* want to be found, and in many cases, the inventors will use language designed to make that patent very difficult to locate. That's why we as searchers depend on a human being skilled in the art, who reads the entire patent, goes "Aha, this is what this patent is really about," and assigns special indexing terms that we can use to find it in the commercial online databases.

Where do you go online, then, when you're searching patents at a professional level? What systems do you search and what do you find?

I search on almost all of the commercial systems. I subscribe to Dialog, STN [121]—which has the Holy Grail for chemists,

Chemical Abstracts—Dow Jones Interactive/Factiva [39], LexisNexis [69], and Orbit/Questel [92] to name a few. Certain databases available on each system contain information that another system won't have. In order to find a particular reference that will invalidate a patent, you may have to use any and all of those systems. In one case, I was able to invalidate a patent by finding an inventor who was looking for an investor. There was an article about his invention in the *Wall Street Journal* [136] before the patent was applied for, because he wanted the money to carry on the research. In that case, that was the damning reference that invalidated the patent.

That's a great example. Is there a place in the patent research field today for manual research?

Oh, absolutely. I still use manual collections. There's information in books that simply is not available online or in the patent office. You have to go to the library and find the information. For example, with techniques that are described in patents, you can find information in, say, medical textbooks that are twenty years old, describing the thing that an inventor is trying to do, which has already been tried. And that may have a bearing on the validity of a patent.

Looking at the USPTO site, I noticed that patents first began to be recorded in 1790. I would think that those old documents would provide a beautiful picture of human intellectual history, looking back at all that we have invented.

It does. And the USPTO site now has every patent back to the very first. You've got to be careful of the numbering system though, because the patent office burned down in the early 1800s, and they started to renumber the patents after that.

The last time I was seriously in the patent literature, around the early nineties, the talk was all about images coming online soon. Is that an important part of a patent search now?

When you get the patent online today, you can download the images. They're extremely helpful. I wish that I had that capability five or six years ago. Images are very, very helpful, especially in instrumentation and electrical circuits. It's very hard, without the picture, to understand just what's going on. The picture truly is worth a thousand words.

Where does a search of the open Web fit into your research arsenal? Is anything out there of value to your business?

Oh, almost all the time I search on the Internet. A lot of times I use it to get background material very quickly. Will I do a true patent search on the Internet? Of course not. But it is very useful. Today I don't think there's a case where I wouldn't go to the Internet to search for information and see what's out there. It may be helpful, it may not. But it's certainly worth a look. I have my favorite search engines and sites just like everyone else, but the Web is constantly changing and we have to adjust to these changes. I would guess that I never search the Internet twice the same way. The way I search depends on what I need and the topic of the search. There are no easy answers.

Does telephone interviewing or primary research have a place in your business?

When necessary, I will call people up, and I have in fact called inventors and asked them very specific questions. Sometimes I will call people who have worked in a particular field for a long time and ask questions related to art described in a patent. It's not a big part of my business. And in many cases my client will specifically prohibit me from discussing my work with anyone outside of my organization.

The nature of your work indeed requires strict adherence to so many client confidentiality issues, Marty, but can you give me a harmless example of a project that might come across your desk?

Well, I rarely deal with an independent inventor. It's not what I do. But one time this gentleman called me and had a new invention and wanted a search done. I sent him to the USPTO page to see if his invention is described in one of the patents there. He really wanted me to do the search and asked again if I would do it. I repeated that I don't do that kind of work, it's costly, and he could do it himself. He said he'd done what he could and really needed my help. So, reluctantly, I agreed to do it. He then sent me a one-paragraph description of his invention. I did the search and found seventy virtually identical inventions. One of them was right on the point of what he was doing. It happened to be a pet feeder—you know, for dog food. After I sent him the results, he said he hadn't found any of these. I asked what he had done, and he told me he'd typed into the PTO site "dog food feeder." Of course, none of the most relevant patents ever used the term "dog food feeder," so he missed all of them. Can I teach somebody to search patents in five minutes? No.

That's funny. I guess he learned something, though.

Yes, that was a good example. But in all fairness, most of my clients are very, very, very intelligent people, and very sophisticated. They're top-notch in their profession, but not at patent searching. My client might be the director of intellectual property for a company where their main asset is their intellectual property. These are savvy people. They know the value of a patent search, they're good at what they do, and they like to hire people who are good at what *they* do. And that's where I come in. In many cases, what I'll do and ultimately find is so far removed from what they had initially anticipated that they come back and say, "Boy, I never would have thought of that approach," or "I never would have found that." One patent attorney called me up and said, "Bless you; you really saved our behind." He was kind enough to call me because, in the patentability search on a test kit, similar to a pregnancy test kit, I had found out that the way they installed one component onto the swab infringed on another company's patent. It was very, very surprising to find the description in the other company's patent. But that's why he said "you really saved our behind," because it was so easy to miss. It was something that's not apparent when you're doing a search, but that emerges when you start to look at the claims of a patent.

Interesting. And fun, too, I'm sure. Now what about the daily grind of running a business—do you do everything yourself, or do you outsource any office tasks?

The mechanics of running the business has never, ever been a problem. I just do everything myself. With the right software, everything's quick and easy and there's really nothing special that I do. I'm not comfortable outsourcing any day-to-day operations.

You undoubtedly have proprietary concerns too, which outsourcing would complicate. Now, what about marketing? Is it still an issue for you after being in business so long?

It's basically word of mouth. I don't do any marketing per se. In a few cases, actually, the opposing counsel for patent cases that I was involved with have called me once the initial case has been resolved. So I get referrals from various people in various ways.

Your Web page contains quite a bit of information on your services. How do you view it in terms of its value?

I think the fact that I have a Web page is really important. I can't say that I get any business from the Web page, but I don't look at it that way. When people call to inquire about my company and say, "Can you send me a brochure?" in most cases I'll simply tell them go look at the Web page; there's more information there than they ever wanted to know. It saves me from having to sit down, type a letter, and send out a brochure in the mail.

And it can eliminate a lot of those initial "this is who I am and this is what I do" kinds of conversations.

I do get those, actually, from the Internet lookers. My regular client base never asks those questions. It's not a question that they would think to ask: "What do you do?" "Well, why did you call me?" It's the other people, who will pick up my name from the Internet; they may or may not have looked at the Web page carefully to get the answers to a lot of those questions.

Is client retention something that you consciously think about, or are you pretty much settled with ongoing business now?

I really don't do anything special in terms of client retention. I like to think that if I do a good job for my clients, they're going to call me back. And, in fact, when another case comes up, they will. I don't make phone calls because the people I deal with generally are extremely busy people. They don't need a call from me asking, "How are you doing?" They bill by the hour. Somebody in the licensing department or the patent department of a large company is usually pretty busy. Companies don't allow much time to chat. So I just don't feel comfortable calling to see how they are doing, and I never have. I don't send out emails either.

When they need me, they know where I am. So I don't do any of those things. It's just not what I do.

With your office at home, is working all the time an issue that you struggle with? Can you shut down and walk away at the end of the day?

I love having my office at home. I operate my business as a business. When I shut the door, the door is shut. I don't answer the phone late. And you know that I don't answer the phone early; I'm not awake. The phone literally does not ring in the house. I have to be in the office to hear the phone ring. I separate my home life from my business life. I have always done that. That's one of the reasons I built the office way in the back of my house; it's a separate space with thick, heavy doors. When I started the business, my son had just started college, one child was in high school, the other in middle school. And they knew that when Daddy was working, Daddy was working. My wife was home, which helped. So that was never an issue for them.

Are you a modern wired person running around with palm devices and various gadgets?

No, no. I just use one of those little books that people send in the mail that has a calendar for the year on it. I put my appointments in there and that's that. I don't keep a calendar on the computer, and I don't use any of the software that schedules your appointments or anything like that. I just write it in the little book, and hope that I'll remember to look in the book. I do have my cell phone with me all the time. That's the one thing I could not live without.

What about staying current, staying updated in your field? I imagine you're watching specific technical fields as well as the information field in general.

I do that in a number of ways. The main way I stay updated is by attending a lot of vendor training, and when there's a class on patent law I'll take that. Fortunately, I live in a major metropolitan area. There are a number of pharmaceutical companies, for example, in New Jersey that makes it worthwhile for every information vendor to offer classes here. I also read a number of computer journals and publications from pharmaceutical associations to stay abreast of new trends and emerging technologies. I constantly read the trade journals to see what's new and novel.

What associations do you belong to?

I belong to the Association of Independent Information Professionals (AIIP) [172], of course. I belong to the Association of Consulting Chemists and Chemical Engineers (ACC&CE) [171], the Patent Information Users Group (PIUG) [155], and I recently joined another organization called the Association of Internet Professionals (AIP) [173].

Do you participate in any electronic discussion lists?

I read the AIIP mailing list [146], the Patent Information Users Group (PIUG) list [155], the Chemical Information list (CHMINF) [149] and, regarding the environmental regulation of laboratories, I read the LIMSList [151].

Do you still have the inventor bug yourself? You must come into contact with so many interesting things in your work. I imagine your kids doing fantastic science projects when they were small.

I'm an entrepreneur; that's what I am. My business is what I have made it. So yes, in that sense, I have the inventor bug. I've recently started another business, StockPricePredictor, LLC, that provides patent valuations via the Web, as well as a list of the "Weekly Top Twenty" most valuable patents from among the roughly 3,000 to 4,000 United States Patents issued each Tuesday. This is available as a subscription-based service.

We all try to make our kids in our image, but it doesn't always work out that way. Except for my youngest daughter, who wanted to be a chemist just like Daddy, none of my children wanted to follow in my footsteps. My response to my youngest was "over my dead body." I never wanted any of my children to be a chemist because, at the time when they were young and talking about what they wanted to be when they grew up, chemists were often exposed to all kinds of fumes and birth defects and all of these horrible things that were associated with chemistry. I don't think I've ever gotten over that as a father, but as it turned out, it wasn't what any of my children wanted to do, anyway.

Fairly recently I was a judge in an elementary school science contest, and I was absolutely amazed at the creativity of these fourth, fifth, and sixth graders. These kids, I thought, were dynamite! They had done very creative things, but each one of them, without exception, had also gone to the USPTO site and done a search to see if anyone else had already invented something similar to their project. I thought that was absolutely amazing. Every one had gone to the library, every one had drawn up a description of their invention, they knew what the invention was, they had pictures, they had the enabling technology to say how they did it, as well as the searching experience. So, I think there are children out there who truly have the inventor bug.

What do you see for the future of the independent information business? You probably have some strong feelings about being a niche researcher.

I see a growing need for the information broker, and I don't have a problem with the term "information broker." It's too bad that others have used the term in an inappropriate manner. People are going to find that the talent of searching is not unique. That is where we're going to need to change; the ability to search per se is not going to be in very high demand. The ability to analyze what we find *will* be. I'm not talking in terms of the reams of information that we get online. I mean the ability to go and focus on a particular issue, and pinpoint what somebody actually wants. People don't want a lot of information. They want an answer to their question.

The people who will make money are people who are experienced and trained both as information brokers and in another field. The problem is that this seems like a job that everybody would want to do. People want to see what an information broker does and make money at it while they still have their original job; basically they want to have their cake and eat it too. I think some people are going into this business with the wrong set of desires, and that bothers me; it always has.

I've told a number of people who have called me for advice, very candidly, that the way to be a success is to be really, really hungry. I was hungry. I left my job voluntarily to start my business. There was no other income. I had a wonderful, loving, supportive wife and I had three young children who were dependent on me, living at home. If I didn't make a living, we didn't eat. It was that simple. One son had just started college and the two younger ones were to follow in a few years.

The fact that you're confident that you're going to make it on your own—that in itself makes you halfway successful. I've seen too many people within our own organization, AIIP, who say that they like to go to the library and read, so they'll become an information broker. By doing that, they're telling me that they're not really committed to the business. They're looking to make it a hobby. That is going to be the key to their demise. I tell people to stop fooling around; quit your job and make the effort. I don't know everyone in the organization, of course, but of the people who started out at night and on weekends "developing the business," as they say, until they're ready to go full time, I don't see a lot of them still in the business. That's why I say that, once you truly make the commitment, you will be successful.

Super Searcher Power Tips

➤ Most people who start a business start it while they are still working. I don't think anyone will be a success if they try to go into this business part time.

➤ I sent out a marketing letter to thirty-eight laboratories detailing how I thought I could help them increase their business. I said "I'm really too busy to call you back and follow up. If you want to talk to me, you've got to call me." Ten of the thirty-eight people called! And out of those ten, four became my clients.

➤ I'm able to predict with pretty fair accuracy what's coming or likely to come down the pipeline. The arrival of certain technologies in many cases foretells the arrival of certain products or services.

➤ Companies change their focus, and one of the best ways to find out how they're changing their focus is by using the patent literature and looking at the patent applications coming out of a company.

➤ What happens if you don't do a preliminary novelty search and you find, five to seven years later, that you're wildly successful, making a lot of money, but infringing upon another company's patent?

➤ People don't want a lot of information. They want an answer to their question.

➤ By letting inventors and others do their own simple patent searching, you're able to show them what they can't do on the free databases on the Web. Most notable is the lack of indexing, which is why we pay human beings to look at patents and find out what they really say.

➤ When people call to inquire about my company and ask for a brochure, in most cases I'll simply tell them go look at my Web page; there's more there than they ever wanted to know.

Lynn Peterson
The Craft of Public Records

Lynn Peterson is president of PFC Information Services, Inc., a public records research firm located in Oakland, California. PFC Information Services provides public records research for law firms, corporations, lenders, venture capitalists, employers, the media, and other information research firms.

lpeterson@pfcinformation.com
www.pfcinformation.com

Lynn, you've always said that if there is anything such as a traditional path in this business, you certainly did not follow one. Your background is unique. So tell me how you ended up in this nice, new office.

There was no grand plan to become an independent information professional by any means. It almost seems like a series of accidents along the way. But I was lucky enough to end up doing something with my life that I really love and feel that I'm good at. I don't think anyone would have deliberately laid out the path that I've taken, but I've been smart enough to know what I like and to seize opportunities as they've come my way.

I was an industrial engineer for ten years in the insurance industry, and that was an accident in itself. I graduated from UC Berkeley in 1974 with a bachelor's degree in history, and somebody that I graduated with got a job with an insurance company. She said, "Oh, Lynn, just get a job with an insurance company." So there I went. I got a job doing time-and-motion studies, which is really horrifying work where you're literally timing people with a stop-watch and trying to develop more efficient procedures for them to follow and determine how many workers are required to do a specific job. It was very numbing, very boring. I was also responsible for management of the documentation department in this insurance company, and so we did all the procedure manuals. I did always like the detail, and my department was responsible for the development of flow charts. And I love flow charts. I just adore them. So that should have been a clue.

Eventually I found myself the mother of one child and pregnant with twins. At that same time, the company that I was working for was merging with another company and my job was going south to LA. I had no intention whatsoever of moving to Los Angeles, nor of committing to a long commute. It just seemed like more than any human being could do.

Our twins arrived very early, and so it was a really hard time. I took some time off and then I had this brilliant idea that I would start my own business and I would have all this free time and flexibility and I could be home with my kids. Oh, brother, was I an idiot. I started a company called Prairie Home Companions, offering recruitment and placement services for nannies, care-givers, and housekeepers. I focused on bringing people from the Midwest out here to California, and while it was successful, it was very, very challenging. In retrospect, I must have been insane. It was hard putting people together in such an intimate way. When you hire someone to take care of your children and live in your home, that's really tough stuff. And as hard as I tried to make everybody happy all the time, it wasn't possible. It drove me crazy.

How long did you run that business?

I had that company for five years. I was fortunate enough to cross paths with a friend of my husband who was a private investigator. He was formerly an investigator with the District Attorney's office and also with the Public Defender, and when he heard about my business and how I was spending a lot of money having my background checks done by a company back in the Midwest, he said I could easily do that myself. I met with him and it became one of the friendships of my life, actually. He became my guru, my mentor, and my friend. He taught me everything I know about public records.

I had really enjoyed the research aspect of my business, and eventually an offer to buy the employment agency came along that I just couldn't refuse. I sold it but kept the quote-unquote "information business," which at that point was just conducting searches under the name of Prairie Home Companions, and decided to devote myself completely to learning about online information and public records. My private investigator friend walked me down to the courthouse and said, "This is where you find this, this is where you find that." So, by the seat of my pants, I started learning about public records. And I discovered that there was so much more out there in terms of information than simply what you might do in the context of a pre-employment background check. I got enthralled with information. But this is not the type of information research you can learn from a book, and there are no classes you could take that would possibly bring you up to speed on the work. Public records research is a craft, and you can only learn it through hands-on experience.

So you saw a different niche emerging, which was a piece of what you had already been doing.

Exactly. I had only been doing it in the context of screening our own applicants for employment. But I thought, wow, maybe there are other companies that would need background checks. That was my initial idea, and then I became aware of all the kinds of information out there, not just on individuals but on businesses. I was also lucky enough that, when I sold the first business, I had some capital so I could coast for a while.

When you started PFC Information Services, you already had the experience of running your own business. Were there any new concerns around setting up an office or needing professional advice?

Physically, everything was already pretty much set up. I worked out of a windowless room off the garage, and I really, really took the big plunge when I bought my state-of-the-art XT computer, and a fax and a phone. That was back in 1989, when this business was launched.

I have always believed that it is as important to know what you don't know as it is to know what you do know. Therefore, when I launched my business I recognized that I needed professional advice. I hired an attorney to draw up our client contract and to review our pre-employment forms for compliance with state and federal statutes. I also incorporated, took out Errors and Omissions insurance, and hired an accountant. I am a Hall-of-Fame worrier; setting up the business properly was absolutely essential to my peace of mind.

What do you recall about those early days and the first types of projects you did?

When I first started out, I was basically providing background checks to parents and other people who were hiring domestic help in their homes. But once the light bulb went off I got really excited about these other kinds of records that were out there. I remember signing up with CDB InfoTek [20, see Appendix], and I thought, "Wow, there's all this other stuff online from different states." I remember going to my hairdresser, and he was telling me a tale of woe about this terrible contractor whom he had hired to remodel his house. The guy took his money and didn't do the work, blah, blah, blah. And I said, "Well, gee, maybe I can help; maybe I could check him out"—because he couldn't even find the guy. And, oh, gosh, I found out that his contractor's license had been revoked, he didn't have a bond, and most importantly, I found out where he was. I thought that was so cool, and it inspired me to want to learn more.

Years later, I crossed paths with another person who was very pivotal in my life, and that was Sue Rugge. She taught me about the business of the information business. She taught me how to make money. And I'll forever be grateful to her. Prairie Home Companions had been a profitable business, but it was very labor-intensive and the profit factor was very small in proportion to the angst that I experienced with each one of the placements. Sue actually felt that I was underpricing my services, and she inspired me to swallow hard and raise my rates.

So tell me about how you crossed paths with Sue and how she became directly involved in your life.

It was in the early '90s, just about the time that the first edition of *The Information Brokers Handbook* [230] came out. Honestly, I was such an upstart, I don't know how I had the nerve to do this, but I found an ad that she had placed for the Rugge Group in a directory of the California Association of Licensed Investigators [175]. I'll never forget it; it said "We know where the bodies are buried—the bodies of information, that is." And I thought, wow, that sounds really interesting. And so, upstart that I was, I called her up, found out that she was in Oakland, asked her out for a cup of coffee, and tried to market my services to her. She turned the tables on me quickly, though, and signed me up for her Information Broker seminar and sold me her book.

How did that change things for you?

It inspired me. I mean, I didn't even know that there was a whole industry of information professionals out there. Here I was offering her my own little isolationist view of things, and she acquainted me with the larger universe. I was most appreciative of her willingness to hire me to do research. She tried me out. She had someone else that she'd been using, but she gave me a chance. I remember the first job that I did for her was locating some missing inventor. They were trying to invalidate a patent position, and this guy had written something fifteen years before about a particular kind of technology. All they had was this guy's name, and very little else to go on. I actually found the guy! She said, "Wow, this is great, I'm really impressed. You saved me an awful lot of work." I owe a lot to her for the help that she gave me, and she went on to become my biggest supporter.

That's a great story of your first business connection with Sue.

Yeah, I mean, who was I? I had no idea who she was. Had I known, I might have been too intimidated to call her up out of the blue and invite her for a cup of coffee.

But that's how she was—very down-to-earth and approachable. I remember calling the number in the back of the first edition of *The Information Broker's Handbook* to order something, and being really nervous when she answered the phone herself. She spent several minutes on the phone with me, though, asking about what I was doing and if I had any other questions for her.

We just hit it off, right off the bat. She spent a whole afternoon talking to me over coffee. She told me all these stories about her personal life. We had a wonderful rapport from the beginning. I'll always be grateful for all of that. And really, it wasn't until my encounter with Sue that things started to take off in other directions with my business. I started to get work from corporate clients, law firms, and so forth. Until then I was primarily just doing little background checks on people.

These many years later, how do you describe your business and the services you offer?

I describe myself as a public records researcher, and people always ask "What's that?" I tell them we do a variety of things. There are so many different kinds of public records available, but the focus in my business is primarily on due diligence research. I do a lot of due diligence for law firms, which entails coming up with a complete picture of a company—its assets and liabilities, any litigation, as well as anything we can find about its owners. Or, in a pending merger and acquisition deal, I might work for venture capital firms and provide the same type of information. I do asset searches, sometimes in preparation for a lawsuit, but sometimes after the lawsuit has been decided, unfortunately, when people start thinking, "Well, I wonder if there's anything to go after." Usually we find out no, there aren't any assets. I do missing persons searches. I do a lot of research on privately held companies, which can also encompass research on the principals of the company, particularly if it's a smaller company.

When you talk about working for a law firm, how closely does your work relate to legal research? If a law firm has a staff already, where do you come into the picture, and how could you help?

Usually the type of work I get is from large law firms. It's the kind of stuff that they don't want to tackle in the library. While law librarians typically know something about public records, searching public records is a specialized skill. They usually don't have the depth of knowledge, so they spin off the more difficult research assignments to me. That's an ongoing source of bread and butter in my business.

What would be an example of something that a law librarian might not want to tackle?

For one thing, research pertaining to an individual. Sure, they can search the newspapers for any mention of a person's name, but when it comes to searching someone's assets or finding lawsuits involving that person, what kind of house they own, their professional license, criminal records—that's over the line from what most law librarians would want to do, or would have the experience to do thoroughly enough.

So there is no question that public records is a niche business, and that it would be really tough for a generalist to offer public records searching as one of their services.

I think that would be a dangerous game to play. I, for one, wouldn't dream of doing, oh, say, a patent search. I don't know how to do that. I would subcontract that research to somebody like Marty Goffman, who understands patent and trademark research. It's not my field.

Marty, incidentally, tells me that he would not touch public records research; he says he would call Lynn Peterson.

Well, you know, he's a wise man. But it's true. It's an area of distinct specialization. There's just no way that anybody can know it all. People think, "Oh, I can do that. I can just sign up with ChoicePoint [23]" or whatever. But the problem is that you don't know what you're getting, number one. You don't know what's included in the search. Two, when you get the information, how do you know you've got it all? And thirdly, how do you know what the information you've gotten *means*? I think it's important in public records research to start at the courthouse, not with the abstracts you get in online research, but with the real documents, which is where I began. You've got to learn what a tax lien looks like. What is a Uniform Commercial Code (UCC) [126] filing? You've got to see the paper. I think that's very, very important.

What type of information is contained in a UCC filing, and how is that valuable to your clients?

It can be valuable in a number of contexts. If we're doing an asset search, let's say someone is a debtor in a UCC filing. Then the collateral that they put up for the loan is encumbered. It's not a true asset. If, on the other hand, there's a secured party in that UCC filing, and the debtor defaults, that collateral may become an asset of the secured party. So UCC filings come into play in situations like that, when you're doing an asset search.

Say you're doing research on a company, and you check UCC filings and you see that they have an awful lot of UCC filings. That means they may be up to their eyeballs in leases and debts. That can be an important piece of information. It may also tell you who they're banking with or have creditor/creditee relationships with.

Sometimes it's a tool to locate people. For one thing, when an individual has a UCC filing, their Social Security number is listed, which can be very helpful in terms of locating that person. Address information is also included. There are a variety of scenarios where these are really valuable documents.

What about verifying someone's professional licenses or academic records?

That would usually be done in the context of pre-employment checking, although if somebody's going to invest in a company, they will want to know if one of the key players really is a chemical engineer or whatever, so they might ask me to check that out.

What about driving records? Where do they come into the picture?

Driving records come into the picture in pre-employment scenarios. It's relevant even if the person isn't going to be driving in the course of their job, because certainly it can point to substance abuse problems. It's also a means of verifying information the person has provided like date of birth, and so on. Typically we find that if someone has a criminal record and they don't want that to be found, they may fudge a digit or two on their date of birth. So the driving record can provide an important piece of verifying basic data.

And real property—is that primarily asset-related searching?

It can be just part of a general profile on an individual. You know, someone claims to be this or that, and when you find that they live in a little house in a bad part of town, you realize maybe they're not the person they're presenting themselves to be. Or, if they own a boat and an airplane, that sometimes presents a different picture, too.

What about in the nonprofit sector, where organizations have even more stringent reporting requirements than the private sector? What can you learn?

Sometimes I'm asked to investigate nonprofits. We may get the IRS 990s, which require disclosure of fundraising and grant recipients, and we may get the 1023, which is their application for nonprofit status. These provide very valuable information about their finances—their income, their contributors, and information regarding their directors. The most direct way to get that information is to actually go to the nonprofit. That information is supposed to be made available to anybody who wants to see it. Usually when you walk in and ask for it they act like they've been shot through the hip or something. "Nobody's ever asked for this before. Why do you want it?" It's kind of funny.

It sounds like your work reaches across many facets of both business and individuals' lives.

It really does. I had a case where a woman—and again it came through an attorney—was convinced that her husband had failed to disclose assets in a divorce settlement. She just knew that he had a lot more than what was being disclosed. And sure enough, we were able to find out that he had set up a company in the Netherlands Antilles, and this company had vast real estate holdings all over the place. The corporation was filed as an alien corporation in Texas, where you have to disclose the president and the rest of the board of directors' names, so I was able to tie it all back to him and find his vast holdings of real estate. If he had incorporated in Delaware or someplace where you don't have to provide corporate records, I never would have been able to find this.

I work on a lot of interesting stuff, for sure. For example, I have worked on many of the Chapter 11 North American Free Trade Agreement (NAFTA) cases that have been filed. This takes place in a situation where, in NAFTA arbitration, if a private company feels that a NAFTA partner country has impinged on trade because of some unfair practice, they can sue under NAFTA and it goes to an outside arbitrator. In these scenarios, I am hired by foreign governments, because it is the American companies that are suing. I am able to go to the ends of the Earth to find information in situations where you can leave no stone unturned. That's kind of exciting, because the budgets for projects of that magnitude are large enough to allow for a free rein when it comes to pursuing any and all ideas pertaining to the research, even the longest long shot.

I have read that only about ten to fifteen percent of public records are available online.

How has digital information changed your business?

More public records are going online all the time. However, we're also in an interesting period in which some public records are being closed. There's a lot of concern about the complete availability of credit headers, for example, which provide an excellent tool for locating people. There are forces out there saying we should be more restrictive, we shouldn't allow this information to be public record. Just recently they deleted address information from the California State Board of Equalization for small businesses.

By the same token, governmental agencies are finding that they can save a lot of money by making public records available online, so they don't have to have employees to provide the information at the courthouse. And in fact, some governmental agencies are charging for access to their records. You can buy units of information with a credit card, and essentially go and retrieve X number of records online for Y dollars. So they are getting into the information business as vendors in that capacity, which is kind of interesting. I don't know how it's all going to shake out. Having a number of commercial vendors, of course, makes things easier for me.

Rolling up your sleeves, now, and actually doing your research—how do you start a project, and how do you decide if you will use online systems or need to locate actual documents?

It's very much like any other research project. You start with the reference interview. Clients come to me, they know they need information, but they don't know what's going to answer their question. Usually they have some problem and they think that maybe there's some kind of information "out there" that can help them. So we talk at the beginning about what might be "out there" that would answer their question or solve their problem. Then we talk about budgets, and we talk about what's feasible and what's not feasible within the budget that they specify. I charge by the hour, plus I charge for any online costs and any costs for manual retrieval of documents. It's not often possible to determine up front how much it's going to cost to do all that research, because we don't know how much we're going to find, and how much we find is largely a function of where the records are. So the client will usually give me a not-to-exceed budget.

Within that budget, then, I generally will start with online research to see what we might find. Often what we find online using vendors like ChoicePoint, LexisNexis [69], Superior Information Services [123], DBT [31], or Pacer [93] points us in the direction of other records. Let's say we find a lot of litigation involving a particular subject; what we get back in terms of content will be very cursory. Though we are able to determine online that there has been all this activity in the courts, we can't get at the details of the cases. So we often have to send someone out to the courthouse to retrieve at least the docket sheet, and maybe the complaint, to find out exactly what was going on.

So, we always start with the reference interview, determine what kind of budget is going to be available, and decide on an approach. If we get in there and find an enormous number of records pertaining to this particular subject, we do as much as we can within that budget. Often it's a multistep process, where the client may extend the budget later if they're interested in what we're finding.

I weave it all together in the end product that I provide. I generally include a summary saying this is what we were looking for, these are the kinds of records we looked at, and this is the period of time we researched. This is what we found, and this is what it means. If there are still question marks and additional areas that perhaps should be pursued, I might add that we should think about doing X, Y, or Z in addition to what we've done in the hopes of finding out whatever it is the client is seeking.

While many information professionals talk about sending nearly everything out electronically these days, I'll bet you still have to provide a lot of actual documents and hard copy reports.

I send out reports electronically, but if there are manually retrieved documents, they're either faxed or shipped directly. And of course we stay in touch with clients by email.

In a typical day, are you generally in your office most of the time? Do you work with people in different locales who go out and do the record retrieval for you?

I'm too old, so I don't go out to the courthouse anymore. I have logged a thousand and one hours at courthouses, at least. But now I have a network of people that I rely on to go out to these various courthouses for me. Every day of the week I dispatch researchers to courthouses or governmental agencies throughout the U.S.

It sounds like you've built up a dependable network, and that is a real value-added service you can offer your clients.

That's right. I know these people. I routinely conduct quality control evaluations by deliberately sending out requests for information that I know there's going to be a hit on, just to make sure—particularly if I'm using somebody new—that they can actually find it.

Because I charge for my labor and then pass along the fee for the court research or the online research at cost, then, yes—the client is achieving considerable savings. I think that's one of the reasons that a lot of law firms choose to use my services. They are probably going to be charged at a higher rate than I am, since they usually do not have the monthly volume of requests required for the discounted rates I receive.

Is there a need in your business to get on the phone with people to interview them or verify information?

I talk with the researchers I'm going to dispatch to wherever I need to send them to get records. Sometimes I might call the courthouse, or whatever governmental agency would have the documents, and find out their availability, where they're stored, whether they are archived, how we're going to get them, that kind of thing. Unless I'm doing a project that specifically involves telephone interviewing, though, I don't have that much need to talk on the phone.

How do you handle the business side of working with local researchers?

It's fee for service. Sometimes different runners have different rates than others, but it depends upon the nature of the assignment. Typically it's just an hourly rate; sometimes I have to send people with a portable copy machine into a particular governmental agency to copy massive amounts of various kinds of documents. Other times I may give them the name of a company and tell them just to check for civil litigation involving this company over the past twelve years. In that case, it's handled on a specific cost-per-name basis.

Do you manage your office yourself, or do you outsource any tasks?

I have two people working with me in clerical support and pre-employment background checks. I'm always trying to extricate myself from those daily support functions—you know, paying the bills, doing the books, ordering the supplies, and all that. It's so time-consuming, and it's amazing how much of the day can get eaten up that way. So now I'm in a mode where I'm going to try to learn to delegate again. That's a new challenge, because I've always had to do pretty much everything myself. My husband has recently retired and is working with me also, so it's exciting to see where that will take us.

That leads me to ask you about your recent expansion, and the move into a larger commercial office suite.

Even before this move, I rented a little hole-in-the-wall space for several years. There were times when I would need to meet with clients and certainly did not want to do that in my home. Sometimes I would work in that office and sometimes I would work from home. I always have a laptop to go back and forth with. Generally when I was involved with a large research project, and it was really intensive and could involve fifty, sixty, seventy hours of work, I might work at home, because I could stay in my pajamas. If I was working on more routine things, I might choose to go into my little office. But once we got into the expansion mode here, we needed more space, and the end result of that is very nice, large offices.

It has made a real difference in my feeling about going to work. I think one of the big problems in working from home is that, for me anyway, it was really hard to have any separation. It's hard to not let every area of your life wash over into every other area. I found it difficult to set limits, to not go down to my office on the weekend and just check the faxes, check the email, whatever. This new office has put more distance between my various roles, and I find that when I'm here, I'm here 100 percent. And it's easier to let go of work when I go home. I think that's a healthy thing for me.

And you did work out of your home for many years, so you've seen the advantages and disadvantages of both arrangements.

Yes, I certainly did put in my time working from home. Then to the hole-in-the-wall office for several years, and now I've got a really nice office that I can bring any client to and feel proud of. It's given me a lift. Maybe it was time. For a long time there were good reasons for working at home. One of the reasons was that I had three little kids. And even with them in high school, I think it was important to be there when they got home from school. That was a really good thing, and I saved money on rent. That was important. But I can't tell you how difficult it was for me to turn the business off at the end of the day, or on the weekend.

I know what you mean. Sometimes I feel like I'm living in a world where nothing is ever finished. My office is about ten feet off the kitchen, and I need to pick up things a little bit in the morning or I swear I can hear the mess out there.

And it bothers you, doesn't it? Or a client calls on a Friday afternoon and they ruin your weekend. They call late, and you're a fool and you pick it up at five after five. So I am finding that this is healthier for me now. I think that for many aspiring information professionals, it makes sense to be at home, because it's a real commitment to lease an office, undergo that expense, and usually you've got to sign something like a three-year lease, and boy, you better make it. And they don't have the capital. So it makes good sense to start at home. But I think that my business has evolved to a point where now I'm much happier with this arrangement.

Reflecting back, tell me a little bit about your marketing and how you found clients over the years. It sounds like you began PFC with some work overflow from your domestic recruitment

business, but what did you find worked best for marketing?

I'm really lousy at it. I'm not a very good marketing person. But what I will say is this: every client that I've ever had has led to two or three more, and my business has grown incrementally and steadily. If I look back five years, I still have almost all of those clients plus many more, and most of them have come through other clients. The primary way that I have grown my business is word of mouth. One of my hopes in having my husband join me in the business is that maybe now I will have more time for marketing. What has always been effective for me is writing articles or giving presentations. I have very little time for marketing, but every time I've written an article or given a talk it has paid off.

What kind of writing have you done?

An article now and then for LLRX [72] or Internet Lawyer [65]. One article I wrote regarding online privacy attracted the attention of a really excellent law firm who used my services for a number of projects and who referred me to another client. Just that article alone has generated probably fifty or sixty thousand dollars in revenue, from people who read it and from word of mouth beyond that. So I think writing is very worthwhile.

I haven't done a lot of marketing because I feel like I'm already at max. How much more can I take on? But now I am in this new mode where I can grow, think about marketing, and continue to do more of the research that I really enjoy doing.

Do you view your Web page as a marketing tool?

I think it's more like having a business card, and it's something you've got to have if you're going to be in the information business. It functions like an online brochure. In terms of people just out there surfing the Net, coming across PFC Information

Services, contacting me, and eventually becoming serious clients—I don't think that's particularly likely. And that's not what the Web page is designed to do. I don't have links and content that are designed to get people to come to my Web site particularly. But if someone calls and they've heard about me from so-and-so and they say, "Tell me more about what you do," I tell them to feel free to take a look at our Web site, and give me a call back if they think I can help.

Probably does a little bit of weeding for you.

Exactly.

I have to ask you about the online privacy debate, and the media's misrepresentation of the need for legitimate and legal access to public records.

It certainly is something that I feel passionately about, not only in terms of my own business, but because I feel so strongly that public records need to remain public. I think there is a simplistic notion that if you no longer make credit headers or Social Security numbers available, you're going to protect people's privacy. There's not been a single case of identity theft that can be attributed to access to online information. It's people throwing stuff out in their garbage. It's going into a store and giving your credit card and the clerk takes down your address as they're looking at your ID. It's those low-tech methodologies, in my opinion, that are responsible for this so-called explosion in identity theft.

It's very shortsighted to remove access not only to credit headers but also to other kinds of public records that are so important to determining who it is that you're doing business with. A lot of the work I do centers around fraud, making sure that if you're going to invest in the company, it's a reputable company or even a *real* company. Who are these people you're dealing with? You can't conduct business on just a handshake anymore.

So the talk of shutting down more and more records is very disturbing to me. I mentioned earlier that the State Board of Equalization here in California has a sales tax permit with address information that used to be public record. Suddenly it's not. Who's making these decisions? A lot of times they're not even a result of legislation, just policy decisions made by bureaucrats. That's disturbing.

I think that it's normal to be concerned about privacy, but we don't hear both sides of the story often enough.

It needs to be balanced, that's right. The need for access to information must be weighed against the desire for privacy. For example, with pre-employment background checks, laws are in place to protect the rights of the applicant. They must provide written permission before the background check can be conducted. If they are denied employment because of adverse information contained in the background check, they are given a copy of the report, a summary of their rights under the law, and the opportunity to rebut the information. I think that is highly appropriate to the situation.

On the other hand, in the context of due diligence research, there is no way to obtain the permission of the subject. In fact, it would not be desirable to do so, as usually a high degree of confidentiality is required. The information contained in public records databases has always been public record. The only difference is that now it is available online. From my perspective, there is no difference between sending someone out to the courthouse to access the information from a public computer terminal and accessing the information online from my computer in my office, except that it can be done more quickly and cheaply.

Here's a good example of why public records need to remain open and accessible. An attorney client of mine had a client who was the adult child of a physician and his wife who had become quote-unquote "members of some investment club." They were putting substantial sums into this investment club. And the promised return on their investment was some ridiculously unrealistic figure, like within six weeks they were to double their money. This was particularly designed to appeal to senior citizens; one percent of their profits would be donated to the charity of their choice, right? And one of the conditions of joining this investment club was that they were to tell no one else about it.

Long story short, the guy who was responsible for this investment club was the one they wanted the background check done on. It turned out he'd been sued so many times it was beyond counting. His name wasn't his true name, it was an a.k.a. (also known as). At one time he had had a real estate broker's license, and it had been revoked. He had moved around a lot. The whole thing was a nightmare, there were numerous problems. This case ended up in the District Attorney's office, where they wanted to prosecute this guy because he had apparently defrauded so many people. There was no investment; he was just taking their money. The clients were not able to get their money back, but at least they were prevented from investing their entire life savings.

Without access to public records and credit headers, I would not have known where to look for evidence and would not have been able to discover his true name. Unfortunately, there are lots of con men in the world, and people need to know who they are doing business with.

A lot of what I do in the context of working for law firms involves getting information about prospective witnesses. Often they're trying to discredit an expert witness for the opposition. Recently they wanted me to dig into a particular physician. I found so many medical malpractice lawsuits—something like thirty-four medical malpractice cases in five years. He was to be a quote-unquote "expert witness." Boy, was my client happy to find all that.

So, there are many, many legitimate reasons why we need access to this information. I think the genie is already out of the bottle, anyway, and you can't put it back in. Maybe the politicians look like they're doing something about the identity theft problem, but in reality they're not solving the problem. They're taking the wrong approach. I think the emphasis should be on stiffer penalties for misuse of information.

How do you stay informed and up-to-date about all these privacy and access concerns?

It's hard to stay current because there is so much going on. Fortunately one of the great communicators in this industry is Mike Sankey of BRB Publications [13]. They produce a newsletter and maintain a Web site with updates about proposed changes in the law that would restrict access to public records, and about records that are now becoming available online. I also network with a lot of people in the industry and try to keep abreast of new services that are becoming available.

What about professional and trade associations?

I am a member of the Association of Independent Information Professionals (AIIP) [172] and the Public Records Research Network (PRRN) [196]. I'm also a member of the Society of Competitive Intelligence Professionals (SCIP) [199], though they don't deal too much with my field. A lot of the vendors are good about providing information, including newsletters that discuss product developments and industry issues.

Are you a high-tech wired type of person?

Actually, I find many of these laborsaving devices to be so time-consuming. I have a calendar, and a pen and paper, and that works for me.

All of your projects sound so interesting, but can you share one of your more unique experiences over the years?

I can think of one birth parent case that is a pretty dramatic story, although I should say right up front that I don't generally take these cases unless I'm working for an attorney or someone like that. If I am working for a private individual, I do not disclose the location of the person I'm seeking unless that person gives permission. I think that's really important, because how do I know the person requesting my services isn't a stalker or whatever. Even in the case of a birth parent or a child put up for adoption, you don't want to wreak havoc with someone else's life.

I sometimes do this work for colleagues if they assure me that it's not a birth parent search. But if a private person comes to me, I'll tell them that I'll take the case, but I won't disclose the subject's whereabouts unless that person is willing to be found and wants to be found. And I tell them that they have to pay me either way. It's amazing how many people that weeds out.

Anyway, this case came to me through an attorney and concerned a woman who had given birth to a child back in the 1940s in Ohio. I had very, very little to go on. Her name was literally as generic as Mary Jones. It took months and months and months of research, sifting through old dusty records to find out whom she had married. Finally I was able to find that. She had given birth to the child many years before, but now she was married and had moved to California with her husband. Well, it turned out that this child who was seeking the birth mother had been adopted by a family in Ohio who had also moved to California. When I was finally able to locate her, we learned that he and his birth mother had been living within about a mile of each other almost his entire life. They probably shopped in the same Safeway and everything. Her husband had died, and she was living kind of a lonely life. It was so wonderful; he had children, so she had grandchildren. And she wanted to be found. She'd always wanted to find him. That was really marvelous. That was one of those great experiences in this line of work where you really feel good about what you're doing.

What would you tell someone who is considering public records research as a career?

People come to me who want to be public records researchers, and I can point them in a number of directions. But I'm careful to tell them that I can't teach them in a few hours how to do this. I think this is a good career if you're really neurotic about detail—I mean to a completely anal degree. If you love research, if the thrill of the chase is really what punches your buttons, it's a great field. But if you're in it just solely for the money, forget it, because it takes a long time to build a business like this. You have to be willing to really work your butt off. At one time two-week workshops in public records were being offered; if you plunked down several thousand dollars, at the end of two weeks you'd be turned out as a public records researcher. It was all bogus. I mean, it takes years of experience.

I think any entrepreneur has to be willing to take risks. I made a bold move leasing these new offices and expanding my business at this juncture. But it's important to be a risk taker—a *calculated* risk taker. It's important to see opportunities where they exist and seize them. When I was starting my business I read a great book by Paul Hawken, *Growing A Business* [227]. He discussed the fact that more businesses fail because they grow too quickly, rather than too slowly. You can't grow overnight without sacrificing quality. If your primary concern is quality, the business will follow.

Super Searcher Power Tips

➤ This is not the type of information research you can learn from a book, and there are no classes that would possibly bring you up to speed on the work. Public records research is a craft, and you can only learn it through hands-on experience.

➤ It is as important to know what you don't know as it is to know what you do know. Therefore, when I launched my business, I recognized that I needed professional advice.

➤ It's important in public records research to start at the courthouse, not at the abstracts found in online research, but with the real documents. You've got to learn what a tax lien looks like. What is a UCC filing? You've got to see the paper.

➤ I weave it all together in the end product that I provide. I generally provide a summary saying this is what we were looking for, these are the kinds of records we looked at, this is the period of time we researched. This is what we found, and this is what it means.

➤ I put in my time working from home. Then I moved to a hole-in-the-wall office for several years, and now I've got a really nice office that I can bring any client to and feel proud of. It's given me a lift.

➤   I'm not a very good marketing person. But every client I've ever had has led to two or three more, and my business has grown incrementally and steadily. If I look back five years ago, I still have almost all of those clients plus many more.

➤   If you love research, if the thrill of the chase is really what punches your buttons, it's a great field. But if you're in it just solely for the money, forget it, because it takes a long time to build a business like this.

Mark Goldstein

Civic Entrepreneur

Mark Goldstein is President of International Research Center, based in Phoenix, Arizona. For the past decade he has provided custom research and strategic support for business, legal, and public policy clients in a variety of high-technology disciplines and arenas, concentrating on telecommunications, information technology, e-content, and the Internet. He is past Chairman of the Arizona Telecommunications & Information Council (ATIC) and serves on the boards of a number of other industry and regional economic development organizations.

markg@researchedge.com
www.researchedge.com

Mark, tell me a little bit about your background before you went into this business.

I graduated from SUNY Binghamton in upstate New York in 1972 with a degree in cinema, where I fell into working with a very active and interesting group of filmmakers. I picked up some significant experience in experimental video, and actually ended up learning enough electronics and engineering to become employed as an engineer and, later, as an engineering manager. I went to work for MicroAge when it was very young; it later became a Fortune 500 company. I was about their twenty-fifth employee when I joined them in 1976, doing R&D around the start of the personal computer revolution. That's when I had my first experience with a modem, using something called a TI Silent 700, which was like a typewriter with an acoustic coupler operating at 110 baud and thermal paper output.

From 1980 to 1992, I worked for Medtronic, another Fortune 500 company, where I managed test engineering for about a billion and a half dollars per year worth of heart pacemakers and other implantable biomedical devices. I ran large teams of engineers and technicians, somewhere around forty-five or fifty people at my peak on projects there, and did some relatively advanced work in computers, networking, and test engineering.

That whole time I had a side business called Advanced Tools for the Arts. I did custom engineering and electronics on contract to local firms including technology research. I also produced a line of products in the '70s, mostly electronic music synthesizers and optical display systems that I designed, built, and sold to Arizona State University and other institutions as well as individual musicians and companies.

So you managed to hold a top-level corporate job, full-time, plus run a business on the side?

Right. It really was just a side business, never more than a project or two at a time. It entailed some consulting, some actual design and manufacturing, all within my home environment. It supplemented my income, but generally just covered my investments in technology, personal training, and other interests. It was almost a net zero game there. You know, I had clients and interesting projects, but it really wasn't a very strong income stream. It was certainly beyond hobby grade activity, as there were real projects with some substantial money, but I more or less considered that play money for me to spend on myself and my interests rather than money I was going to live on.

With so much success in a corporate environment, how did you come to leave that world behind and go out completely on your own?

I probably always wanted to, and I suppose it was just a matter of timing and a leap of faith. I worked in a very intense environment those last twelve years at Medtronic, and they were always very performance-, very task- and deliverables-oriented, and very rough on people, frankly. However, we consistently delivered the goods to support the testing of new advanced biomedical devices, often in inventive and innovative ways.

In any case, I really wanted to go out on my own after about eight years there. I stuck it out for another four years, somewhat to my detriment in terms of getting my new enterprise going, as well as in terms of my health and sanity, because I really was ready to be gone. But I did one last, very big project for them. As much as I wanted to leave during those last four years, I also felt bound by my own ethics and interest to finish that project. So by mid-'92 when that project had actually achieved a successful and stable level, I gave them six weeks notice and left. What a relief and a change that was!

Sounds like you wanted to bring closure to a big part of your professional life.

Right. I really did feel I needed some closure. In a sense it was just a job and I should have been able to walk away with two weeks' notice at any time, but on the other hand I really did feel I was doing something important. I was the primary architect of their new generation of test systems, so it was my baby and a part of me really wanted to see it through.

At that point I felt I had several options for self-employment. I could try to build my electronic design business; I could become one of the early computer consultants for networks and integration into the business environment; or I could dig into the market viability of researching technological products and markets, tracking both historical and current trends of certain technologies. I named my new enterprise International Research Center and began from there.

When I began researching my career options for myself I discovered and joined both the Association of Independent

Information Professionals (AIIP) [172, see Appendix] and the Society of Competitive Intelligence Professional (SCIP) [199]. I went to my first AIIP conference in '93, and that really helped me find the heart and soul of the independent information professional world as well as a strong support group for those managing their own research businesses.

Was attending that first AIIP conference a turning point for you?

I had already turned, and it was in that process of researching what resources I had, what things I should learn to do this, that I found AIIP. It was certainly crucial early on to building my understanding, my network of peer professionals, and my resources, but I had already made the commitment and begun down that path.

Logistically, you already had the experience of running an office out of your home, but you must have had to shift that into high gear.

I did spend some substantial money over those first few years building out a more elaborate and better equipped office environment. I had to go out and buy what was at the time a reasonably expensive fax machine, filing cabinets, more bookcases, and resource materials and start squeezing all that stuff into the house. Since bringing my full-time employment home almost a decade ago, this house has become a little small and crowded, and we're working toward a new house that we're designing and hope to build before long on some wonderful land on South Mountain Park here in Phoenix. Now everything my wife and I are doing is working toward that—it has become a driver when we look around the place we're in. We're comfortable but a little cramped and have big ideas for our new abode and the surrounding desert property.

What do you like about having your office at home? Did you ever consider leasing space, maybe for increased visibility?

I considered it, investigated it, but never wanted to be based outside the house. My work habits are more nocturnal than diurnal, meaning I often push into, and occasionally through, the night in my work, and I really didn't want to be away from the house that much. I also like to take breaks and go play with the cats or make my lunch or tidy up here and there. I'm comfortable here, and I'd rather drift in and out of my workday, or night, as I'm able to readily do in this environment.

When I meet with clients, I do occasionally meet them here, and in fact I sometimes facilitate a strategic session over lunch in our family room. I'll set up the enormous Post-it notes that go on a stand, and put them on the wall as we're working on them. But more often than not I'll meet with clients and prospects in a semi-social coffee or lunch setting, or alternately at their site or inside their facilities.

Did you use outside professional services in setting up this business?

I've always had an accountant. I'm now on my third in twenty years. I was already doing schedule Cs, self-employment income and expense reporting, since the mid-'70s on my tax returns, and I had a system for everything. Obviously I ramped it up a little when I went out on my own. But frankly, there wasn't so much business at first that it was all that different. The expenses were skyrocketing, but not necessarily the income.

In terms of an attorney, no; I set up as a sole proprietorship. I did get some business insurance, but I didn't need to consult with an attorney to do it. I'm sure if I had decided to set up as a corporate entity, a limited liability corporation, or a partnership, I would have, but as a sole proprietorship I didn't really see that much difference from the way I had handled things as a side business.

What about any small business or online vendor training?

I didn't seek any general small business training, but I did actively engage for the first eighteen months or so in what I considered a strategic program to do vendor training and attend conferences. Dialog [35], for example, would conduct search classes at our university library. The university itself ran a search service, and they were open and willing to share their experience and welcome a new member to the community. I attended perhaps six or eight conferences in that first eighteen months. In addition to AIIP, I went to Online World [91] for the first time in '93, which gave me good exposure to the vendors, and took some additional training there including Sue Rugge's Information Broker's Seminar [230].

A very important and, for me, very critical conference at that time was Computers, Freedom, and Privacy (CFP) [26]. That was a real cyber-scene with a melange of some 500 people held in the San Francisco Bay area in the spring of 1993. It was organized by people from the Electronic Frontier Foundation (EFF) [43], including Mitch Kapor, who had started Lotus, and John Perry Barlow, who is still known as the Thomas Jefferson of cyberspace and was a lyricist for the Grateful Dead. They started kind of an ACLU for cyberspace, really. The conference drew everyone from an alphabet soup of federal agencies like OMB, CIA, FBI, DOJ, FCC, and FTC, as well as hackers and crackers and everyone in between. It included people from large companies like Sun, Apple, and others who had a vision of computers and networking and the social transformations that would occur. Moreover, it included science fiction writers like Bruce Sterling, journalists from a great variety of publications including *Mondo 2000* and *Wired* [140], which was just starting, and cyber-libertarians of all persuasions. There were very intense sixteen-hour days of immersion in the cyber-culture that was certainly beyond my experience to date. It drove some crucial transformations in my own understanding of the importance of the computer and the network to social transformation and the impact it was going to have, and certainly energized my personal interest and commitment to being in that space.

Cyber-cultural immersion—it's so interesting how these things were going on in that period of time. Tell me about the early days of your research business, or perhaps your first client?

At that time I didn't yet know quite how to serve a client, so the first thing I did was basically develop about a half-dozen projects over a period of four to six months that I did for free. I don't even know that I had a paying project in that time. I paid for the database access, or I did project-style work during training opportunities. Besides proprietary online databases, there was a nascent and growing Internet where you could use tools like Gopher, WAIS, Archie, and Veronica to search textual content on computers around the world. I asked friends and business associates what they would like to know.

I had been well paid as a Fortune 500 technical manager and had laid away some significant reserves, had paid down or off all my debt, and was prepared to spend tens of thousands of dollars, as I eventually did, investing in my own education and start-up. Of my earliest projects, one had to do with ATM security, regarding bank machine security and the liabilities to banks. Another had to do with coffeepots and product liability. I had another product liability project dealing with a specific ladder model and type. So, those were a few of the early ones, but I did all those for free.

But there was value in that because you were testing your market and you were testing people's appetite for information.

And I was learning what a project and a package looked like. I had done really serious project management with large staffs and responsibilities and budgets, but I still had to understand the steps to characterize a client's need, to size a job, to bid and come to agreement on budget and deliverables, and then to deliver and satisfy that need. In doing this, I learned about interacting with a client, particularly performing a reference interview, defining the scope of work, what deliverables could and should look like, and what would answer people's questions. People will ask for a lot of stuff and you have to be thinking, "Well, what is it you really want to know?"—but more than that, "If you learn that, what does it mean for your business?" Because they may not be asking the right questions. You want to challenge the presumptions behind the questions they think they should be asking. I also found it extremely helpful to learn what sources they use now and how they value them.

I still use those same basic lines of questioning in reference interviews today: What is it you think you want to know? Why is it you want to know it? What does it mean to your business if you find out certain things? And lastly, what do you already know today and how do you know it?

Interesting how your experience starting out with pro bono projects really worked for you. Now, bringing your business up-to-date, how do you describe yourself if you're meeting a potential client?

I bid on and receive large public policy work, generally projects in the ten to fifty thousand dollar range. They often result from a publicly released request for proposal (RFP), for which I have to prepare formal proposals and bid and compete with other vendors, and hopefully win. Those projects tend to be on telecommunications policy and information technology, often for government agencies or industry trade groups. For example, I've done a lot of work for my state Department of Education. I've also done work for other state agencies, as well as for counties and municipalities on strategic planning for the telecom environment. Some of that work has had national reach and implications. I did a very comprehensive universal service study for telecom that got national play and use in the debate over the Digital Divide. Last year I did another study for an industry trade association on multitenant building access in the telecom industry.

So that's one whole category of larger public policy projects. They usually range from four to eight months in duration, and they're generally large and complex endeavors. One thing I really like about them is that the client wants the results to be publicly visible with whatever reach and impact they can achieve. My work often results in a Web site with associated content that the client may mount or that I may mount for them, or a report that's given wide circulation. The work is kind of branded by my firm because I have authored or contributed to it. This, of course, is unlike a lot of client work, which is usually proprietary and confidential, and where you may name the clients but you certainly can't show your work.

What a great concept—a client project that the client publicizes!

The next category is perhaps more traditional information brokering activity, which I would categorize as market research, business intelligence, and technology or market trending. In business intelligence, I may research and lay out a competitive landscape or certain other factors in an industry, or perform prospect identification for sales organizations. I do a range of projects of that sort. Some of them are ongoing with particular clients, others are one-offs. I consider these to be more in the range of the traditional information broker, which frankly is a term I've never liked. I've always described my business and what I do simply as research and consulting.

Yes, the ongoing battle with words and professional identification. But we are an opinionated bunch if nothing else—some

like the term *information broker* because of its roots, and others feel that the media has done too much damage by using it incorrectly.

I never really liked it from the get-go. I may have used it in some very early promotional literature for my company because of its familiarity, but I've always avoided the term as best I could. I never felt that the word "broker" truly represented the value-added nature of what we do at our best. Certainly though, a significant segment of my work falls into that traditional information professional category of research, filtering, and analyzing information for our clients, whatever we choose to call it.

There's yet a third category, which I call "smart-guy" stuff. It's really consulting, backed up by a research component, where I have a variety of clients, many of them ongoing, for whom I do smart-guy stuff. I sit in on marketing or strategic or team meetings at the customer's site, with their people, on a regular basis. I'm really considered kind of an ad hoc team member or an employee on call, as you might have in a matrixed organization. I do that with some fairly large and substantial companies on an ongoing basis.

I also sit on the board of advisors for several high-tech companies including AeroGen Broadband, which provides wireless broadband services, and Opnix, which is pioneering intelligent bandwidth routing and traffic management. And I often have several start-ups that I may advise and assist for a modest equity consideration; it's really sweat equity work. It yields a sense of participation and is usually an interesting and exciting experience, win or lose.

As far as industries are concerned, rather than trying to be everything to everybody, you focus on a few core markets, primarily e-commerce, telecom, and high tech.

Absolutely. My early interests were in telecom and cyberspace as I've described, and over time my personal investment in learning about those things and being involved in them led to me being known as and considered a smart guy in those arenas. Part of that also has to do with my ongoing pro bono public policy involvement, which is part of my marketing or public giveback.

Beyond telecom it often goes to information technology issues like e-learning or technology and education, which often encompasses the hardware, the software, the connectivity, and the human and organizational components. I wouldn't even call my work telecom per se, as that's a little too limited to the transport layer, when really the action can be most exciting at the application layer. But that's certainly a core focus area for me, reflected in my clientele and projects.

Speaking of your clientele, when I looked at your Web site, what really stood out was an impressive client list. I wondered about your rationale for including this, since client lists are sometimes closely guarded.

I've never been closely guarded. I prefer to be known for what I do and what I do well, and am perfectly willing to take my chances with some competition. If I lose a job here and there to someone else, that's fine; I'm busy enough. I see the presentation of a client list as an announcement of the range and variety of companies that I do work with, everything from start-ups to Fortune 500 companies. Overwhelmingly, my clients have been very happy with me and my work, have used me time and again, and, if they don't, it's because times change, people change, needs change, and I take my chances on that and go with the flow.

I thought it was an interesting marketing angle, though I assume you need to obtain permission to use their names.

Right, and I actually do have clients for whom our engagement agreement specifically says I cannot name them. I have clients I would *like* to have on my Web site, but don't because of that specificity. Their active concern is that they don't want to reveal to anyone else on a Web search who their service providers may be. But that's the exception rather than the rule.

Tell me about your civic involvement, and in particular the Arizona Telecom and Information Council.

ATIC [170] is a Governor's task force on telecommunications infrastructure and information technology. I am the past Chair of that organization. I had been on the board of the preceding organization as well as the current version of it since 1993. Back when I was getting started I called my old boss from MicroAge, Alan Hald, who was a futurist and a visionary when I worked for him in the '70s. I knew he was involved in regional public policy work, and I asked him what was going on in Arizona with all this stuff. Well, he said, a little bit, not so much yet, but you need to talk to this guy, Ted Kraver, because we have something called the Governor's Strategic Partnership for Economic Development (GSPED) [186] and he is trying to form an information technology group. I met with Ted and helped him build that group and I later chaired it after it transformed from AICI, the predecessor organization, to ATIC in the mid-'90s.

Under GSPED, I also sit on the boards of the Arizona Software and Internet Association (AZSOFT.net) [168], and the Global Arizona ELearning cluster (GAZEL) [185]. I often attend, but am not a board member of, GSPED's High-Tech Industry Cluster (HTIC) [187], Environmental Technology Industry Cluster (ETIC) [181], and Biotechnology Industry Cluster [174]. I'm also on the board of a very exciting new group called Tech Oasis [202], working to build and promote Arizona as a core location for high-tech industry and its stakeholders.

In the higher education community, I sit on the Dean's Advisory Council for Arizona State University's College of Engineering and Applied Science [10], a group chaired by Craig Barrett, CEO of Intel. And I'm involved with the Maricopa Community College District [75], especially their ACE Entrepreneurs Program and their new digital television station MCTV.

I've also been involved with a number of national and international organizations, and was on the Board of Directors of AIIP from 1998 to 2000. I served as their Inter-Industry Liaison, meaning I negotiated on behalf of some 800 members with online database aggregators and other content providers. The experience I gained really turned out to be significant for me, as I built a strong network among top content industry executives and learned a lot about the content industry and its value chains that I am using today in my work with several content distribution and digital rights management clients.

Wow. I imagine all that takes a significant amount of time.

We have a term here for people who really invest in the development of their community in this way. We call them civic entrepreneurs. I know a number of people I respect and love and have learned from, especially over these last ten years, whom this term describes. It means you not only have built a business, but you're involved deeply in the community and its development. I customarily don't view my community involvement as marketing in a direct way, but I know that I'm out there, I'm doing good things, and people know me from that. People whom I first met three or five or seven years ago all of a sudden have a need, and you come to mind as someone who works in that area, who's smart and generous with their time and resources.

It does create some conflict, as you might imagine, between billable hours and pro bono hours. I spend a lot of time on the pro bono stuff, but I enjoy it. If I didn't enjoy it, it would be onerous to spend that much time. But I'm a night owl. And I don't have—well, I do have a life. But I am accused of working too much, and part of that is to get the billable or project work done, in addition to the pro bono and community work.

I hear an important aspect of marketing coming out of what you're saying. It's not as though you wear it on your chest—"Hi, I'm Mark and I'm looking for clients." You don't need to do that. But you're out there, you're working with people, you're visible, and the business just naturally follows.

Right. I remember an early AIIP conference where Paul and Sarah Edwards [96] gave a workshop on how to market yourself. It confirmed what I felt I already was doing and I came back with a sense of validation and recommitment to it. The two primary things I learned from them can be summarized as this: One, don't be a generalist, be a specialist. A specialist is going to be more highly valued and will help define the communities in which you invest and make yourself visible and market to. You can try to be a generalist, but then you don't know who to sell to and what to do. If you're a specialist you can value your time more highly as you build credibility in that community, and you can always still do generalist work that happens to come your way.

The other point they made was that the only marketing that works is network marketing. I had already been finding that to be true, as I continue to do. I do have a hard-copy brochure, which I've had since I started my business. I paid a very good independent graphic artist a fair amount of money, and had a high-quality printing job done, multicolor on good stock with scored folds. I had three thousand printed, of which I still have a few hundred. I've stopped using it, though, because it's a little dated and not necessarily the way I'd go now.

I remember Sue Rugge saying that she had always regretted naming a company after herself. She felt your company should look like it's more than just you, so it can go on and continue without you, or grow beyond you. Thus I came to choose the somewhat presumptuous name International Research Center, which I thought might indicate the scale and scope of work I wanted to do, though perhaps not where I already was.

Do you do anything you would call formal marketing or advertising?

I've got myself listed in a variety of directories, including AIIP, the Software and Information Industry Association (SIIA) [200], and some export and industry directories. In total I'm probably listed in more than a dozen directories, some national and the rest regional. What I find they bring me, mostly, is either people wanting to sell me something or, come May of every year, a slew of resumes of graduating students who would like employment. They go to their library, correctly, to do research and then generally spam everyone in various directories that seems to make sense with a copy of their resume. I can think of only four or five jobs in my nine-plus years on my own that have actually come from a directory inquiry.

I've never done any cold calling. I do have listings in the Yellow Pages under Information Services and also Market Research, but hardly anyone ever reaches me that way. Nearly all of my marketing is done by public visibility and networking, referral from clients or associates, direct engagement, or people finding me through my Web site.

How do you view your Web site? Is it a marketing tool for you or is it something that just needs to be there?

I do believe it absolutely needs to be there. We're offering services of an advanced nature regarding telecom and the Internet and e-commerce and so on, and it would certainly be odd not to have some Web presence. I view the site in several ways. One is as brochure-ware, in that it lists the basics about the company, our clients, our personnel. But I also try, as I know a number of other people do, to have lists of useful resources available and maintained on the site. People sometimes say, well, if I go there I can find resources myself and do my own research. That's great. I always encourage people to do what they can on their own, and to use me when they run into a brick wall or need research beyond their expertise, time, or means.

I also host the ATIC site as an independent site under mine, so that brings traffic through, too, though I don't overtly redirect visitors to my site.

What about speaking at conferences? Have you found that to be valuable?

Yes, that has led to some client work, but I also consider it perhaps more than that, as part of my own ongoing professional development. When I speak at a conference I'm committed to attending, I get to schmooze with the other speakers as well as the attendees. I have some visibility and credibility as a speaker and moderator within that environment, so I absolutely do look for opportunities, within reason, to present at conferences through the year. I've presented at Online World and the inaugural Web Search University [139], and done preconference workshops and a presentation at eContent Expo [41]. I present at some legal seminars about telecom policy regulation and research for Law Seminars International [68], and at other venues for e-commerce and telecom, often out of state. I also occasionally provide training on various topics such as the Internet, research techniques, and telecom technology and markets. Finally, I do a lot of in-state public speaking, often on Information Age transformations and public policy implications, mostly pro bono.

And writing? I have an old copy of your *Internet Resource Guide for Research and Exploration*.

That's actually now out of date and the revision frozen; I think the last version was November '99. I wasn't able to continue with it, but it is an interesting historical note in that what I did was develop a hundred-plus page, very dense, Internet resource guide that many people used for quite some time. I both gave it away and sold it as a book, and additionally mounted about forty percent of it on my Web site, as a public resource and to encourage visitors to buy the other sixty percent contained in the book. That did work somewhat for several years, but I decided there were so many big Internet guides published professionally and nationally, and I couldn't afford the time to adequately keep that one up, so I did let it kind of go away.

I do some other things now that are of that ilk. I've developed some specific and detailed subject resource guides that I share readily with people. I have one on telecom resources, one on market research related to new economy and e-commerce issues, and a general Internet Resource Hot Sheet. Those are three of my current ones. I usually have a couple of those as well as recent conference and training presentations on my Web site. That's a kind of outreach marketing.

Which professional search services do you use?

Dialog, DataStar [30], LexisNexis [69], and Dow Jones Interactive/Factiva [39] are core, although I'm most comfortable with Dialog and tend to prefer it as my general transactional data provider. There remains for me a familiarity and precision in utilizing their command mode, doing Boolean searching, and working from precisely defined data collections and result sets. But I also use sites like Northern Light [89] and Hoover's [56], which have done a bit of information-gathering and organizing beforehand. There's another great resource called Knowledge Express Data Systems (KEDS) [66]. They have information on technology companies, supplied by CorpTech [28], available under reasonable terms, but they also have some unique resources like university research for technology transfer that I use for some of my clients. I'll use MEDLINE [80] for access to the medical literature, Questel-Orbit [92] for scientific searching, and ChoicePoint (formerly CDB Infotech) [20], with which I have a subscription for public records. But I'll also use KnowX [67] for public records and pay by the record. I have a direct Dun & Bradstreet [40] search account for checking credit ratings of companies, and an account with InfoUSA [62], which is useful for creating lists of companies by industry sector; those are some of the boutique search services that I commonly use. I'll also pick up and then drop other specific niche services as needed, on a project basis, or pay for an on-demand search in a proprietary database from an information provider's own in-house research service.

Let's go to the Internet. What do you actually search for on the Web? Any sites you particularly rely on?

I should send you my personal Internet Research Hot List, which is five pages long in two columns, so it's probably more than 500 URLs. If I'm doing company research, there may be ten or fifteen primary sites I end up using in the course of a project, but it depends on what I'm looking for. If it's intellectual property, again, I have my favorite twelve or fifteen sites, including the U.S. Patent and Trademark Office (USPTO) [129] and Thomson and Thomson [125]. If I'm doing company research I may use FreeEdgar [49] or other online access points to Securities and Exchange Commission (SEC) [130] records.

I'm a great fan of hierarchical directories. The World Wide Web Virtual Library [143] organizes topical directories of resources on a variety of subjects. I will often check there to find who maintains the relevant topical directories and use those as resource starting points. I'll also check out resources linked from other hierarchical directory sites such as About.com [4], Google Web Directory [54], or Yahoo! [145].

I use a number of general search tools—AltaVista [8], HotBot [57], and Google [53], among others—and quite a variety of hierarchical directories. I'll read some of the electronic newsletters on search engine developments, such as Search Engine Watch [114], to keep current.

I also use some market research aggregators like AllNet-Research [7], First Call [47], IMR Mall [64], Market-Research.com [76], and MindBranch [83]. I often use Multex [84] for accessing investment house research. If I want to get what Salomon Smith Barney [110] or Standard & Poor's [119] are writing about public companies, I'll often go to Multex to buy from their extensive aggregation of company and industry segment research reports.

And then the invisible Web is increasingly important, where you get beyond what the general search engines will pick up. Certainly a lot of what I've already mentioned goes beyond the visible Web. The investment and market research reports I want on Multex don't come up in a Google search. I have to know to go to Multex. I may use something called Mighty Words (formerly FatBrain) [82] as one source for what we call gray literature, publications that didn't get ISBN numbers or general distribution. I utilize a search PDF function on the Adobe site [5], which indexes millions of PDF documents that aren't otherwise indexed. Most casual Web searchers tend to rely on the visible Web, if not exclusively focus there.

I have a lot of experience, as I'm sure we all do, with clients who say "I searched the Web already, it wasn't there." And I say okay, fine. Then the first thing I do is go search the Web and I find them exactly what they needed, for free. They couldn't find it themselves. So experience tells me that, unless I really trust a person's searching skills—as part of the reference interview I find out a bit about that—I'm going to go back and search the visible Web in my ways, to complement what they tell me they've already done. I do that before I go to transactional sources, like Dialog, and the invisible Web.

How has the growth and maturity, if you will, of the Internet affected your work in the last few years?

Five or six years ago, I'd tell people, well, I'm only getting ten or fifteen percent of my projects' result-oriented information off the Web. Three years ago I might have said that had risen to twenty-five or thirty percent. Today, I'd say it's probably closer to forty percent from the visible Web, varying significantly, of course, from project to project. That doesn't mean my clients can necessarily find that same forty percent; often they can't. But beyond that, I probably get another thirty percent from transactional sources like Dialog or Dow Jones Interactive, that are protected from general access by either credit card or subscription or password access. And then I get perhaps another twenty or thirty percent from libraries in hard copy and from direct human contact—finding the author of the article, finding the executive director of a trade association, finding people who know. I still do a fair amount of shoe-leather research, going down to the library and looking at books and periodicals.

Tell me about how you use manual research in your projects.

I have a great university here, Arizona State University (ASU), which has at least six libraries on campus. Of them, I frequent the general university Hayden Library and the Noble Science and Engineering Library. A lot of reference books have no online equivalent. You can find books listed in the online catalog, but you go to the library to actually get your look at a copy, assuming you're not going to buy it outright.

I use quite a number of reference books on a regular basis—industry statistics, association or industry directories, the Gale Encyclopedia of Associations [225], five-volume backbreaking tome that it is. There's still a tangible satisfaction in handling hard copy that I don't know if I'll ever outgrow no matter how great the online world becomes. I still appreciate seeing someone come to Captain Jean Luc Picard's ready room or quarters in *Star Trek: The Next Generation*, and he is reading a physical book even though the text is undoubtedly available from the ship's computer.

I also go to the library to look at periodicals. A lot of periodicals are simply not archived or available to nonsubscribers online, but the university still subscribes to several thousand periodicals in print. They have a nice big room with the last year or two of those periodicals on the shelves. You pull them, you look at them, you put them back, there's no gatekeeper; you just can't take them out of the room. There are copy machines and so on. And there's a separate area for bound volumes of back issues of those periodicals.

Those are some of the reasons I go to the library, but there are two more. One is that they have quite a number of database products licensed on their network. If I were a student or faculty member, I could access some of those databases remotely, but I'm not. I do have a community library card, and my associated privileges only allow me to access those databases in-house. So I will often do some searching that would be expensive to do on my own transactional accounts. The library's licensing terms do not allow you to deliver those results directly to your client, but I can type up a bibliography from the items I found, or go look for them on the actual magazine or journal publisher's Web site and create an active hotlinked bibliography or Webliography for my clients. If I want them to see certain articles I've discovered, I may go back to my own Dialog account, or whatever, and pull those articles for them.

The final reason I go to the library is there are smart people there and they are my friends. I know the reference librarians in science and in business; I go up to them and I chat. I may not have a question that day; it may just be what's happening of interest in our community, but they're an absolute resource when I need them. I go to the librarians as I would go to the AIIP mailing list, to post about a research problem or a dead end or a success that I wanted to share with people. One of the many pro bono things I do is I sit on the state library association's legislative affairs committee, because I can help forge a link between the library community and the technology community on some joint interests like UCITA [127] or other information liability or information theft issues.

Now what about primary research, as perhaps a final piece of your research methodologies and sources. Do you do primary research yourself, or do you sub that out?

I have had public policy projects that involved significant survey activity. For example, I did work for a very small town where we had to interview probably 500 households out of a community of 4,000, a pretty significant sample. I engaged some people to do that for me, but I often survey what some people call VITO, very important top officers, myself. I have one assistant half-time, Daryl Mallett, who sometimes does some of that. I have a strategic partner, Richard Gooding, with a management consulting firm of his own, who does high-level group facilitation. We're not doing focus groups at a consumer level; we're doing them at a very high level with managers, directors, and executives, or the leaders within a government entity. Sometimes it's more of an extended reference interview, and I often lead up to it with several individual reference inter-views. But I may really need a cross-functional team of the client's personnel involved to help agree on the most impor-tant issues at hand and examine potential courses of action. I'll often do a focus group with them to arrive at a refined scope of work once a project is underway.

I'm also collaborating with Oris Friesen, who was a senior database scientist for a large computer company for some thirty years and is now also a telecom policy wonk. I'm doing a project, the Arizona Telecom Directory, which involves creating an online portal directory to several hundred telecom providers active in Arizona. He's a crucial partner in designing the data-base component and the surveying. Bill Neumann, an instructor at the University of Arizona at Tucson who teaches business communications, is having thirty student volunteers from his class interview these telecom companies. Each student was assigned about a dozen companies to interview. It takes a lot of preparation and management for me to deal with this contributed resource. In fact, it might be cheaper for me to pay three people to do this than to take the time to manage thirty students who don't have quite the same interest or responsibility. But it is part of their class grade, and they will be co-managed by their professor. However, I'm also doing it to help build a relationship between the telecom organization that's sponsoring the study and the University of Arizona.

Do you have structured formal partnerships or do you just go on a per-project basis?

It's per-project, but I sometimes view it like the old *Mission Impossible*, where you know what your task is and then you sit there with the portfolios and the pictures and background on the people you know whom you've worked with, or wanted to work with, and you ask who has what skills and who would work well together.

Last year I bid for my largest project ever, a quarter-million-dollar regional wide area network (WAN) assessment for a consortium of two dozen municipal governments. I failed to get that project, but I presented a team of nine people, six of whom I had worked with before, three of whom were new and specific to that project, but who were people I knew. I didn't have the opportunity to build that team, but it was an interesting exercise for me in generating the proposal with two other core participants and all the additional players.

Most projects are not that complicated for me. They may involve myself, my assistant, and maybe one, two, or three additional people. My Web designer, Alan Levine—and his company Dommy Media—is another active participant in my organization and one of my ongoing strategic partners. He's an integral element in the implementation of the directory project, because my deliverable to my client is not infrequently a Web site implementation of the results.

I myself have often become a member of other consultant or organization project teams as a subcontractor, not leading but contributing as necessary and appropriate. At times I have done a substantial amount of subcontracting. I remain quite comfortable joining such an effort and bringing what value my skills and resources can to the process. I've learned that I don't have to "own" the job, and this has led to a variety of interesting opportunities and work over the years.

Do you have any tricks of the trade or timesaving devices to help you keep track of those really large, complex projects? Are you a Palm Pilot kind of guy, do you have any live-or-die-by software? I have a feeling you go way beyond a calendar and a pen.

I actually still use a physical calendar, but my contacts are all on mobile and desktop devices. I run a Sharp Mobilon, which is a fold-open, color screen, Windows CE device with a little touch keyboard, because I prefer a real keyboard to the cursive writing styles and chancy handwriting recognition on a Palm. It does have a built-in modem, but I don't yet have wireless enablement for my email. I am looking at new PDAs (personal digital assistants) that are wireless-enabled, so that I can do some limited Web surfing, at least, and also get and respond to email while I'm mobile.

On the desktop I use a standard Microsoft Office Suite with Word, Excel, PowerPoint, and Access. I also use a number of special applications, such as the full Adobe Acrobat [5], which allows you to edit and create Acrobat PDF files, PhotoShop for photos and graphic editing, and Corel Draw for vector drawing, as well as some utilities for image capture and file conversion.

I have a fair amount of graphic output at times. I've moved most of my personal and business photography to digital, so I have to manage digital media assets, and I'm still struggling a little with selecting comprehensive cataloging and desktop searching tools.

I have file structures and a regimen I'm very comfortable with for organizing my documents on a per-project basis, be they email, word processing, visual images, rich media, spreadsheets, or databases. I maintain a very specific project structure and hierarchy. I've created a numbering system so that, while all projects occur chronologically, my file names have that embedded identification and they're organized into appropriate directories. There are big management issues with hard drive organization, and if you're not on top of it—you know, if you just have a "My Documents" directory—you're going to get into a lot of trouble before you're done. I use some specific tools to back up hard drives, such as Adaptec CD Creator.

I have four desktop computers and one high-power laptop computer as well as my PDA. I have a networked environment in the home and a cable modem for Internet access. My wife's computer and mine both have very good laser volume printers. I have a third work station for my assistant in his work area in my house, and the fourth desktop machine is back in my electronics lab.

We've been talking about the information professional as somebody who helps others stay up-to-date in their field. How do you yourself stay current with information?

I'm clearly an information junkie. I have a voracious appetite for information and knowledge. I've always taken an enormous variety of hard-copy periodicals going back over twenty-five years. Today I have close to 200 hardcopy subscriptions. About sixty percent of them are free trade magazines. The other forty percent—maybe eighty magazines I pay for—run about $4,000 a year, a significant though essential personal investment.

The periodicals I take are all over the board. They're not just technical; they're not just on the information industry. They range from esoteric to popular culture and all sorts of things. I'm a very broad minded guy, able to find synergy and draw connections between often seemingly unrelated material. I may have a techno-focused business, but I believe part of my value is my ability to synergize even popular trends that I find in a broad range of material and bring that to the task at hand.

With the Web, I now subscribe to more than 300 different e-newsletters. I may open them immediately or shuffle them off to a holding zone if I'm busy. But I always scan the tables of contents before I save them in their own little subdirectories. Some are weekly, some are monthly, and some are every business day. Email management is certainly a problem in terms of the time it takes, but that's where I've extended my information appetite.

I call what I do "processing." I look at the material and I ask myself, is there anything interesting here for me on a general interest basis? Is there anything interesting for past projects that I might push to a client, or print and file because I'm still interested in some of the issues that I have researched in the past? Is anything here relevant for current projects? Beyond that, I look for anything for business acquaintances as well as friends and family; we shouldn't leave them out, either.

I try to cull out a part of my day where I push stuff to people. If I see an article in hard copy, I may go find the online version and then push the URL with a little note to somebody. My retained clients get a pretty good flow of such messages from me. For example, I've been on retainer to Cox Communications, a very large cable company, here at their Phoenix division, for four years. They get stuff from me basically every day. There are fifteen or twenty people in that organization with whom I maintain active contact. I've created little submailing lists of those people in a Word document, organized by the categories of information I'm likely to send them. So when I find something of interest for people at Cox, I drop into a Word document that tells me that, for consumer data modem access, here are the five people that I should push this to. For business broadband connectivity, or regulatory issues, here's the little subgroup. Someone's name may appear multiple times, depending on their interests.

Mark, that is just an amazing amount of information you process.

I find more and more online now, and I'm in a quandary on how to deal with the volumes of print that arrive daily in my mailbox. I have stacks of back issues, and I love it. One of my favorite things to do is to go to the post office—I still have a post office box and get most of my mail there. I pick up my mail and go a block away to a place called the Coffee Plantation and sit for two hours and read fifteen or more magazines. That's about what it takes me, five to ten minutes per magazine, because I just scan—or to use my word, process—looking at the table of contents for items of interest. Or I may flip through it page by page, but I may only actually read one article in a magazine, or cull something from it for later use. I'm also known to haul a whole bunch of magazines along on my travels and discard them as I read, processing them along the way.

One thing I've done in the course of reading this strange brew of print and electronic media is brainstorm about good domain names and actively acquire the best I come up with. I often build a group of related names around a theme and have ended up with more than 600 names in an interesting intellectual property portfolio. There are some inquiries already about my domain names and sales, and some challenges to them. For example, I've just prevailed at the World Intellectual Property Organization (WIPO) [141] in a legal challenge to my ownership of the domain name CrucialTechnology.com by Micron Technology, a large public company. And hopefully there will be many more interesting stories yet to come. I'm currently preparing to offer at auction some 150 or so biotechnology-related domain names.

Do you have a good story to tell me of a funny or unusual project you've worked on?

I used to be listed in a motion picture industry directory of resources. I'd get an occasional call on movie ideas to research for writers or production groups, and I did a couple of interesting projects in that arena. So I got a call one day, and they said, we're from so-and-so studio—I'm always impressed to get a call from Hollywood, still the heart of American cultural content—and we were wondering if you could research vehicles that run on unusual fuels. I say, sure, unusual fuels, you mean like electricity or methane. And they said, oh no, like strawberries. And I thought, strawberries, that's pretty weird. It was something like a Flubber story, where you end up powering the car on something unlikely. In the end we couldn't come to terms and the project didn't happen. I knew I could find information in the technical literature about corn that had been converted to alcohol, but I didn't think I would actually find articles about things like strawberries. I was willing to give it a shot, though.

You do a lot in 24 hours. I'm wondering about maintaining your personal balance, and how you keep it all together.

Well, we are DINKS—dual income, no kids. And that means my wife, Liz Warren, who teaches at South Mountain Community College, has her own very active life deeply involved in storytelling as a pursuit and passion. We often travel together to storytelling festivals and related cultural events and places, so part of my recreational life is involved in her interests.

We are able to give each other a lot of space, and there's also a difference in our schedules. She gets up at five A.M. or so, and has the house to herself until I manage to struggle up at 7:30 or 8:30 in the morning. Then I, in turn, have a quiet house later in the evening. She'll go to bed at ten or so and I'll usually work until two or three in the morning. So each of us has a three- or four-hour block of absolute quiet time within the house that makes for good work time.

Beyond that, I find a lot of my recreational value in my pro bono work, going out and engaging with people, working on regional economic development issues. That's a lively part of my life. I don't view it as work per se, that day-to-day engagement with people on interesting matters with interesting ideas and interesting interactions.

And I imagine lots of lunches and dinners.

Yes, lunches and dinners. I belong to a number of groups whose dinners I just go to as social and schmooze-fest stuff, or for their content with local and national speakers. That to me is an integral part of my life, not my business.

And your three cats, because we've talked about those before.

Yes, the two girl cats, Guinevere and Caer, are very lovey and fun and playful and cuddle all night. Caer often goes purposely about the house and yard pursuing her important kitten business. Then there's this weird old guy Ming, who is my inheritance from my great, now deceased, friend, David Campbell, who had been a dancer for Martha Graham in the forties. Out of my film background I also have a number of friends who are working artists who don't do anything like what I do. They're print artists, photographers, dancers, and gallery owners. As you may have been able to tell from my earlier company, Advanced Tools for the Arts, that was a company designed to mostly bring technology into artistic environments. I maintain a lively kind of artistic subculture life too, and we attend many openings, concerts, and cultural events.

Tell me your thoughts on the future of the independent information professional. Wide open, or tough market?

Well, you know, I'm not sure. My business has become very diverse, as we've discussed, and my preference these days is always for what I call smart-guy stuff. It's good work when you can get it. That's not quite the traditional information professional career path, in that it integrates my core competency in certain industry segments, with research, into a consulting relationship. They think of me more as a consultant than a researcher, but a consultant who happens to deliver a broad range of information and, hopefully, value.

I don't know if I'm qualified to speak on the future of the profession, but to me the research and the other traditional information professional skills remain an absolute core and essential competency. As artificial intelligence and smart personal agents come to do a better job of information retrieval, filtering, and preparation, they may automate and displace some of the research tasks we do today. I would hope to learn to use those tools effectively for my clients and, further, to consult to others on their applications and implementation.

I've begun to work with several interesting clients whose products enable content distribution and digital rights management. With the far-reaching transformations in the content industry driven by the advent of rich media, ubiquitous networking, and broadband connectivity, I'm looking forward to staying on the cutting edge of our content industry in the interesting times yet to come.

What advice do you have for somebody looking to build a consultancy or an independent business? Do you think some time in industry and the corporate world is important?

Well, you know I spent my last twelve corporate years with a biomedical device manufacturer. I've had very few projects in that realm. I learned more about the discipline and the skills required to work with teams and manage complex projects than about any specific content areas I'm involved with today.

It can go either way. Industry or other enterprise experience—and that can be at the university or government level too—is a core place to learn those people skills, those organizational skills. But the content area that you work in may or may not end up being the content area that you specialize in. I've always had some strategic plans for myself. Not a formal business plan, just a roadmap of the things I thought I would like to do. But I've always allowed myself, as on any good road trip, to be diverted by interesting and/or lucrative things that came along. I've always had a general direction that I would pursue, but I've left myself open to those serendipitous events, the things that come to you.

My friend and mentor Alan Hald would say that luck is a combination of preparation and opportunity. The serendipitous events don't happen to you, in all likelihood, unless you, one, prepare yourself for them and, two, open yourself up to them. If you sit in your office, they're not usually going to come. It's really that combination of self-development, of professional development through client activities and community, and being ready for opportunity, that makes for luck.

Super Searcher Power Tips

➤ I use a basic set of questions in reference interviews: What is it you think you want to know? Why do you want to know it? What does it mean to your business if you find out certain things? And lastly, what do you know already, and how do you know it?

➤ I've always welcomed, and in fact have cultivated, my own competition. I've always enjoyed meeting with others in our business and see that as a way to find subcontracting or cross referrals as well as being supportive to the greater community of researchers. I've never been closely guarded.

➤ All of my marketing is done by public visibility and networking, referral from clients or associates, direct engagement, or people finding me through my Web site.

➤ People say, well, if I go to your Web site I can find lists of resources myself to do my own research. That's great. I always encourage people to do what they can on their own, and only use me when they run into a brick wall or need research beyond their expertise, time, or means.

➤ Public speaking has led to some client work, but I also consider it perhaps more than that, as part of my own ongoing professional development. When I speak at a conference, I get to schmooze with the other speakers as well as the attendees.

➤ Unless I really trust a person's searching protocol and skills, I'm going to go back and search the Web in my ways to complement what they tell me they've already done.

➤ There's still a tangible satisfaction in handling hard copy that I don't know if I'll ever outgrow no matter how great the online world becomes.

➤ My clients think of me more as a consultant than a researcher, but a consultant who happens to deliver a broad range of information and value.

Chris Dobson
Serving Corporate Libraries

Chris Dobson is president of F1 Services, Inc., a Dallas, Texas-based consulting organization that helps clients gather, manage, and use information. F1 Services designs corporate libraries, develops taxonomies for portals and knowledge management systems, creates specialized databases, and supplies on-demand research services. Chris is a frequent speaker at information industry conferences and is the author of the ezine, The Shelfless Librarian.

chris.dobson@f1servicesinc.com
www.f1servicesinc.com

Chris, tell me something about your background before you became an independent business owner.

I was a corporate librarian for nine years at Core Laboratories, American Airlines, and then at Infomart, a market center for high technology, where I ran a fee-based library service. I have a master's degree in library science from Texas Woman's University. I also have a master's degree in history, but that turned out to be not too useful when it came to earning a living.

What did you do in these positions that helped you as an independent business owner?

Infomart was unique because we basically did information brokering, so obviously that was a big help. I think that being in a corporate library is good experience for information brokers because most corporate libraries are essentially small businesses. Typically, they're billing back their costs, they have to keep track of how they spend money, who they spend it for, and what they spend it on. They tend to operate as very self-contained units. And that's all useful. If you can run a corporate library efficiently, you are going to have a step up when it actually comes to running your own company.

The move to your own business, then—was that something you spent a lot of time planning, or did it just kind of happen?

No, I did not plan for it. My boss showed up one day and said, "We're closing the library. Would you like to be an information broker?" And, I said, "Okay, fine."

You were already operating a fee-based information service, but were you aware of any other independents out there?

There was actually a small group of information brokers in Dallas. We had a meeting when I was at Infomart; I think there were maybe five of us. We only had one meeting, though, because shortly thereafter two of the people took real jobs. I was aware of the field, and we were part of it because, even though we were a corporate library, we were open to the public. We operated as a privately funded public library, and a lot of people thought we were actually part of Dallas Public. I was hired at Infomart specifically to set up the fee-based part of the business.

So your boss at Infomart approached you and basically asked you to continue doing the same work as an independent?

Yes. Their idea was to move the library service to the upstairs of the building we were in, which had a lot of empty space. They did not want to lose the corporate library research capability, and they were also concerned about the bad press they would get by closing the library. We had 20,000 people a year coming through. So what they did was offer us office space in exchange for services for a certain period of time, and sold us all the equipment at a very reasonable rate.

That sure is an interesting way to begin! What did you see as advantages or disadvantages to being in a commercial office as opposed to working from your home?

The visibility was good, and I think that people viewed us as more of a "real" company because we had a "real" office. In 1988, the home office craze hadn't really hit. The other factor was that my husband has his own business and he already had the home office. There just was not room for two of us to work out of the house. But when we told people that we were at Infomart, that gave us quite a bit of credibility because it was known to be a high-class, expensive building. Now, had we just started out and decided to go lease an office, we would have had difficulty because we would have had no credit rating as a company. So that was one of the advantages—we were at Infomart for three years, and then when we decided to move into a different space, we had a track record, so someone would lease to us.

What about setting up as a business entity and seeking professional advice? How did you do all that?

My business began as a partnership, so we had an attorney draw up a partnership agreement. And we had agreements with Infomart. Later on, when we started doing temporary library staffing, we had agreements with clients. Now, most of the contracts we accept we tend to handle on our own, but every now and then we still have to call an attorney in because we've got some screwball contract that somebody has presented. I think that when you're starting out, there's no point in trying to figure all that out yourself. And your needs change over time; eventually the original partnership was dissolved and I incorporated the business, so, again, I needed legal advice for that.

We set up our own accounting and decided to use QuickBooks [104, see Appendix]. There weren't a lot of accountants back then who knew anything about QuickBooks software. We've gone through a couple of CPAs over the course of twelve years, but now we have one with whom we have a good relationship. If I had to do it over again, though, I would get more professional help. One of the reasons we didn't was that we basically just mapped the system we had at Infomart, since we did our own accounting in the library. We kept our own accounts receivable and payable. Infomart corporate wrote the actual checks, but we kept very close track of everything. So it wasn't that difficult to convert the system we were using over to our own business.

In the early days, it sounds like you walked right into an established client base. How did you stir up more business?

We were lucky again, because we had a client list. Basically what we did was a management buy-out, though there was not a lot of money involved in the library operations. Obviously we weren't loaning books anymore, but we did get the client list and did a mailing to everyone saying, okay, the people you knew and loved on the first floor are now on the fifth floor. We can still do the same wonderful things for you but you can't check out books. I would say that, in maybe two and a half to three years, that client list turned over completely. Very few of the people who were on the client list when we were with the library remained on it. But that did give us a few months of not having to start from ground zero.

What type of research were you doing when you first started out?

We did a lot of corporate profiles. There was no Internet, so we did a lot of what I call the easy stuff. We did a few more complicated projects, but most of it was "find me what's been written on this or that." We had one client that was an oil company selling partnerships for horizontal drilling. We did a weekly update on everything that had happened in the previous week having to do with horizontal drilling. We worked with a lot of PR firms doing similar current awareness assignments. The work was definitely easier than what we do now.

Your business model and your services are much different today. Can you tell me about the transition and the changes that you've gone through?

Today I own the company, and I have someone who works with me very closely. We make joint decisions, but we are both employees of the corporation. A lot of people I have talked to over the years who have been in partnerships agree that it tends to not work, because usually one person is more committed than the other. I think it's a lot better to have one person take the lead or have majority shares in the company.

As far as the work goes, when we first started out, we did research. After a year we started doing temporary staffing for corporate libraries. It was a case of the phone not ringing and sitting there thinking, "Okay, what have people paid me to do in my life before?" One of the things they paid me to do was be a corporate librarian. So I sent letters to all the corporate librarians in the Dallas Metroplex and said, "Hey, if you have somebody out on vacation or maternity leave or whatever, call me and I will come fill in." Originally, I was the temp, and now we have a group of professional librarians working for us. I don't need to go out on jobs too much anymore.

About the time I incorporated, I hired Carolyn Ernst, who had more corporate experience than I had, as well as a complementary skill set. What we have done together is to really try to emphasize the consulting. We set up corporate libraries, we do taxonomies for corporate portals and knowledge management systems, and we do information audits. These services are a lot more lucrative than research. We tend to do big projects, and we continue to do basic research for the clients we've had for a long time.

Tell me a bit more about your work in setting up corporate libraries. Having worked as a startup corporate librarian myself, one thing that really caught my eye on your Web site was that you actually work on marketing campaigns for the libraries within the companies that you're consulting for. In one case you described a grand opening, complete with an "Information Menu" for patrons.

We'll get calls from companies for various reasons. In one case they had extra money in their market research budget and they needed to spend it or they would lose it the next year. So I said, that's enough to set up a corporate library. In other cases, they'll hire an employee who just can't believe they don't have a library because he had a library in his last company and he has to have one here. Usually there's some sort of champion involved who gets the ball rolling.

We go in and do an information audit to find out what kind of services they need, what kind of collection they need, whether it needs to be a physical library or if it can be all virtual. Then we create a collection policy and set up all the procedures. I think that's one of the most valuable things we do, because one of the mistakes a lot of companies make is that they'll decide, well, they need a new library, they can hire a new librarian. They'll hire somebody right out of library school, and the problem is that the person doesn't usually know how to set up all the procedures— things like keeping track of the money and what's been ordered. Making sure that stuff that was ordered comes in. Figuring out what kind of cataloging system to use. What kind of software they need. How to justify expenditures. How to deliver the research. There are just dozens of areas where, if you've never done it before, it's a major hurdle. We've set up and run enough libraries ourselves that we can pretty easily figure out what particular mix of things is going to work.

Once the procedures are set up, we document everything so that they can hire someone with little or no library experience, generally an MLS but sometimes not even that, to come in and basically keep it going. And then, depending on what our arrangement is with the company, in some cases we've actually stayed on long enough to get the library operation going, train the person and do some marketing. That's where we'll do things like hold open houses, print brochures, and set up email alerts.

So you're there from the beginning, even getting the word out within the company about their new library.

Sometimes it turns out that we staff the library too. We can provide them with a librarian from our pool of professionals. We basically outsource the whole thing. It's a turnkey operation.

What kind of feedback do you get from companies? Do you track your success, so to speak, go back and see how it's functioning later on?

We don't really measure our success in terms of whether or not it's still functioning. A lot of factors go into whether or not a library makes it. In the case of the one we set up where we plugged the "information menu," they eventually decided that they couldn't justify the library and no one was going to pay for it. That was a situation where one fairly small department was responsible for the library, and when they tried to spread the load, no one else was willing to take them up on it. It was also sort of a strange corporate culture, one of those places where people are running so fast that they're not working smart, they're just working more. As a result, a lot of people didn't think they had the time to use the library. We couldn't convince them that it would save them time. In other cases the library has been very successful. But once we set it up, even if it's just six months down the road, we can't really take credit or blame for it. The company will either realize its value and support it, or they won't.

Your temporary staffing services provide paraprofessional staffing as well as degreed librarians. How big a portion of your business is that?

It's a pretty substantial portion. One of the nice things about it is that it has taken on its own momentum. We don't have to market it anymore; it just goes. We have a limited geographic area in the Dallas vicinity, though we do staff as far away as Austin in some cases. We have no competition, and every librarian in town knows about us. We also have two library schools nearby, and most of the people who are getting ready to graduate know about us. We just collect resumes and people call us, and we go through our records and see who fits.

You hire these folks as your employees and handle all their benefits and taxes, so what you can offer to a company is a preselected, qualified candidate to walk in and work on-site without their having to watch the business side of things.

Yes. There are a couple of reasons, basically, why companies will hire people through us. They don't want the salary to come out of their payroll account; they can't add a head but they've got the money to pay for somebody, so they'll hire a contractor. The money comes out of a different account. It's one of those corporate things that companies can do. The other reason is that they can hire somebody from us for a short-term project, and they don't have to worry about their unemployment rates going up when they lay that person off.

Turning to the research services that you offer to your clients, what online systems do you subscribe to?

Just about everything. We subscribe to Dialog [35], Dow Jones [39], Disclosure [37], LexisNexis [69], Research Bank [107], Investext [107], STN [121], and DataStar [30], to name a few.

How has the growth of the Internet and of better search capabilities there impacted your business? How much do you use the Internet as a research tool?

Because of the Internet, we don't get any easy projects anymore. When people call us up and they're looking for something that should be simple, like, gee, I need an address for this company, well, it's not simple. It's because they've already looked on the Internet and haven't been able to find it. A lot of the requests we get are for bigger projects where they need to track down a lot of companies. They need some analysis and they need it in a real simple format. They don't want to read a ton of stuff. They want it already digested.

In the early '90s one of our primary clients was an outplacement agency for whom we did $20,000 per year worth of corporate profiles. Well, we hardly do anything for them anymore because they can get it off the Internet. It has changed the business. It's made it more challenging. There are times when it would be nice to do something that we don't have to even think about. But unfortunately we have to think about just about everything we do now.

As far as actually using the Web is concerned, once in awhile we'll still get a project where the sources are publicly available on the Web. I had a project where the client was interested in some kind of educational trend, so everything that we needed was right there. ERIC [42] is free, and I could get a lot of papers that way. I managed to do ninety-five percent of the project without ever going to a source I had to pay for.

The problem I have with using most of the public Web sites, other than for corporate propaganda, is that often you can't figure out the source. If I'm going to give a client a summary that says this is the status of this particular technique, or whatever, at this time, I can't use as my source a paper where I can't figure out who the author is and when it was written. A lot of times you'll find the perfect paper, but who knows how long it's been out there? We just can't use that stuff.

The other reason that I don't like using the Internet is that, even for things like press releases, time is money and I'm charging for my time. If I have to go onto Dow Jones and pay three dollars for a press release from PR Newswire [98], it's worth it, because it would cost me more than three dollars worth of my time to try to find the thing on the PR Newswire site. If I can spend a half an hour on Dow Jones and download ten or fifteen articles, it's a much better use of my time than if I spend three hours trying to find a needle in a haystack.

Good point. What about the search engines? What do you like to use?

I usually start with MetaCrawler [81], and I like Google [53] and HotBot [57]. There are searches where you know that something like a recent company announcement is not going to be in one of the commercial services like Dialog yet, and it's not going to have been picked up by any of the industry periodical sites, either. Then I will use all the search engines I can find.

Do you ever use special collections or do manual or telephone research for your projects?

No, and we hardly ever did. That's just one of those cases where there are certain things that we don't like doing, and one of the advantages of being self-employed is that, within certain parameters, you don't have to do things you don't like to do. In the past, if we needed that kind of research, we knew people in town who did it, and we either farmed it out or referred people directly to them. I would not have wanted to be a librarian before computers.

We may occasionally do a tiny bit of telephone research. How far I will go depends on the situation. I did a project last year where a company was trying to find trends in several different industries that they worked with. I did wind up calling several associations and some government agencies, but I wasn't asking for anything that anybody should not be willing to tell me. I don't do competitive telephone research. I would not call companies and try to find out about their strategic marketing plan or their pricing. One really important consideration when you're a generalist is knowing what areas you are not good at and what areas require expertise that you don't have.

Slightly related to that is your work with focus groups. I know you do focus groups in the context of setting up libraries, but do you also offer them as more of a broad research service?

When we do a focus group, it's a tool. We're doing it to gather data that we're going to use. But if somebody needs primary market research, we're not the people to call. There are people who specialize in that.

We begin most of our consulting projects by doing interviews or a focus group. It's usually a combination. We like interviews better because you get a lot more usable information.

We recently set up a taxonomy for a corporate portal. We did interviews, and then after we had the taxonomy drafted and outlined, we did a focus group to make sure the categories we had selected were going to be meaningful to people.

Basically, there are three techniques you can use to do an information audit: the focus group, interviews, and a survey. We usually start with the interview. For this corporate portal project, we interviewed twenty people, and from that we could get an idea of what information they use and how they use it. That was enough for us to come up with a preliminary taxonomy.

The reason for using the focus group was that the people we interviewed tended to be middle managers, and the focus group was primarily the workers, clerical support staff, and people who did not supervise anybody. That gave us a chance to make sure that what worked for one tier of people was going to work for another tier, without our having to go and do another round of interviews.

We did one library project where the interviews helped us figure out what the collection needed to include and some of the services they wanted. Then we did a focus group to determine what role the librarian needed to play. This was a case where the company wanted to set up a library, but they wanted it run by a paraprofessional. They had already decided who was going to run it, so one of the things we wanted to do was find out what people's expectations were in terms of research and how the information was going to be delivered to them. We had to make sure their expectations were going to match with the paraprofessional's abilities.

We've occasionally done surveys, but we don't like them. People don't think when they're filling out a survey. They're just checking off the boxes and the results you get tend to be not all that valuable.

What about pricing your services? Do you have a different model for consulting projects vs. an hourly rate?

For research we have an hourly rate that is based on what the market will bear. People in our profession sometimes go into great detail about how much they want to make, what their overhead costs are, how many hours they think they're going to work. As far as I am concerned, all that's nonsense. Just find out what everybody else in your area is charging and pick a number. If you're doing something different from everybody else, you can pick a higher number, but not a lot higher.

The problem with selling research services is that it's usually not viewed as essential, and so people are going to be very price conscious. We basically just pick a number and then every few years we raise the number. We used to announce when we raised the number, but now we don't, because when people call us they are not interested in our hourly fee. They want to know what this particular project is going to cost.

We really try to get the client to tell us how much they want to spend, because if you haven't done the research before, you don't know in advance how hard it's going to be, so it's difficult to come up with an accurate estimate. Sometimes we can get the client to pick, and other times we just give them a number and hope it's right.

For consulting, we actually sit down and try to figure out how many hours we need to spend on the project. We usually multiply that by three because we know we always underestimate. Then we decide that is probably more than the client will pay and so we cut it down a little bit.

What is a typical timeline on these larger consulting projects?

We set up a virtual library for an association a few years ago and spent about nine months on that. That's probably been our longest project. Usually when we set up a library it takes two to four months.

What about some of your office logistics, like delivering results and keeping everything running smoothly?

We almost always email client correspondence and project results. We haven't done a hard-copy project in a long time. The office is completely run by Carolyn and myself. I'm not a gadget person. I carry a calendar and two pens, in case one of them runs out. I used to have one of those little things where you put all your names and phone numbers in it, but the problem was when the batteries went out you lost everything. If I win a Palm Pilot one of these years I might use it. I don't carry a cell phone. In fact, one of the things I have discovered about cell phones is that they have made life a lot easier for those of us who refuse to get one. The last time I was at an airport where my flight was going to be delayed by many, many hours, I had no problem getting a pay phone. Everybody else was shouting into his or her cell phone and there I was in this quiet little phone booth area, which was very nice. Back at the office we use Call Notes [19], which is a great voice mail management service, and come to think of it, we've got music on hold.

Tell me about your marketing and what you have found to be most effective over the years.

Basically, I hate marketing, which is typical of a lot of people who go into this business. They like to do the work but they're not really into sales. I don't think advertising as such works at all. There's no way you can adequately communicate what you can do for people in an advertisement and be able to afford it. We used to have yellow-pages listings and they worked very well for generating calls, but in the last few years we've pretty much let them go because I don't think people are using the yellow pages as much anymore. They're going to the Internet, and that's basically where most of our marketing efforts have gone. In the fall of 2000 we finally took the time to put together our Web site. We had one before but we had somebody else do it for us. It was ugly, and we had never bothered to write the content. So, during a slow period, we finally took the time to do it right.

We pay to be listed on Yahoo! [145], and that's how we got the portal project; if you search on "taxonomies" on Yahoo! you get us and one other company. If you put in "taxonomy," singular, you get a lot of listings, but plural, you get us. We pay to be on LookSmart [73] and the Verizon [133] online yellow pages where there's actually a link to our Web site. We try to get listed everywhere we can. I used to feel that the people who were going to pay us to do research were not going to be surfing the Web. I think that's changed. Everybody surfs now. They just don't do it effectively. When they get frustrated, they may find us.

We used to send out a newsletter, but that was to build the research side of the business, and I think it did help. We sent it out every couple of months and it reminded people that we were in business. If we were going to do that now, we would probably do it electronically. But at this point, we are not trying to build the research business, so we just don't do that anymore. And with the consulting business, we don't get a lot of repeat business.

I was going to ask you about client retention. If you go in and set up a library, then that client is probably not going to need you again.

Well, not until a librarian quits, and then they're going to need a temp. Some libraries that we set up will use us for overflow research. But we're really trying to create an image that we are your one-stop library company. Our printed brochures are targeted toward libraries. You get some of that on our Web page too. We'll set up your library, we'll staff your library, when your librarian gets overworked, we'll help her out. We're trying to sell all three services to the same market.

What about professional associations? Do those memberships serve as a marketing vehicle?

I belong to the Association of Independent Information Professionals (AIIP) [172], of course, and the Special Libraries Association (SLA) [201]. I also belong to some regional library associations. We've moved from marketing to end-users to marketing primarily to librarians. As a result I belong to the Dallas Association of Law Librarians [178]. I'm on the local arrangements committee for the Medical Library Association (MLA) [190] 2002 conference, even though I am not a member of MLA. We're pretty active in SLA, not so much on the national level, but on the local and the state level. And my feeling is that this is a marketing technique that fits us because we are librarians and librarians hate to market. On the other hand, librarians hate to be marketed to. It works out well because all we do is go to meetings and talk to people. It's pretty much all networking.

And you're speaking the same language, peer to peer.

Yes, we're just talking. We ask them how they are doing, and they ask how is your business, and we say, well, we've got this great project. We're not really trying to sell anybody anything and that works for the people we're trying to sell to. Librarians as a group tend to be very sales resistant. It's not the approach that would work if we had a different group as our core clientele. It's so low-key that it's almost nonexistent. As the business evolved we figured out whom we were comfortable with, and whom we did not need to do a sales job on, because we didn't like doing sales jobs. Finding the market that fits you the best takes a while, unless you really sit down and do a lot of self-analysis, which of course we didn't do before we went into this.

That's a great point. Now, I want to ask you about your book, *Information Brokering:*

A How-To-Do-It Manual [229]. It's very thorough; you left no stone unturned.

My co-author Florence Mason is also a consultant, primarily for public and university libraries. She teaches at Emporia State and at the University of North Texas. She had been doing a course in Information Brokering for Emporia and one of her problems was she didn't have a textbook, so she got the bright idea that we should write one. That was the initial reason for doing it. I had been teaching an adult education course for three to four years called "Opportunities as an Information Broker," back when the economy was bad and people were getting laid off and there were all these "you could make money as a ..." courses. We took some of the notes that she had been using in her class, took the notes I had been using in my class, and based on those notes, we wrote the book. It's not something I would want to make my living doing. It was fun in some ways, and a lot of work in others. I had a lot of frustration with the editing process. I've talked to many people who have written books, and none of my experiences were unique. But I'm glad we did it.

How do you handle staying informed and up-to-date? We routinely do this for clients, but we need current information ourselves.

Carolyn reads for me, and I subscribe to the AIIP discussion list. We get *Searcher* [223], and I'm usually a year behind on that. We get *Information Today* [217], and I'm usually four or five months behind on that. We get *Library Journal* [218] and *Information Outlook* [216], but quite frankly, Carolyn just reads for me. She skims all the stuff on the email lists, and we get a bunch of magazines like *Business Week* [209] and *Business 2.0* [207]. If there's something I need to know, she tells me or she marks it and I have to read it.

That sounds like a great system. After many years as a searcher, you must have a great story or two to share, or a funny client request.

You know, I've done so many of those, and I always say, "This is one that we need to remember so that when people ask us about kinds of research we do, we can pull this one out." And then somehow I still forget. Sometimes I can't remember what I did research on last week! Once it's done, it's done. We do have one client for whom we were doing a current-awareness update over a long period of time. It was a PR agency and their client was Trojan, the condom maker. So we know a whole lot more about condoms than most people. They come in lots of different colors and flavors. There's a restaurant in China decorated with them, you know. It's a big market over there with that one-child-per-family law.

Most of our research requests are pretty cut-and-dried, though. "What's new about my competitor?" "I heard that so and so said this …" "Somebody told me about an article in the *Wall Street Journal* …" "I need to know about this market …" "What are the trends in X?" We don't do a lot of exciting stuff.

What do you like about what you do? What do you like most about owning your own business?

I like the fact that I'm not just doing one thing. I can't even do research for eight hours a day. I have a short attention span. I don't have to go to any unproductive meetings. If I don't like my boss, I can choose to not work for them anymore. We have had clients for whom we did projects and decided that, if they called again, we were not going to be available. We have other clients we've been working for since 1988, and it's been great to watch their businesses grow and to keep in touch with them. You have more control when you own your own business. Not a lot of control, because you are still at the mercy of your clients and, to a certain extent, the economy.

Corporate librarians in particular feel that they are performing a valuable service. When there are cutbacks, the budget for the corporate library will get cut in half at the same time the president's conference room is being remodeled. My experience in having worked for companies, from 60,000-employee firms to six-person businesses, is that a lot of corporate decisions are not based on any kind of logic. That can be very frustrating when you are suffering the consequences of one of those decisions. When you're running your own business, your decisions may not be based on logic, either, but they're your own decisions and so it doesn't matter. We've probably made decisions in the last thirteen years that haven't made sense to anybody else, but they made sense to us.

How do you keep your life in balance so that you're not working eighty hours a week? Can you shut down and go home pretty easily?

One of the problems is that you do not control your workflow. Right now, I am working a lot more hours than I want to. I was in both days this weekend. Last February, when I didn't need to be mowing my lawn and I didn't have my garden to work in, I was going home and I could take the whole weekend off, because February was slow. But, since the beginning of March it has not been. So, you work when you have work to do. One of the problems with being self-employed is that you either have time or you have money. It's very difficult to take a vacation. If you have the time to take a vacation, you can't afford it. And if you can afford it, you're too busy to leave.

We sat down and actually did goal planning about five years ago for the first time, and one of my goals at that point was to work fewer hours, because I was working most weekends. And I have done that. That was one of the advantages of moving the business more toward the consulting side, because the projects are bigger, they are much more rewarding financially, and they tend to have a cycle and then a gap. There is time between one project and the next where you can regroup and relax and get to see what color your house is because you're going home during the daylight.

What do you see for the future of the independent information business?

Quite frankly, I don't think anybody can make a living just doing research. I think that companies have been following the trend in recent years of focusing on core competencies and out-sourcing the rest. That is a good trend for information professionals because they can go in and do something for a company on a short-term project basis.

This company that we've been working with that's putting in a portal has consultants coming out of its ears. They've bought the software, so they have the software company working on the installation. They have another set of consultants working on business practices. And then they brought us in to do the taxonomy and the metadata.

I think one of the ways information professionals can grow their businesses is to identify services that people need on a short-term basis, that they don't need every day. I still feel that companies are better off with on-site employee librarians. I don't think you get the same level of service when you outsource the library. On the other hand, there's no reason why librarians can't outsource a lot of project-related research. When you're doing competitive intelligence and that sort of thing, you've got a lot better handle on it if you're part of the company. You know what new projects and products are coming down the pike, which they don't tell somebody who's working on it from the outside. But when a project does get to a point where, okay, now we need to know everything we can about this industry or this technology—that's the kind of thing that can be easily outsourced. I think a lot of opportunities still exist for people to work independently.

What advice do you have for somebody interested in the independent information profession? Do you think some corporate experience is a good idea?

You certainly cannot do this right out of library school or as a fresh MBA. You have to know how business works. You have to know how to do research. You can't learn on your client's money. You have to already know. And the best way to learn is to get a job in a library or in a marketing department where you're doing research. The advice that I always, somewhat tongue-in-cheek, gave people who took my course was to have a spouse with a high-paying secure job. I still think that that's true. My husband and I are both self-employed, and that makes for some really exciting months. But it's also what has made us successful.

I can relate—needing to make a living is a great motivation!

I do think that the more variety of experience you have, the better off you're going to be. I also think that if you haven't had that experience, you need to take some small business administration courses. I see a lot of people who are great researchers and have a terrible time in this business because they can't cope with invoices. As far as I'm concerned, doing the invoicing is the fun part. You can be the best researcher in the world, but if you can't keep track of who owes you money and get them to pay you, you are not going to succeed. Being able to run your business efficiently is absolutely essential, because you can't spend loads and loads of time dealing with the overhead. The time you spend writing checks and sending out invoices and dunning people for money is time you can't bill.

Also, it's important to pick a niche. I think people have to do that now. We didn't have to pick a niche because, when we started out, there were so few resources that we could handle them all. We can't do that anymore. You need to pick a type of service, like telephone research, or you need to focus on certain industries. We have said we don't do case law research. We don't do disease-of-the-week research. We don't do patent research. As we've gone along, our list of "we don't do's" has gotten bigger. You just can't keep up with it all.

That's a good point.

As I said, we're not trying to build the research side of the business at this point, but we've got maybe half a dozen key clients for whom we still do research. We try not to farm out their work because we know their industries. But we got one project recently for a client we've had for a while that I had to farm out because we didn't have time to do it. And we got a new client, and I just turned around and farmed that research out, too, because there was no way we could handle it.

One of the problems with doing consulting is that when you're in the middle of a project, you often can't do anything else. And with this last project, the time frame was much tighter than we would normally go along with, so it meant that we had to farm out all the research that came in. It's not something we like to do, but it brings up another one of the important things in business—pick your subcontractors carefully.

How do you handle working with subcontractors?

If you're an experienced research person and you subcontract something out, I think the best way is to have the other person send the results to you, at least for the first couple of times. You look at the results and then send them on to the client. That's how you find out whether or not you're getting what you're paying the subcontractor for.

If you're just starting out in business, a great way to learn how to do research is to have somebody else do it, send it to you raw so that you can see what their search strategy was, and then you pretty it up and do the analysis and send it on to the client. That way, you get to see how it's done, and when the client calls, you can answer their questions. It always amazes me when someone calls me up and says, "We're a brand new information broker company and we're looking for subcontracting work." I say, "Give me a break, I'm not going to give you any work when I don't know you at all!"

"Will you pay for my learning curve?"

Yes. For people who are starting out, it has to be the other way around. They need to be doing the marketing and getting the clients and having somebody else do the research for them, so they can learn and still deliver a quality product. It benefits everyone involved.

Super Searcher Power Tips

➤ Clients need some analysis and they need it in a simple format. They don't want to read a ton of stuff. They want it already digested.

➤ One of the advantages of being self-employed is that, within certain parameters, you don't have to do stuff you don't like to do. If we need manual research, we know people in town who do it and we either farm it out or refer people to them.

➤ It's important to know what areas you are not good at and what areas require expertise that you don't have.

➤ I don't think advertising as such works at all. There's no way you can communicate what you can do for people in an ad and be able to afford it.

➤ I used to feel that people who were going to pay us to do research were not going to be surfing the Web. Well, everybody surfs now. They just don't do it effectively. When they get frustrated, they may find us.

➤ Companies have been following the trend in recent years of focusing on core competencies and outsourcing the rest. That is a good trend for information professionals because they can go in and do short-term projects for a company.

➤ We have said we don't do case law research. We don't do disease-of-the-week research. We don't do patent research. As we've gone along, our list of "we don't do's" has gotten bigger. You just can't keep up with it all.

➤ You certainly cannot do this right out of library school or as a fresh MBA. You have to know how business works. You have to know how to do research. You can't learn on your client's money. You have to already know.

Crystal Sharp
Canadian Business Information

Crystal Sharp is the owner and director of InformAction, CD Sharp Information Systems, Ltd., an independent research company based in London, Ontario, Canada. InformAction offers business intelligence, marketing research, grant proposal writing and coordination, and consulting services for the healthcare industry.

crystal@cdsharp.com
www.cdsharp.com

Crystal, tell me about your background, and how you ended up running a business from your home in Canada.

I was raised in India and after high school spent a couple years in the Middle East where my father took a job. During that time I met my husband, who is British, and soon after we were married we moved to the States, where David enrolled in a Ph.D. program at the Sloan School of Management at MIT. I decided to go back to school as well, and enrolled in a junior college studying travel and tourism. I then decided to continue for my B.A. and transferred to Wellesley College, where I majored in economics with a minor in French. I really got interested in research when I did an independent research project for one course, and when I worked in the summers as a research assistant.

After I graduated from Wellesley, I worked in a travel agency for a while and then took a break when our first son was born. When Andrew was a year old, I decided to enroll in Boston College for a master's in economics. After that, I got a job doing contract research at the Harvard Institute for International Development (HIID). That's what introduced me to the idea that I could work on a project basis and didn't have to be working full-time somewhere. The research aspect of the job was great, and I really enjoyed the variety of the work.

Tell me a little more about the types of projects you worked on at Harvard.

I worked on many different projects, often involving library research, writing, finding and compiling statistics on various aspects of developing countries, and some analysis. I was part of one team project that worked to develop indicators of openness for developing countries for the United States Agency for International Development (USAID). The agency had some discretionary funds to spend, and decided to use them to reward a country that was opening up its trade policies or becoming more liberal with social policies. Our task was to come up with indicators that would help them decide where that money should go. Another involved looking at economic trends in certain African economies, as my boss was doing some consulting to government officials on their financial policies. I also helped in the development of summer workshops for developing country officials that HIID ran annually.

We moved to Canada in 1992, with Andrew who was five and Christopher who was one year old, and I was expecting my youngest, Joseph. Two years later, I began to think about entering the workforce again, and fortunately I discovered the library and information science program at the University of Western Ontario, which, after many name changes, has now settled on the Faculty of Information and Media Studies. You could take classes in the evenings, which was very convenient for me, and it was an opportunity to learn emerging technologies, because by that time the Internet and World Wide Web were coming into use. While I had been quite technologically savvy two years previously, I found I had fallen behind considerably!

As I progressed through the program, my main goal continued to be to work independently, and various ideas kept going around in my mind. I hadn't a clear idea of how I was going to do it, but knew it would be research related. As I got closer to graduation, I really had to think about the business aspects too, because that was something I hadn't had to worry about before. So I started doing research and discovered the Association of Independent Information Professionals (AIIP) [172, see Appendix], and joined the Business Librarians discussion list, BUSLIB [148], because my skills and previous experience lent themselves quite nicely to business librarianship. I also read Sue Rugge's book [230], which I thought was fascinating reading, and definitely decided that was the way I wanted to go. I took a course called Information Entrepreneurship, which I found very interesting because marketing information services is quite different from marketing a product.

Joining AIIP was the best thing I ever did because the discussions on the email list were so practical. Whenever someone posted a research problem, that became my practice time, because I would take that problem and see whether I could come up with answers to the questions that were put forth.

That's funny; I did the exact same thing. I would challenge myself with AIIP-L [146] queries, up to the point of not spending money, but at least identifying databases and thinking about how the search could be structured.

It's a confidence booster, isn't it, because if you haven't had experience with that range of questions, it sort of tests your ability.

And it was always a real-world business question that somebody needed to answer, so it was practical. Now, once you received your MLS, it sounds like you moved directly into setting up your business.

We incorporated CD Sharp Information Systems in 1996. We had to use a lawyer and go through the articles of incorporation in order to do that. The name of *my* research business is InformAction, which I registered in 1998. CD Sharp Information Systems is the parent company, you might say, and its revenues come from both my husband's consulting work and contracts that we work on together. The names of the business are a mouthful and, in retrospect, perhaps not the best choice. The CD Sharp bit is okay (Crystal & David Sharp), but the Information Systems bit brings to mind computer sales or something, judging from the queries we often get. David is a professor at the Ivey Business School at the University of Western Ontario, and teaches accounting and international business. The consulting that he does is of course on his own time.

What about the logistics of setting up an office?

The first thing I did was to get a computer that was state-of-the-art at the time, but now I see that my kids' computer is more efficient and higher-powered than mine, and it is definitely upgrade time! My office is in the basement, where it's quiet and away from everything. We found some great office shelves, cupboards, and a steel filing cabinet at an auction sale. I've got it set up with everything that I need. My reference section and newsletters are arranged in boxes, but not catalogued the way they should be. I never have the time, but I have great intentions.

I set up accounts with database vendors, and there again AIIP was tremendously helpful, not just in the special deals that they negotiated with vendors, but also in the free vendor training sessions they arranged in conjunction with their annual conference.

I have a Web site and my own domain name, but that's one of the areas that I really do need to work on. Again, I have all sorts of ideas, but need to take the time to put them into action.

Do you recall the first project that you worked on, maybe something in the early days that really validated what you were doing?

It's a scary process, actually, getting your first bit of business. A lot of the early months were spent thinking and setting things up. And then I thought, well, how do I go about getting my name known out there? So I talked to people a lot, went to local business meetings, but I didn't get the sense that the local business community was where I wanted to market. I developed a little questionnaire, called around to local businesses, and while some were really helpful and wonderful, others just didn't have the time. And I didn't even know if I was targeting the right places. I went to the Small Business Development Center (SBDC) [198] and spoke to people there, and tried to come up with a business plan. But the problem was that I really didn't know how to market my services. I figured from this that I needed to educate people, and a one-to-one marketing plan would work the best.

My first break came with a professor who had taught me in library school, who is an entrepreneur and library consultant as well. He also headed up the Canadian Library Association (CLA) [176] recently. I met him at one of the librarian functions, and when I mentioned to him that I had started my own business, he gave me my first project. It was a document retrieval project, looking for resources on everything to do with services for the blind in libraries, because he was working on this issue. He just subcontracted the bibliographic research portion to me. I've worked with him on a few other projects over the years, and he's wonderful because the information exchange is good, he's very clear about what he wants, and he understands the pricing side of things without my having to justify every detail! It was really good for a first experience, and it gave me confidence to take things further.

It's great to work with somebody who appreciates and understands information. How do you describe your services today, if you're meeting somebody at a business function, for example?

I tell them I am a researcher, and then they usually ask, what kind of research? I say, I do secondary research and some primary research, and go on to explain what that is. I am a generalist; I don't have a well-defined niche, and that probably makes explanations a little harder than if I specialized in a particular kind of research. These days I'm doing a lot with health and medical research and grant proposals, helping people to write the big proposals, especially, that involve a large research component. I find that an information professional can play a very useful role in this process. I work with consultants and with small businesses. I work on market feasibility studies, competitive intelligence, and various writing projects. On one of my last projects I facilitated some focus group sessions in a workshop looking at rural development strategies in Ontario.

So the work is varied, and I love that. All of it is information- and research-related, and a lot of it involves writing too. It's really funny how projects come about sometimes. I struck up a conversation with a person on a train a year or two ago. In the course of talking, I mentioned my business, and he was quite interested, as he did not realize that anyone did the type of work that I do. He felt he was suffering from information overload, had all these papers that were half-written and that he could use help with pulling together. We exchanged business cards, but I didn't hear from him for quite a while. However he did call eventually, and I've since worked quite a lot with his research group. Most of my marketing tends to be done that way, just talking to people about what I do.

Getting out and interacting with people is really the bottom line, isn't it? Do you do any advertising, newsletters, or more traditional marketing?

No, and actually I should. It's really tough, though, to find the time and the energy to get down to it. However, I think if I had tried that even two years ago, I would have been very discouraged, because I wouldn't have known where to start. Now I've got a better sense of what my strengths are and what services I can offer. I also have a sense of who I can target.

I'm interested in hearing some particulars about Canada. Do you find that people understand what you do? Is working from home accepted in the Canadian business environment?

It tends to be acceptable for people to work from home these days, and it is generally acceptable for women, I find, because of family demands. If you say you're doing professional work, maybe because this is more of an academic community, people accept it. I don't get a sense that it's unusual at all. Telecommuting is the way a lot of things are going. It conjures up a familiar image in people's minds when you say "I have my own business and I work from home." They understand that I can manage my own time better this way. With most of my clients, email and phone communication is enough. I am happy to meet with them face to face if they need me to. We usually meet in their office or at a coffee shop or restaurant.

When I was working in Harvard Square, there was such a space problem that I realized very soon they actually welcomed the fact that I could work from home and just come in for meetings and things like that.

What about within the information profession? Do you find other independent researchers when you go to functions of the Canadian Library Association? What is the level of recognition for what you do?

When I was first starting our business, I thought one good thing I could offer was business research services through the public library. I know for a fact that the librarians are really busy. It would have been helpful to them, and also they were really uncomfortable with marketing, as I understood it. But I found out that you run into union problems there, so that wasn't workable.

The CLA is in the process of revamping its membership policies and what it offers its members. To be truthful, they don't offer that much for the independent professional, because the CLA mainly serves public librarian needs. I think the Special Libraries Association (SLA) [201] caters better to our needs as information professionals. The problem I face, being in London, Ontario is the geographic spread of Canada. The country is wide, and London is a small town, so it is difficult to network and share ideas with other information professionals. Toronto has a very active Society of Competitive Intelligence Professionals (SCIP) [199] chapter, as well as an SLA chapter, but it is far enough away that it is not worth my time to drive two hours for a dinner or breakfast meeting. In the next few years, the situation in London might change, however, as service industries and biotechnology are really taking off here.

Another problem as an IP is that, when visiting trade shows or exhibit areas at large conferences, vendors tend to ignore you. Perhaps it is just that they do not understand what IPs do or what our needs are, because they tend to home in on the big companies to whom they can sell their Internet products and enterprisewide licenses. You tend to feel rather left out of the loop as an independent. Since I need to keep current and know the information sources out there, I do need to talk to the vendors and see demonstrations of their products. Most often the products are priced for large companies with fixed annual fees for access, and sometimes I feel awkward asking for a demonstration when I know I cannot possibly afford enterprise-type fees.

As far as day-to-day operation and research tools are concerned, what online systems do you subscribe to?

Dialog [35] and Dow Jones Interactive [39]. I've found Dow Jones to be the most useful for me, because of the way it's set up with free searching and paying only for what you use. I find the ERIC [42] and LISA [71] databases on Dialog very good for my library science projects. I also use Hoover's [56], but I tend to concentrate on health and medical information, so more often I'm in MEDLINE [80] through PubMed [102], and CINAHL [29], the nursing and allied health literature database.

I have various favorite sites on the Internet that are starting points for further research. Some are pay-per-use sites, and others offer free searching and pay-per-document retrieved. I tend to use a variety of search engines to get what I need; my general searches are conducted on Google [53]. I use different meta-search engines for different topics, such as Vivisimo [135], Query Server [103], and SurfWax [124], but I never limit myself to just these.

How else do you use the Internet in your business?

I monitor and participate in various discussion lists to keep current. I frequently use the Internet for directory information. With most projects these days, I go to the Internet to do a general search first, because I have to look for very current information. For example, as I did with a recent project on gambling research, I start off looking at association Web sites, because the current issues, trade press, and conference proceedings are found there. And then I would search for bibliographies through various gateways, like the Librarians' Index to the Internet [70]. I would do a careful search in the psychology and social science literature through online databases and in online public access library catalogues (OPACs) [90] to see what else has been published. I often do a search on the names of the major writers in the field, and see what that points to. It might lead me to research they are currently engaged in, which might not have made it into the published literature yet. And then I often call or email some of these people, just to make sure I've got the facts straight.

Do you always do your own telephone interviewing, or do you subcontract out parts of projects?

I haven't subcontracted work to anyone, actually, and I think it has to do with the fact that I just don't know how to delegate. Because my projects tend to be so specific, and I invest so much of myself in learning what the clients actually want, it seems like it would take a whole lot more energy to explain it to someone else. There are times when I have considered subcontracting; I just haven't done it yet.

Does your research take you into any special collections? Do you still use libraries at all?

Yes, I do, particularly in the mental health literature. I have a part-time job at the Lawson Health Research Institute, under whose auspices I am co-authoring a paper on the history of the mental health system in Canada in the last four decades. I am currently working on a literature review on the prevalence of mental disorders in developed countries. The job keeps me in the research environment, which is good. Actually, right now I have moments when I question whether I should be doing this or not, because there are lots of things that I need to get done with the business. But I started at this job in the early days of my business in order to have a regular source of income to finance the ideas I had about developing the research business. It is hard to make the decision to take myself away from the project, just because I've invested so much of my time and knowledge in it.

Tell me about some of your other projects.

I've been working on quite a few grant proposals in the past year. When people approach you for help with writing a grant, one of the first things you must consider is whether you can work within the defined time frame; that is crucial before progressing any further. Everything takes much longer to do than you think, especially on large national grants that are very competitive and involve input from researchers in various locations. You need to know who's on the team and how you're going to negotiate the information exchange, especially when some of the investigators are scattered geographically. Then you need to define the topic, and what exactly is expected from the research. Look carefully at the published guidelines by the funding agency. If something looks unclear, know who you can contact to clarify points. Establish whether you have access to someone who is going to provide you with feedback on a regular basis. Your fee must be discussed early on to make sure it's acceptable to the client.

Once you get past that point, then you've got to really focus on the application and see what's required. You're working to a deadline, and it generally involves a research component. As the researcher, what I provide is a different set of eyes, to see whether the proposal is consistent and if any research is missing, and whether the research approach follows the guidelines laid out by the funding agency. That's the grant proposal side.

Feasibility studies are completely different. I do a quick Internet search to see what else has been done and what people are talking about. Then I go into the databases, such as ABI Inform [3] on Dialog, check Dow Jones also, and isolate the keywords that look like they'd be relevant. Learning the vocabulary of each project is a big component, because I deal with so many different types of projects. I do this by using a thesaurus or through reading articles and identifying words that might describe what I need to zero in on. Then, through talking to people, sometimes I discover that a word might mean something quite different in one discipline than it does in another discipline or in normal use. In many cases, defining the questions is the hard part. If that part is done correctly, locating the answers is easy.

Do you deliver most of your results in hard copy or electronic format?

It varies. With grant proposals, a lot of the information exchange is electronic, but at the end, it's got to be hard copy. You've got to check for all the proper papers, the number of copies, and all the signatures. With a feasibility study, a lot of it is electronic, but if I find a book that would be useful I might order that for the client as well. I always provide a summary that lists exactly what I've looked at, ideas for further study, and an annotated bibliography. With something like Medline or PubMed it's easy to provide abstracts, and I use Reference Manager [106] to format those. If people want the full-text articles, then I provide those as well.

Do you think of yourself more as an information provider or an analyst? I imagine that with your economics background you could wear either hat.

I prefer the information provider aspect, and that's how I bill myself. I often say analysis is negotiable. But generally, with most of the projects I've had so far, clients have needed the sources, very often the articles, and a summary. Actually, I'm really happy with that. It is less time consuming, and it is easier to estimate the hours for billing purposes when I don't have to do the analysis as well.

How do you handle your pricing?

An hourly fee or a per-project basis is the way I work. For the grant proposals, people generally prefer to know up front what they will be paying, and I think that's reasonable. It's tricky coming up with a pricing structure for that, because the projects are extraordinarily time consuming, and I find that, in order to get the job done and get it done well, I put in more of myself than sometimes I think is necessary. But whatever it takes to get the job done, I do it.

It's a constant learning process. You've mentioned women's career issues as one of your topic interests. What kind of work have you done in this area?

A couple of years ago a group of professional women here in London, Ontario, had a sense that women who'd made it to a senior position in their companies and were heading for the CEO-type jobs were deciding to leave at the peak of their careers to do something else, often volunteer work. This phenomenon was described in an article in *Fortune* magazine at about the same time. The group decided to fund a project to examine if this was the case in Canada generally. They approached our company, and I was quite interested in it, and my husband and I actually worked on the project together. We conducted a telephone survey involving fifteen senior women managers across Canada. Based on the results of that survey and a review of the published literature on career choices, the glass ceiling, and various gender surveys, we designed a questionnaire. To save costs, we sent out the survey with a newsletter, *Women in Management* [224], which has a circulation of over 20,000. We received about 700 replies and the results were very interesting. The study generated quite a bit of interest internationally, and was quoted in various publications including the *Globe and Mail* [214] and the *Financial Times* [213].

It's noteworthy that this was a large primary research study, completely different from the kinds of secondary research you do.

Yes, it was different. I really got a sense of what organizations are like and what they are focusing on. About thirty percent of the respondents indicated a strong possibility of leaving their organizations. The main reason why a lot of women were leaving was they felt that they weren't appreciated by their organizations, and that their skills weren't being used adequately. This was an interesting finding because it is generally thought that women leave mainly due to family commitments.

That leads nicely into asking how you keep it all together as a parent of three children, and how you divide up your time between work and home.

It's hard to maintain a balance. There are times when it's really, really hectic. When I have a project to work on, it generally is not short and quick. It tends to be really intense, and I have to work to deadline. I think the boys have come to realize that when I've got to work, I have to work, and it is a hard slog and they've got to help out. Sometimes they do; sometimes they don't.

But it also puts things into perspective for me. The end of the day, when they come home from school to when they go to bed, is usually their time. I really try to keep that for them and their activities, so we spend that time together. I often work late into the night or during the day, of course, when they are at school. But there's always laundry, and groceries to be bought, and sometimes you put all that aside because you have this huge project. It's all a mess at times. I do have a weekly housecleaning service, so if things pile up, they are cleared at least weekly.

I think we're learning to manage better. It's tough; there's no doubt about it. However, I don't think I would be happy doing it any other way, like working a nine-to-five job. I like the flexibility of knowing that, well, if I don't do this now I can do it later tonight, or I can do it over the weekend, and I don't have to be away from the household. It's a balance, and it's not very easy sometimes.

As you told me earlier this morning, you were over at the school helping to tie ice skates for a class recreation period. You don't have to ask anybody if you could go tie ice skates. You just do it, and you know you'll make up that time. Do you have any timesaving gadgets to help you keep track of everything?

I do run a Palm Pilot, but I don't use it intensely the way some people do. What helps me most is my cell phone, because I'm accessible anywhere. People can contact me wherever I am. For projects I use Reference Manager [106], which is great for creating a database of citations and abstracts, for producing bibliographies, and for citing in the required citation format, which varies depending on the subject area I am currently doing research in. It's a great time-saver! And I use little sticky notes a lot. They're wonderful things, I've got them all over the place, and I color-code them, and that tends to help a great deal.

How do you handle the need to stay current, stay updated professionally?

I was reading an article recently about knowledge, and it challenged me to think as to whether mine is a mile wide and an inch deep, or whether it is an inch wide and a mile deep. It is so necessary for the work I do to try to keep my knowledge base both a mile wide *and* a mile deep! There are so many areas to watch— the technology, what's happening in information aggregation, the changing content of the various proprietary databases, Internet search engine developments and sites, new developments in various subject areas. It is overwhelming at times.

I use various methods to keep myself current. I try to attend at least three conferences a year. I keep an eye on key daily newspapers, the *New York Times* [219] being one. I read the *Economist* [211], *Searcher* [223], and *EContent* [212] whenever I can. I subscribe to the email discussion lists of AIIP, BUSLIB, and the SLA

Toronto Chapter [201]. The electronic newsletters I receive include Free Pint [150], Search Engine Watch [114], ResearchBuzz [108], The Scout Report [111], various NUA newsletters [154], GDSourcing [51] for Canadian information, and whatever Gary Price [134] writes about, to name a few.

For health and medical information I also monitor Psychiatry-Online [101], I get the *British Medical Journal* [14] table of contents, and various other alerts that I set up on Northern Light [89]. And I check various sites from time to time that cover new books in what might be an area of current interest, or that look like they deal with an interesting topic in technology.

Do you have any thoughts on the future of the independent information profession? Do you see growth? Opportunity? Any advice to someone who might be interested in the field?

The more I look around and see the information overload, the more I see a growing role for information specialists in the "new economy." A few years ago, there was an article in the *Economist* after an international chess champion played the IBM computer Big Blue, and lost. The opinion in the *Economist* was that, although chess is a highly intellectual game, the various moves can be computed; the alternatives can be evaluated using algorithms and calculated decisions can be made by analyzing patterns. The implications of that, according to the article, suggest that even high-level jobs, if their components can be computed with reasonable predictability, can be taken over by computers. But when I think of what information professionals do, I don't believe that the thought processes involved in defining a problem, thinking about a process, creating different approaches to solving it, organizing information from disparate sources, and using various information management strategies can be replicated by computing techniques, at least not yet.

For people aspiring to be independent information professionals, it's still a hard field in which to get established. You've got to start out with a realistic idea of what's involved. It's not as easy as they say in some of the books that I read before I started my business—you only need a computer and a modem to get started in business! No, you need much more than that. You need to attend conferences, you need to invest time and effort in establishing and maintaining your knowledge and skills and in identifying customer needs. You need to be able to market yourself and keep your current customers happy so that they keep coming back to you. All that costs a considerable amount. You don't recover any of that immediately; it takes time.

What about getting some experience in an industry or an organization rather than trying to go right into business from college?

Hmmm, that's a tough one. I had a lot of experience behind me when I started. I don't think I would have had the confidence to take on certain projects or market my skills adequately had I not had that knowledge and experience. On the other hand, when you're young and just out of college, you feel you can do anything, and such a lack of inhibition might be a good thing. However, you also need to be able to deliver what you profess to, and without experience, that's not easy. Experience helps me feel the confidence I need to project to clients.

I sometimes wish I had been a practicing librarian for a while before I went into the independent information profession, because there are so many things I might do differently, or at least approach differently. On the other hand, the research experience I have had allows me to take on very different types of projects. This is the way my life choices have taken me, and I'm really enjoying how it is working out.

Super Searcher Power Tips

➤ If you say you're doing professional work from your home, people seem to accept it; I don't get a sense that it's unusual at all.

➤ I usually go to the Internet to do a general search first these days, because I have to look for very current information.

➤ I may do a search on the names of the major writers in the field, and see what that points to. It might lead me to research they are currently engaged in which has not made it into the published literature yet. Then I may call or email some of these people to make sure I've got the facts straight.

➤ On team projects, everything takes much longer than you think, especially on large national grants that are very competitive and involve input from researchers in various locations.

➤ Learning the vocabulary of each project is a big component, because I deal with so many different types of projects. I do this by using a thesaurus or reading articles and identifying words that look like they might describe what I need to zero in on.

➤ I like the flexibility of knowing that if I don't complete my work now I can do it later tonight, or over the weekend, and I don't have to be away from the household.

➤ Getting started is not as easy as they say in some of the books that I read before I started my business— you only need a computer and a modem to get started in business! No, you need much more than that.

Margaret Metcalf Carr

Value-Added Research

Margaret Metcalf "Peggy" Carr is principal of Carr Research Group, an information research and analysis firm based in Baltimore, Maryland. She specializes in value-added primary and secondary research for the defense, aerospace, electronics, and telecommunications industries. Before starting her own firm in 1990, she was a member of the competitive intelligence team for the business development and strategic planning departments of Martin Marietta Corporation.

pcarr@carr-research.com
www.carr-research.com

Peggy, tell me something about your background and how you came to operate your own information business.

I started working in libraries in 1970 when I was a sophomore in high school. Since I had some free time after school, I thought that being a library aide would be a cool thing to do. I was very fortunate in that the head of the library at Wethersfield High School in Wethersfield, Connecticut, saw that I was interested in research and became a wonderful mentor. In addition to the basics of shelving books, she taught me how to catalog with the Dewey Decimal System and the *Sears List of Subject Headings* [115, see Appendix], and some of the basic reference sources in the library so I could also help out students and faculty. Even in the tenth grade I was starting to use my research skills, which was a lot of fun. She also told me what educational background I would need, and that if I were going to do anything in the library science field, I absolutely had to get my masters. So four years of college just became a means to an end, to get to graduate school.

Sounds like you were one of those people who knew very early on what your direction in life was and what you wanted to do.

Yes, very much so, and I realize to some people that seems unusual, but I had an older sister who knew from the time she was five that she was going to be a nurse, so maybe it's a family thing. I went on to college and majored in history, as it had been recommended that I get a broad background. I attended a small liberal arts college, which I think was a wonderful underpinning, and since I absolutely loved learning, I decided to do a double major with the addition of communications. I focused on European history, and complemented this with speech and media studies. I worked at the library at Muskegon College, doing everything from repairing books to serials check-ins to weekend reference, and again had a wonderful mentor and senior advisor who helped me with the scholarly research aspect of a mini-thesis that I had to do as a history major.

I marched through my four years, taking every single course I could, and went to graduate school at Syracuse University two weeks after I graduated. They had a concentration in information retrieval, which meant that not only did you have to take the basic courses of reference and cataloging, but also systems analysis, computerized reference, and computerized online research, which meant Orbit [92], Dialog [35] and BRS [15] in those days. I got a job after school working in the Upstate Medical Center Library, where I was a shelver during the week and the reference librarian on Saturdays. I learned all about MESH [79] headings and *Index Medicus* [58]. I later received an internship where I worked at Gaylord Library Systems for twenty hours a week. That included working on their automated circulation system, which back in those days was still fairly novel. My job was to test the systems, update the user manual, and train the librarians in the Liverpool library system on automated circulation. So there are many bits and pieces in my background, but they all had to do with library systems and seemed to follow a pattern.

What about your first employment experiences after grad school?

My first employment was as a bibliographer for Raven Systems and Research Inc. in Washington, DC. It was under a contract with the Environmental Protection Agency (EPA). My specific job was in quality control. We would receive documents that had to be filed by the chemical companies for all the pesticides they had to register, and had to go through each document and come up with a meaningful citation and abstract. These were not formal journal articles, but backup documents. In effect we had to make them more official to receive certification from the EPA. The information ultimately was used for pesticide labeling, which consumers would read in the stores.

Lots of attention to detail, I'm sure.

Lots of attention to detail, and a lot of reading, because while some documents were fairly easy to create a citation for, others were maybe seven pages long and still had to be boiled down to a small, concise paragraph summarizing what the material contained.

And from there?

From there I moved to Baltimore and took a job as a technical information specialist, working in the library, for Martin Marietta Laboratories. It was an R&D laboratory, and my primary responsibilities there were interlibrary loans, taking care of the patent collection, and doing the online and manual reference services for the scientists. I was one of two professionals in the library, and we also had a full-time paraprofessional who did serials check-in and the daily operational tasks. I held that job for five years, and then was promoted to manager of a new business information center at Martin Marietta Corporation, the corporate headquarters. After years of hodgepodge ordering and relying on the operational sci-tech libraries, corporate was able to justify an on-site library that would cater to the head office and to the business development department. They brought in a consultant to do the hiring and assist with the setup and acquisitions. I basically had to create the center from the ground up based upon the consultant's recommendations. For the first year and a half, I was the only person in the library, which meant I had to do everything from periodicals check-in to collection development to all the manual and online reference services, plus packaging and delivering the product to the executives.

Plus introducing the concept of a library within the company, I imagine.

Right, including marketing and putting together a monthly report for the senior vice president, to whom I reported. I had to be able to quantify everything, look at the cost of the center and do some basic return-on-investment reports. I worked with a fellow who was the head of the strategic development department, on how we could translate library figures into meaningful presentations. It was a very good learning experience. We went from working in a room that was 400 square feet to another area of the building that was more than 1,200 square feet. So we tripled in size within the five years that I managed that information center.

That's very impressive growth, yet something else was churning around in your mind. How, and why, did you make the move to opening up your own business?

Well, during my ninth year with the company, I realized that my heartstrings as a mother were being pulled. I had two children at home who had been in day care, but once my eldest son went to kindergarten, I found that there was a whole new parameter opening up in the afternoon, and that was when he wanted to go play with Billy after school and I had no idea who Billy or his parents were. I was thirty-six miles away from home, easily spending fifty-five to sixty hours a week on my job. I found that I just couldn't do both any more. I couldn't be both a full-time mom and a full-time on-site worker. I absolutely loved my job, and the people I worked with, but Human Resources insisted that I be at a desk from eight to four-thirty Monday through Friday. I simply could not balance being at an office desk, being present at parent-teacher conferences, and cutting and pasting in kindergarten.

So I started exploring independent consulting options. In my job at Martin Marietta I had outsourced projects to two independents who were members of the Maryland chapter of the Special Libraries Association (SLA) [201]—Jan Goudreau and Beverly Gresehover of Information Crossroads in nearby Columbia, Maryland. I had also met another independent through chapter Board duties, Mary Park of the Information Consultancy in Baltimore, and my conversations on how to become an independent started with Mary. I did some research on the subject, and spoke to my husband about our options. We made a one-year plan for how I could bank some of my vacation pay so that I would have a nest egg to start my business. We bought a computer, and I actually fell into a project for my first client. One of my former bosses had left to join another company as a vice president and found he didn't have an on-site library, so he called me up and asked if I would do research for him in the evening. I jumped right into that, and then he put me in contact with someone else who needed the same thing. I worked in the evenings at home for these two clients, so that's how I knew that I could actually set myself up in business.

I took classes from the Small Business Administration (SBA) [118] and a series of free seminars from the Service Corps of Retired Executives (SCORE) [197]. I inquired with the State of Maryland about how to become a valid operating business, and basically started putting all my ducks in a row. I worked with my sister and brother-in-law to set up my books, created a company name and logo, and ordered stationery and business cards at the local print shop. I took a course through SLA taught by Alice Sizer Warner on how to offer fee-based information services so that I knew how to price my services and draw up contracts. I also engaged a lawyer, based on a referral from a lawyer I had worked and carpooled with at Martin Marietta. I got the ins and outs of being a sole proprietor vs. a corporation in the state of Maryland, and decided that a sole proprietorship was the best fit.

We decided on a date; I was going to start working from home when our son Patrick started first grade in September of 1989. We had also decided that, since I was going to be home, we could have another child. And lo and behold we found out I was expecting twins, so I delayed opening my business until January of 1990.

What kinds of research were you doing with these early projects?

It was mostly just online research back in those days. Fortunately, one of the gentlemen that I had done work for had gone out on his own and had a contract with the Library of Congress. He had to do a big project for the Senate and needed somebody to do very specific online research on selected countries. So, for the first few months, I was doing nothing but this one big project as a subcontractor through him. It was all online research, using both Dialog and LexisNexis [69]. Back in those days I couldn't afford a LexisNexis password, so I was using their in-house reference service, which you hired at an hourly fee. They would give me a data dump—just a massive amount of raw information from the databases, which I would then go through and massage, and present as a report to my client. I was not asked to do a lot of packaging. I put some headers and footers on things, but did little or no writing, and no analysis.

My second client was a publisher who needed somebody to abstract government data that they pulled from Department of Defense records. It was a seasonal project, from May to October, but it was wonderful because I could do it during the hours I was available. It didn't matter that I was working while the children were napping, before they were awake in the morning, or when they were asleep at night.

Now, these many years later, how do you describe your business and the services you offer?

We provide tailored results for business information needs. The requests we get nowadays are very specific questions that need targeted answers. It is not a data dump anymore, and it is not just a matter of performing online research. Normally it's performing a secondary literature search, sifting through the research results, conducting primary research interviews, and then going back to review the data, writing a concise executive summary, and creating a bound report.

It's a very different package than what I was providing eleven years ago. Most people can go out on the Internet nowadays and get a company annual report if that's all they want. They don't need to ask us to deliver the data that they can find through a simple Internet search. We are getting calls for the complicated searches and the hard-to-find statistics that are only found by wading through lots of material or conducting telephone interviews. We offer time, resources, anonymity, objectivity, and expertise that most of our customers don't have available in-house. Not only that, clients are requesting a very concise report at the end of the research. They don't want to be reading twenty or fifty pages of data. They want a three-page executive summary.

Tell me about your collaboration efforts. When you talk about the Carr Research Group, you're

obviously not doing everything yourself anymore.

No, I'm sure not. We have formed a group of six professionals who work very well together. Each of us has our own area of expertise, and therefore our work is divided on big projects, depending first upon who's available, and then by what they're most comfortable doing. Jan Goudreau does online business and technical searching. She's also very good at manipulating databases and abstracting data. Jill Gardner and Ann Sentinella enjoy doing the primary research and requesting reports within the client's industry where a third party is needed for client confidentiality purposes. Liz Farley is very comfortable doing the online research on the commercial systems such as Dialog that either I don't have the time to search or where I need to double-team because of time constraints. Cheryl McAfee helps out with Web and intranet interfacing issues. She prepares information for Web readability/mountability. For example, she created an online form so that potential clients can request a quote or more information right from our Web site. She also assists with the evaluation, selection, and installation of software that interfaces with client intranets and Web sites, such as library cataloging and search engines. I usually spend most of my time going through the research results, the interview data, massaging it, putting it into templates, and then writing up the executive summary.

Do you remain a sole proprietor and just cooperate with these other researchers on projects, or has your business model changed?

No, I remain a sole proprietor. I find that, due to wonderful things like the IRS, state and county regulations, Social Security benefits, and all the related tax law issues, it works out best to subcontract. I work exclusively with Association of Independent Information Professionals (AIIP) [172] members and use the template services agreement that AIIP has created. We function on a project-by-project basis. Sometimes we actually do requests for proposals (RFPs) together, each giving input to the scope of work to be performed, fees, and realistic deliverable dates. It really is a collaborative effort. Most clients request a W-9 form for accounting purposes. I am a woman-owned firm and a sole proprietor. My tax ID is my Social Security number. And I have no problem presenting myself, or our group in that manner.

It's hard to be everything to everybody in the marketplace today. Tell me about the industries you serve and that you've identified as core competencies.

Because of my background in working at Martin Marietta, it's primarily defense, aerospace, electronics, and telecommunications. I stick with those industries because I'm most comfortable with them. With all the research I've done I tend to know something about specific companies that participate in those marketplaces. Of course, nowadays, that changes on a daily basis, but those are the industries that I try to keep up on and read about on a regular basis. Anything falling outside of those industries, I subcontract out or totally refer the project to another person. I won't handle it unless it falls comfortably into a category close to those industries. Sometimes I will do something in manufacturing but not explicitly electronic, like industrial burners. But it's got to be familiar enough for me to put my arms around.

I know you do on-site client work as well.

Yes, I do. Actually, for the past nine years or so, I've done on-site contracting for three different clients at various times. I have one client that's been very steady, and that's my past employer, now known as Lockheed Martin since a 1995 merger. It's a very interesting perspective, doing something like that. They have insisted on my coming on-site because my showing up and meeting with people on a weekly basis reminds them that they can off-load that data-gathering task sitting on their desk. I always have my backup team in place when I am on vacation. They don't always need to go on-site, but I do need to leave a telephone number to make the client comfortable. That way I manage to cover them fifty-two weeks a year.

In what capacity do you function when you're on-site? Are you working in a corporate information center?

Actually, my title is contract research analyst for strategic development, so I totally support that particular department. I submit an activity report monthly, as all contractors and consultants have to do. The types of requests they get are not just internal to their own department; they also have to field questions from executive communications, from the business development department, and from other operating units. So in essence, I support the units they support.

That seems like it would create a nice balance in your workweek. You're "out there" yet still on your own.

Yes, I'm out there two days a week, which means that I have to get dressed in the gray pinstriped suit and wear pantyhose—very different than sitting at home in my Dockers and loafers and sweater. But I think it's very good. It gives me adult contact. It also gives me exposure to an information center where I have access to up-to-date hard-copy resources that I don't always have available in my own office. It helps me keep up on the needs of the corporate environment. I think it has a lot of benefits on both sides. They get someone who is helping not only them, but also other corporations. I have to constantly look at the latest and greatest information retrieval systems, Web sites, and clipping services. With our extended work network, we're able to compare notes. I bring in an outside perspective on what I'm seeing in other corporate environments, and the lessons that others have learned.

Let's shift gears a bit here and talk about the research process itself, and about commercial information services vs. the Internet.

I maintain accounts on the three major services, Dow Jones Interactive [39], LexisNexis, and Dialog. I use each of them for very specific purposes. I find that when I need to search the trade literature my two best bets are LexisNexis and Dialog. I use Dow Jones for a quick and easy search to find out how much is out there, and to start getting my teeth into what is available on a particular industry or company. I always go online first because I have to find out whom the best sources are to contact for my primary research. I specifically look for experts in the literature, and the watchdogs of the industry. Then I use investment reports to find out how the Wall Street analysts are viewing the industry or the company, which leads me to the specific analysts and firms that are following that particular industry or company. I've learned not to hesitate to pick up the telephone and call the analyst to get specific information I need. Digging into the market research side can complement what I've learned from my initial company or industry search.

How has the growth of the Internet impacted your business, especially in the last several years with more useful content appearing?

I'm using it more than I used to. The Internet has become much more of a research tool than it was, say, five years ago. It has become valuable particularly for what companies post on their Web sites. When I'm researching smaller companies, even private firms, I find that the venture capitalists who are giving them money are following them and talking them up in public. The wealth of information on the Internet has also impacted my mode of access. I used to dial up through a Delphi [32] gateway for text-only access, and went through a menu to get through to the World Wide Web. I also used CompuServe [25] and their early version of the Mosaic browser. Then I went to having my own ISP, and now I have broadband access. I don't go a day without being on the Internet at some point, doing some of my research there. It provides me with leads to trade shows, speakers, company literature, and all sorts of things that I never would have gotten so easily before.

What about the invisible web, those specialized sites that the search engines usually miss? Do you have any favorite sites that you've found to be really valuable?

Hoover's [56] and 10K Wizard [1] have been absolutely phenomenal for me. I'm also very happy with what the U.S. government is putting up on the Web, primarily with FirstGov.com [48]. But as Chris Sherman and Gary Price are quick to point out in their book *The Invisible Web* [232], unless you know what sites to get to, it's very difficult to know what's out there. Sometimes I fall into a useful site through one of the meta-search engines like HotBot [57], but more often it's by reading about it or going with a colleague's recommendation.

I find that I don't have to do an immense amount of research reading myself. I subscribe to *Searcher* [223], *CyberSkeptic* [210], and Gary Price's Lists of Lists [99] in order to keep up-to-date on what valuable Web sites are out there. I find a lot of leads through AIIP-L [146], which is AIIP's private electronic forum, and I also participate on the SLA solo librarians' list [161]. Both of these are extremely helpful.

Before we leave our discussion of research, at times I've heard you mention going to the library. Tell me about how you still do manual research and use good old-fashioned books.

That's still very much a part of my work, and I don't think we can ever get away from that. I've been fortunate in that I have worked for three different corporate clients, and I sometimes get their year-end editions of reference sources when the new ones come in, so I've been able to build a mini-reference collection in my own office. There's a big difference between searching and browsing, and I find that for browsing purposes I still need to go to the library. Browsing can be a very valuable exercise when you are not sure exactly what you are looking for, as one idea builds upon the other. I use several local collections. I'm very fortunate to be in Baltimore with several universities nearby, each with its own subject expertise.

The search of the day, or week, determines which collection I travel to. For instance, there is a very good telecommunications collection right at the local community college. When I need business resources, I tend to go to the business school at Loyola. When I need information-technology references, I go to the University of Maryland, Baltimore. Being in the quasi-DC/sub-urban area, I've been able to tap into special collections for some projects, such as the National Agricultural Library. I have used the Library of Congress, although I try not to go there because it's difficult to get to. And the University of Maryland College Park has a full government document collection. I'm sorry, but when you want documents from pre-1980, you will end up going to a library collection. Some of the information that we look for can only be found by reading print material.

Good point. Now, looking at your Web site, I noticed that you have named your products. You have CRG reports, CRG briefs, and so on. That leads me to want to ask about your deliverables. Do you still send hard copy out at all, or is it all electronic?

Clients get what they ask for. It used to be that the more sophisticated clients requested their results on a diskette. That was before you could do easy attachments in email. As the technology has evolved, it has affected how reports are requested and delivered. Most of the time now I send a PDF file by email, particularly when the client has to share the report internally with others, and then we FedEx a backup in hard copy with all the attachments, backup documentation, index tabs, and colored stationery. For a report in which secondary and primary research is involved, we're likely to send along our typed-up interview notes, screen shots from Web sites, articles we've photocopied, results of our online research with bolded headlines and portions of text. I use a cover-binding system to package all the reports. I have very special stationery—three colors on white linen. We do put out an entire family of publications, so everything that goes out is consistent with our image.

Could you take a guess at the ratio of information retrieval to analysis you do today, with maybe a little perspective from the early days?

Years ago, it was 100 percent information retrieval. Now, I would say it's eighty/twenty, eighty-some percent analysis and twenty percent just plain information retrieval. Lots of our clients can do their own data gathering nowadays. All they need to do is get a password on one of the online systems. Several of the analysts I work for actually go out and do their own preliminary data gathering, and when they run into a problem, or they're not getting at what they feel they need to get at, that's when they call me. They tell us what they've done already, and we can pick up the ball and carry it on.

I like the fact that I'm working with an educated consumer. They can do their own Internet research. They can certainly hop on Yahoo! [145] or HotBot [57] or WebCrawler [138] just as easily as I can. They may not be able to search as sophisticatedly as we do, but at least when they call me up they know how to tailor their questions. They're not so broad that we can't start with a focus. They've already spent several hours getting frustrated, and they know that whatever we can do for them will be better than what they can do themselves. We're giving them the resources, the expertise, and the time that they don't have.

We've touched on some aspects of marketing, but I want to ask you about any specifics that you have found to be effective. You've certainly worked hard to establish a corporate identity.

I've found that you have to work several avenues at the same time. I've taught seminars; exhibited at trade shows; offered to speak at local client sites, Kiwanis, and Chamber of Commerce groups; and joined the National Association of Women Business Owners (NAWBO) [194]. I'm very active in the local chapter of SLA and also in the solo, engineering, and library management divisions of SLA. I'm a member of the Society of Competitive Intelligence Professionals (SCIP) [199] and attend many local chapter meetings as well as the annual conference. I find that you need to be visible in many, many ways.

In addition, I've started developing a series of research tips that we put on our Web site in PDF format. We only have a few subscribers now, but as time goes on I'm looking forward to adding content to the site. I try to put it out on a quarterly basis, and I hope to go to bimonthly, or even monthly.

I speak at as many industry conferences as I can. I enjoy speaking opportunities and find that I'm doing that more and more. I put my speeches and papers, at least scaled-down versions, up on my Web site. I don't necessarily give out the entire presentation, because I feel people have paid a lot of money to go to those sessions, and I don't want to undervalue their attendance. But it does help promote the areas of expertise that we have within the group.

How else do you utilize your Web site? Do you track visitors?

The Web site is there to establish our presence and provide more visibility. I hope to do much more with it as time allows. I personally do not track visits to the Web site but outsource that to Ann Sentinella, who has been working with me for eight years. She comes into my office on a weekly basis and updates the Web site, answers the phone, mails out all the information packets that people have requested, and does general office support. I would definitely recommend to any business owner that they hire somebody, even if it's for only six to eight hours a week—whatever you can afford—to come in and focus for you at least one day a week. I've been very comfortable with Ann. She's my alter ego in many ways.

You obviously reached a point where you knew that, in order to grow the business, you couldn't do it all yourself.

Yes; that happened at the time when I had to be out of the office two to three days a week with corporate clients. At one point I was spending four days a week out of the office serving three different corporate clients, doing on-site work. Yes, I was in my office for two to three hours in the morning, but then I would have to pick up a briefcase and go on-site with the client to do whatever they needed me to do. But I was not physically in my own office to do the administrative work, and that was the first thing I contracted out.

Then I contracted out my marketing to Chris Olson and Associates [24], who helped me write a brochure, and I eventually moved on to other marketing pieces, including Rolodex cards, the Web site, and our "Research Tip" newsletter template. Since then, it seems, every year or so I have them design a different piece for me. The next thing I'm going to have them do is develop a piece on card stock, so that after I speak at a training seminar or a conference, I can send a follow-up note to the attendees who were in my session, saying, "Thank you for coming; if you have any questions feel free to contact us here," and give them three bullet points to remember from the session. It's one more way to remind them that we're out there. Marketing is never a done deal.

With this entire operation running now, you still maintain your office at home. What are the advantages of that?

It's rare, but when there's a need for me to be with children who are sick or out of school for whatever reason, I have a way to totally operate from home. I also am a very early morning person. I may be working in my office at four o'clock in the morning; I don't know anybody who would want me showing up at that hour anywhere else. I can be very productive in my own home office. I have a separate room that has been specifically outfitted for my business. We hired a firm to come in, and Ann and I worked with them to explain our workflow during the day and demonstrate our work surface and book shelving needs. This office is only nine feet by nine feet. But it's floor to ceiling work surface, shelves, file drawers, and equipment, and it works great. I can have two people working at a time, and we've got it set up with everything we need. I have a laptop and a desktop computer, two different printers, a fax machine, scanner, and photocopier. I'm very happy with the arrangement.

Any timesaving tips, techniques, software, or devices? What helps you stay organized and keep it all together?

I have a Palm III that my husband gave me for my birthday, which I absolutely love. I like it because I can keep my current events on it, use it for daily task scheduling, for keeping reminder lists, and sometimes just thoughts that I pen in there. As far as software tools are concerned, I use the Microsoft Office family, which I find indispensable. I also use Calendar Creator [18] for keeping track of schedules—not only for myself, but also for my group, so I know when people are on vacation. I keep charts of tasks and workflow on a monthly basis, and prefer a year-long calendar on the wall for that. I also have PowerMarks [97], a program to help track bookmarks for a project. I use the full Adobe Acrobat [5] program, so that I can create my own documents as PDF files. For Web applications we use Allaire's HomeSite [6] and WS-FTP [144] for updating our Web site. We use QuickBooks Pro [104] for accounting and Paintshop Pro [94] for screenshots.

How do you price your services?

We actually publish our hourly fee on the Web site, but more often we price by the project. We find that most people are more comfortable with that. We do respond to RFPs and we sometimes find that's the best way to work it. If the client can provide us with a one- or two-page description of what they're looking for and what results they're hoping to get, we can turn that around quickly, and that way we have no surprises on either end.

We also find that providing progress reports to the client in between, particularly if it's a project we're working on for a month or more, is helpful. Getting back to them after the first two weeks and telling them what we've found so far gives them confidence that we can provide them with the final product. Communication with the client along the way is very important.

Do you have a funny story to tell about an unusual request you've gotten, something that was particularly memorable?

The funniest request I've ever had was the time I got a phone call from overseas saying, "Oh, you're Carr Research. What do you have on automobiles in your office?" They thought I had off-the-shelf research reports on *cars* sitting around my office. Automobile market research reports on Toyotas and BMWs sitting here, totally done, that I would be able to just pluck off the shelf and mail to them.

We've talked about AIIP and SLA, and you mentioned that you're also a member of SCIP. Having had the pleasure of serving on the AIIP Board of Directors while you were president, I have to ask how AIIP has helped you and why you've devoted so much time and energy to this group.

I joined AIIP the first year I was in business, so I was very fortunate in that respect. I'm also fortunate to be based in the mid-Atlantic region, because I'm part of a very active group of information professionals in this area. We call ourselves the I-95ers, because we're all along the Interstate 95 corridor. I have a tremendous amount of support not only in my own geographic area, but also via AIIP's electronic discussion list. I can't say enough about AIIP; it's composed of people who have been there, done that. They have experienced your pain. How do you deal with a client who doesn't understand that they're paying you for your efforts, not just for the results? How do you guarantee that the client is going to be happy with the work that you do provide? How do you write your contracts so that there are no questions later? You name it. Whether it be a business-related issue or a subject stumbling block, there's always, always, another AIIP-er out there who can help you. The support system is absolutely outstanding and awesome.

Owning your own business and having an active family can be overwhelming at times. What do you do to balance your life and keep it all together?

It's very important to try to keep a schedule. I realize the client work doesn't always allow this to happen. When I've got a report that has to be on the client's desk at 9 A.M. on Monday morning, I know I've got to have that puppy ready for shipping at the

FedEx kiosk by 7 P.M. on Friday night, or at Staples by 4 P.M. on Saturday afternoon, which means that I may be working through dinner on Friday night, or up working at 5:30 on Saturday morning. But I try to make those the exceptions, not the rule.

My official work hours are 6:30 A.M. to 3:30 P.M. Eastern Standard Time. I may be in the office earlier or later than that, but I do my best to be out of my office by 5 P.M., so I can cook dinner for my family and check up with the kids on how their school day has been. I have an open-door policy in my home. My children are free to come and go in my office with the following understanding: If my door is closed, they know I'm probably on the phone and they need to knock. If the door is open, they know that they can come in and talk to me. We just work it with some flexibility. I do try to literally get myself out of my chair during lunch. I go out and walk the dog, or I go to the gym. It may be 11:30 in the morning, it may be 2:30 in the afternoon, but I do my best to take a break in the middle of the day, because otherwise by 3:00 in the afternoon I'm exhausted. It's a way to get my energy back. I also enjoy gardening and yard work. I find that it's important to get out and do something outside of the four walls of my office. We plan our family vacations way ahead of time. Every August I know what my schedule is going to be for the entire fall and the next spring and summer.

Tell me your thoughts on the future of the independent information profession, and what opportunities exist for people interested in this business.

Our clients will be even more savvy and knowledgeable than they've been in the past. We're going to continue to see more complexity in our projects. Along with that comes more hours, therefore more money. My days of having to respond to "I need it in ten minutes and I want you to spend under $100" are gone. The clients are doing that kind of work for themselves. I'm finding that my projects are longer, more sophisticated, more intellectually rewarding, and more lucrative.

I think that anybody looking into being an independent information professional needs to be able to define a market for their services. They need to keep their eyes and ears wide open. They need to talk to their clients. They need to be active in some trade and professional associations, in their clients' industries as well as in the information industry. You've got to keep reading up on what's going on in the world. You have to constantly survey your clients to find out where you need to evolve to continue to fill a need.

What about education and experience? What mix of information and business study do you think is a good fit?

I don't think there's any clear plan anymore. I have seen many successful independents, and they've all had very diverse backgrounds. They might have a master's degree in a specific scientific area, so they do research in that subject area. I have found others who have a master's in library science, as I do, who take the research route and then gain their subject expertise in their work environment. I've also worked with MBAs and found that their skill set was a great complement. It all depends on who your target market is. I go after the folks who need industry and company research, because that's where my background is. I try to stay with the subject areas where I have practical work experience. I feel very comfortable doing information retrieval, whether it be manual, online, or primary research, and I stay on that path. I've found a market there, so that's even more reason to keep doing it.

Go with where you have experience, don't try to do something different. I think it's absolutely necessary that you have the work experience behind you—not only to be competent doing what you're doing, but also to establish credibility.

Super Searcher Power Tips

➤ One of my first clients provided a seasonal project, which was wonderful because I could do it in the hours I was available. It didn't matter that I was working while the children were napping, before they were awake in the morning or when they were asleep at night.

➤ Clients today don't need to ask us to deliver data they can find through a simple Internet search. We are getting calls for the complicated searches, and the hard-to-find statistics that are only found by wading through lots of material or conducting telephone interviews.

➤ Due to my background, my niche lies primarily in defense, aerospace, electronics, and telecommunications. I stick with those industries because I'm most comfortable with them.

➤ I use investment reports to find out how the Wall Street analysts are viewing the industry or the company. That leads to the specific analysts and firms that are following that particular industry or company.

➤ Books are still very much a part of my work, and I don't think we can ever get away from that. There's a big difference between searching and browsing, and I find for browsing purposes, I still need to go to the library.

➤ Years ago, our work was 100 percent information retrieval. Now it's 80/20, 80-some percent analysis and 20 percent just plain information retrieval. Lots of people can do their own data gathering nowadays.

➤ If the client can provide us with a one- or two-page description of what they're looking for and what results they're hoping to get, we can turn that around quickly, and that way we have no surprises on either end.

➤ We're going to continue to see more complexity in our projects. Along with that comes more hours, therefore more money. My days of having to respond to "I need it in ten minutes and I want you to spend under $100" are gone.

Chris Sherman

Search Engine Analyst

Chris Sherman is President of Searchwise, a Boulder, Colorado-based Web consulting firm, and Associate Editor of Search Engine Watch [114, see Appendix], a Web site devoted to tracking developments on the search engine front. He is a frequent contributor to *Information Today* [217], *Online* [220], and *EContent* [212], and his published work includes *The Invisible Web* [232], co-authored with Gary Price. His primary focus is analyzing search technologies and applying them to competitive intelligence research on the Web.

csherman@searchwise.net
www.searchwise.net

Chris, tell me a bit about yourself and how you ended up in this niche of Web research.

My background is a little different than most information professionals. I came to searching and the Web because I was a site designer back in the early days of the Web. I remember when Yahoo! [145] first popped up, and then AltaVista [8] and Lycos [74], and the amazing things that you could actually find on the Web instead of having to use these so-called link lists of cool sites. When search engines started coming out, I was fascinated by the concept. I was doing tutorials for clients on how to find information on the Web, got more and more into the technology, and started to focus on the Web search aspect rather than site development, which I eventually gave up altogether. When the Web Search Guide position opened up at About.com [4] in late '97 I applied for it, was fortunate enough to land it, and spent the last three years doing that and writing for *Online* and *Searcher* [223], among other things.

What about your education?

I have a BA from the University of California-San Diego. It's a double major in communications and visual arts, with minors in psychology and writing. As it turns out I do a tremendous amount of writing in various media about search engines and sites that I analyze, so the formal training has been invaluable. The psychology aspect also comes into play because searching is really something of a psychological game—trying to figure out how to do it, what works, and so on—as well as the cognitive issues behind finding things on the Web. It's a very interesting process. I also have an MA from Stanford in interactive educational technology, which is a little more related to what I do now, but originally I went there because I was working for a company developing interactive video training programs, and wanted additional credentials in instructional design, systems integration, and computer science.

When did you first begin working on your own, and how did that come about?

The first time was when I was laid off from my job as an instructional designer in 1981, and as many people do in that situation, I went back to work for the same company as a consultant. They realized they'd made a mistake and tried to hire me back immediately, and I said no. Some time later I accepted a position with another company, and they were pushing me in areas that I wanted to go, but I lacked the formal credentials and background to really do what they wanted. So that's when I decided to go to grad school and get the credential, or the pedigree, as I called it.

After that I was on my own for another two years out of graduate school, doing independent consulting, contracting, and design work for CD-ROM and interactive video programs. One of the clients that I worked for, a global management consulting firm, decided to bring me on board to head up their own in-house development group. I ended up becoming their Vice President of Technology and got to travel all around the world. I was exposed to many different cultures, which I think was also valuable background for finding stuff on the Web.

And have you always maintained a home office?

Other than the times I've worked for other people, I've worked out of my home. With our recent move to Boulder, Colorado, however, I am leasing a small office space for the first time. In the past I didn't have a family and small kids, and could set my own hours and do what I wanted to do. I'm finding now that the kids want to be around when I'm around, and I think that's fair, so I want to return the favor. But it doesn't leave a lot of time to get stuff done, as you know. There are perks to working at home. You get to set your own schedule and do your own thing. But on the other hand, I do miss the day-to-day contact with people, the interaction, and the interplay of ideas you find in an office environment.

What about your choice of business entity? Did you get any outside professional advice in deciding to work on your own?

I'm a sole proprietor and did not consult with an accountant or an attorney in the beginning, though I probably should have. In the past couple of years, I have worked with an attorney a little bit more, primarily in negotiating contracts. The main areas of concern I have are two: One is nondisclosure, because I talk with people who are actually developing search engines, and I have to balance their need for confidentiality with my need for information. While I'm not necessarily going to spill their secrets, I need to have a good understanding of what the latest developments are about and how they fit into the overall landscape. I need a certain amount of information and I need to be able to use it.

That's a delicate balance. You hear about new technologies much sooner than I would as a search consumer, and you have to decide how far to go with that information.

That's right. And most companies, when they ask you to sign a nondisclosure agreement, essentially what they'd like is to rip your vocal cords out. They don't want you to say anything to anybody about anything for X amount of time. It's way over-reaching. So I've actually had an attorney draft up my own nondisclosure agreement that specifies how far I will go in agreeing to these things, and I don't sign anything that comes from *their* attorneys because it's usually unacceptable.

The other area that I'm concerned with in writing for publication is omissions and oversight. You can be sued for overlooking or not saying the right things. That's an area I constantly monitor, and one that any independent professional should be aware of.

About.com bills itself as the "Human Internet." Tell me how you landed the Web Search Guide position there.

About.com has a very formal multistep process to select and train subject area Guides. When one of these positions becomes available, you send them a letter expressing your interest, background, and so on. That's the first level of screening. They write back and say, okay, and then put you in a process called prep, which is a twelve-week process where they give you increasingly harder assignments that are all related to building the different parts of a Guide site. There are articles that you have to write, there's the link section that you have to maintain, there's the community chat, bulletin boards, newsletter production, and all these things that you need to do to become a Guide. During this twelve-week process, you actually build a prototype site, it goes live in a staging area that's not public, and the staff evaluates it as you go along. If you make it all the way through the twelve weeks, you're typically in competition with one or two other people. They're doing the same process in parallel. It gets down to the wire. If you miss even just a small deadline, you're out. They're really rigorous with this. They want only the most committed people who are really good and passionate about what they do.

In my last week of prep, we had planned a family vacation to go skiing, and this was right after our son was born, so we decided to drive. On the way, I got hit with the worse plague I have ever had in my life. I could not even get out of bed, let alone go skiing. And I didn't have access to a computer. I finally was able to find a community online access terminal and retrieve my mail through Hotmail. It was totally pins and needles; literally all I did for a whole week was get up for about fifteen minutes, drive to where the terminal was, check my email to see if I got this job, and then go back to bed. So it was certainly a relief when word came through that I was actually going live with my site.

At About.com, what were your duties?

Well, I was the Web search guy. Basically my charter there was twofold. First of all, to write about searching and how you find things on the Web, and, second, to provide guidance to Webmasters who wanted their sites to be found. Since I have a site development background, I really enjoyed this and would work to get the best placement possible in search engines. I divided my time more or less equally between those two areas. I wrote an article a week at least, usually more like two or three, and a weekly newsletter. It was a wonderful learning experience, and exposed me to a lot of different perspectives on the online information scene.

You answered people's Web search questions, which I understand ran the gamut from very amateur to quite challenging.

Yes, but the model changed over time. When The Mining Company—which is what About.com was originally called—first started, we were expected to have a tremendous amount of one-on-one interaction with users. But the site—both the property as a whole and then our individual Guide sites—grew to be so heavily trafficked that our email got out of control. It was unbelievable. So we moved away from the "ask us" model and tried to get people to post their questions to the forum, and the Guide would answer there so all the other people in the community would benefit.

The questions were all over the map in terms of subjects. Some were really interesting; some were really funny. One of the most common things that people would ask me was to help them find a person. Quite often it would be, "I knew her maiden name, I don't know what her married name is, she got divorced four times, she moved out of the country, and all of her ex-husbands are dead. Can you help me find her?" And that's all the information they would provide. And I would say, no, sorry; I think you need a professional detective for that.

You were doing this between 1998 and early 2001, a time of phenomenal growth and development of the Internet. Did the About.com community pose more intelligent questions as more sophisticated search tools became available?

In a sense, there were fewer questions. What stood out more was the evolution of the forum community, which took on a life of its own. There was some lively interchange, with people having very interesting discussions and mentioning other interesting sites they found. There definitely was an increase in sophistication. There was also a simultaneous growth in new users who kept coming onto the site all the time, so you had this continual flow of newbie questions along with an expanding overall user base where the sophistication was also increasing. I think that's still occurring on the Internet as a whole. We're at 300 million Web users now, and we still have a ways to go before we get to six billion.

In another interview you described an observation you came away with from About.com, namely that people were using the Web to solve a problem or to fill a need. They weren't really thinking that much about searching.

I honestly feel that most people, other than information professionals, don't really search. What they have is a pressing need. They need to know something. They need a fact or some bit of information. They don't want to go out and talk to a search engine and be confronted with a list of three million results, and here are the top 100. That's not satisfying an information need at all. I think very few people want to take the time to really master the search engines and the tools so that they can get past all that and find what they're looking for.

I'm seeing some new systems and new technologies that combine things like natural language processing with the ability to search both structured and unstructured sources of information. I think that, in the next two or three years, the concept of a search engine as we know it today is largely going to go away. We are going to have something more like an electronic reference librarian to which you ask your question in natural language and it will come back and actually provide you with an answer. It's going to be different from Ask Jeeves [11], which really isn't a natural language search engine. Most people seem to think it is, but it actually is a question database. You ask a question, and it tries to match it to a question in its database. Then if one of the questions it presents is similar enough, you click on it, and it returns a document that a Jeeves editor has determined answers the question. But you still have to look at that document and figure out whether it really is a match or not.

The newer systems won't do that. You'll ask a question like "How did Cisco's stock do today?" It will go out, query a real-time database, and build a table for you showing, here is Cisco, here is its price, number of shares, and so on. Now, the neat thing about these systems is that they'll probably also have context understanding, so you can further say, "okay, compare it to its competitors." That's the basic answering-questions model that many people on the Web want. But there's still going to be a need for information pros who can really get in and do sophisticated queries and authoritative-type searches, so we'll still have search engines.

Tell me about what you're doing now with Search Engine Watch.

I'm writing a daily newsletter called *SearchDay* [113]. Essentially I have an open portfolio to write about anything that catches my eye. I'm doing pretty much what I did with About.com, scanning the horizon, identifying the new tools that are out there, what's new in the whole search engine arena. My task as associate editor is to complement what Danny Sullivan, founder and head of Search Engine Watch, is doing. Danny has a phenomenal encyclopedic knowledge of search engine technology and how Webmasters can get their pages placed highly. I think that's really his true love, whereas my perspective is more that of a searcher—here are the kinds of things that you should be aware of, here are the new tools that are coming out, here are some tricks and techniques, and here's how you use Boolean logic on AltaVista.

How in the world do you find the information that you write about? You are essentially

writing what other searchers read to stay current. How do you stay current?

It's kind of a chicken-and-egg problem. What's made it a lot easier is that, as people become aware that I write about this field, they tend to come to me. I get a lot of press releases and companies saying, "We'd like you to write about us," so I have an information conduit that way. But I also love to get out there and find out what's going on in the research labs. I check various university computer science department sites and find the research projects, and then start tracking the people and what they're doing as they move out and get venture capital.

So you're doing a form of competitive intelligence on your own field.

Yes. I maintain for my own use a pretty extensive database of people who are working on search technology, what they're doing, and the players involved. It's my own personal tool that I can tap into. And then I read everybody else. Obviously Search Engine Watch is quite important, and ResearchBuzz [108], Neat New Stuff [88], the Librarians' Index to the Internet [70], and the Scout Report [111]. There's a great site that's primarily for Linux and open source hackers called Slashdot.org [117] that often has very articulate debate about search and other Net technologies. I also like to track a few Weblogs, like Jorn Barger's Robot Wisdom [109] and Gary Price's Virtual Acquisition Shelf [134].

Sometimes I will scan some random unknowns because Weblogs tend to extensively link to each other. They're great early warning systems, though you have to be prepared to wade through a lot of inaccurate information or self-indulgent navel gazing. But that's just the nature of self-publishing on the Web. The absence of editorial control is both boon and bane.

How much of your time on a typical day is spent just educating yourself through searching and reading?

It's hard to say. I don't really have a typical day. If I'm working on a short piece of writing, just a quick article or something, then I'd say most of my day is dedicated to just being out there and absorbing. But if I'm working on a more in-depth piece or an article that requires a lot of interviewing, then I can go through the entire day and not even read, which drives me crazy. It quickly becomes "Whoops, what happened to today? I missed it." But you just have to let go sometimes. There comes a point where you can't absorb everything or do any more, and you can only hope that your searching skills are strong enough that you'll be able to find something that you missed when you need it.

Tell me about the other side of your business, Searchwise, where you work as a research consultant. Would that be a fair term?

Yes, I think so. I mainly work for search companies who are interested in competitive analysis of their product vs. who's out there in the marketplace. "Tell us what you think of what we're doing, do we have a market here, are we going to be successful in this, are our strategies the correct ones?" That's where I'll bring in some of my management consulting experience to try to help them position themselves in the market. I also work as an analyst in the information technology industry, and basically look at individual companies and products.

So your end product is a written report?

Yes, usually in the form of a white paper, a bulletin, or sometimes quite an extensive report. It's really whatever the client requests. I have some nice arrangements where I function as a consulting analyst and have access to my client company's internal research, except that as an external analyst I can offer a fresh perspective.

You've developed something of a brand for yourself with the "invisible Web" and the work that you do with Gary Price. Can you tell me about that concept, and how you are presenting it in a number of different venues?

The invisible Web is something that I became interested in very early on. I might actually have written one of the first papers describing it in 1998. I'm not taking credit for inventing the phrase; it's been around for a long time. But nobody really had quantified it or talked about it or written very much about it, and the interest seemed to be immense. So, I started delving into it as a personal interest, and then Gary said, "Hey, I'd love to work with you, because I'm essentially doing the same thing."

How did you two first connect?

We were both speaking at a conference, and once we started talking we realized that we shared a lot of common interests. We started speaking together about the invisible Web, and realized we should probably write a book as well. So that evolved into a separate project, and *The Invisible Web* was released in the last half of 2001. It's such an interesting subject, and there's such a demand for information about it, that we have limitless possibilities.

On the other hand, I see search technology eventually catching up with some of the problems that give rise to the invisible Web, so I'm not so sure that it's something that will be around forever. At this point we're both approaching it from the standpoint that we just enjoy talking about it. People seem receptive to the presentations that we make, and we like sharing the word.

Even outside of the information professional community, everyone feels overwhelmed by

the Web, so the phrase itself has a lot of marketing power.

We hope so! Speaking about the invisible Web has become a good marketing tool for the book, but the speaking itself is great. Speaking to groups is hard for some people, but invariably, anytime I speak somewhere I end up getting work out of it. There are two advantages to giving presentations. One is, you generally don't have to pay to attend the conference. Secondly, even if you have to pay your own expenses to get to the conference and stay there, you get exposure to people. After a while, you get used to talking to large groups. Your confidence level improves. It's a great thing for anybody who's in business on his or her own to consider doing, because it pays off multifold. It's one of the most effective marketing tools you could possibly have.

Information professionals commonly tell me, "Why would I spend an hour looking for something on the Web when I can get what I want in five minutes in a commercial online service?" I imagine you have a different view on that.

It's an interesting comment, and when I hear it, I'll often follow up by asking, "Well, what tool are you using to search the Web?" Almost invariably the answer comes back, a general purpose search engine like Google [53], AltaVista, or Yahoo!. Those are all good tools in their own right, but this is the whole reason that we focus so much on the invisible Web: The invisible Web technologies, by definition, are almost always going to deliver better results for many types of specific queries that information professionals tend to demand.

The analogy we make in our talks is that invisible Web resources are much like reference works in the library. They tend to be very focused, they're on a particular subject, and they're quite often produced by extremely authoritative sources. So when people say, "I don't want to waste my time searching the Web," to me it's like they're saying, "I don't really know what's available on the Web, and I don't know how to use search engines to find it." I consider it to be kind of a cop-out. No criticism intended, but you really do have to spend some time in, as Gary likes to put it, your own acquisition development on the Web. You have to go out and find these resources and bookmark them, get to know what they offer, and learn how to use them, just like librarians would have a knowledge of their own reference collection in their library. You as a searcher may not be able to have quite that breadth of knowledge of the realm of Web sites out there. But if you were a reference librarian, you certainly would. I think an information professional should be in the same sort of position in respect to online resources.

People always seem amazed at the invisible Web resources that Gary and I present. But I'm likewise in awe of the searchers who can say, "well, that's easy to find on File 7, Social SciSearch" on Dialog [35], or "just do a forward search on Social Science Citation Index to find the latest research based on citation analysis." They're all just tools! I really think it behooves any information professional to take the time to get out there and investigate. Particularly if it's a narrow area of interest rather than a broad spectrum, you can come up to speed pretty quickly with the ten or twenty or fifty key information sources that are available on the Web. Once you've familiarized yourself with them, you won't be wasting your time, first of all, and secondly you'll be getting this information for free, or for very low cost. And it's going to be just as high quality as the stuff that you'll find on the proprietary services. You'll lose some of the searching capabilities. You'll lose some of the neat features that are built into the proprietary online systems. It's not a total substitute. But on the other hand, there's a lot more out there on the Web than people are willing to give credit for.

What about copyright concerns on the Internet? Sometimes I don't want to use information from a Web site for a client project because its terms of usage are just too fuzzy. But the general public, at least, seems to assume that if it's on the Web it's there for the taking.

Copyright is such a contentious subject. On the one hand, it protects the rights of content creators to realize some kind of return on investment for their works, and protects them from charlatans who would steal their work. On the other hand, copyright law was never intended to establish perpetual monopolies. Content is no different than other products—once it's out in the public domain it's meant to be used, not hoarded.

Napster [85] blew the whole issue wide open. The recording industry's narrow-minded focus on protecting "copyright"— read "profits"—has exposed numerous flaws in existing copyright law. What's ultimately needed is a balance between protecting the rights of content creators and the rights of information users. Draconian regulations won't work—we'll likely see Al Capone-like figures appear to circumvent Prohibition-era type laws if Napster, Gnutella [52] and their kin are outlawed. Cybergangsters!

As a Web content creator myself, I'm torn between wanting to be adequately compensated for my work and letting the greatest number of people possible access my work. It's a difficult issue, because "free" content on the Web facilitates so-called viral marketing. It's similar to public speaking; offering "free" content on the Web leads to intriguing business opportunities. But I don't want everything I create to be free; I need to provide for my family! I'm optimistic that a balanced solution will be found soon, one that won't make information professionals feel like thieves for quoting a paragraph or two, but will also adequately compensate content creators for their efforts.

With your broad perspective on the Internet, where would you search if you were working on a general IT (information technology) industry project?

There are some sites specifically dedicated to information technology, and they tend to be metasites. They have not only a lot of really good content themselves, but links to other sources of information. Bitpipe [12] is one that comes to mind; another is InformIT [61]. There are so many sites like this that are very narrowly focused on their industry, with professionals creating the content, finding links, and building directories.

One of my favorites, which only recently did move to a subscription model, was what used to be the IBM patent server and is now the Delphion Intellectual Property [33] server. It has the full text of all U.S. patents back to 1973 or so, and it has extensive searching and limiting capabilities. It's a phenomenal tool. Grateful Med [55] is another one, for medical and health information. The list goes on and on, depending on what you're looking for.

So much of the authoritative information that is repackaged by the proprietary databases comes from government agencies, and more and more government agencies are becoming much more sophisticated about putting information online. First of all, they're mandated to do this by the Paperwork Reduction Act. As time goes on, more and more authoritative sources of information are going to be out there, and because they're government-sponsored, they're going to be free.

I had an ongoing project a couple years ago that involved searching the Web for studies that various government agencies were putting out, but the client wanted the studies in print. It got harder and harder, and pretty soon it just wasn't happening.

The real problem is that government agencies are not coordinated with each other, and the systems they use for putting information online are all over the map. Some of them will use simple HTML, some will have sophisticated, dynamic databases, others publish in PDF format only. There's a project underway called FirstGov [48], which is attempting to be a one-stop portal for information services. I have talked to the people who are working on it, and they are so eager to do the right thing. They really want to have a killer search engine for government information. They're highly motivated, and they are going to find the resources and the people to do it. It's just a matter of time. It's really encouraging to see that kind of stuff. The fact that they were able to get those government agencies to talk to each other and coordinate even on a basic level was, I think, remarkable.

And government information itself is just amazing. There's seemingly no end to it, and when you know where to look, you can find such good stuff.

Now, thinking about functioning as a consultant and working on your own, do you outsource any business support services or research work? Do you do everything yourself?

I don't have everything automated, and I don't outsource. Those day-to-day details are a major pain. I probably don't have the best system, but right now my business is not very complicated so it's not too much of a problem. But if it looked like my business were really going to expand or change, then I would definitely seek help.

How do you keep everything together when you travel so much? Are you a gadget person?

I'm actually a borderline Luddite. I don't have a cell phone. I have a Palm Pilot that I think I turned on a couple years ago. I keep contacts in Outlook on my laptop, and I've got this wonderful program called 80/20 Retriever [2] that makes everything on your computer searchable. It's a search engine for your personal information. It indexes email, attachments to email, your phone directory, and all that kind of stuff. It's such a powerful search engine that you don't have to worry as much about deleting or filing. You have all the different folders, and then you click down through the hierarchy as you need to. Or you just type in the keywords and boom, you've got it. That's really what I rely on.

I have all the computers in the house networked together; if you count the ones for the kids, that makes six. I like to have a good computer as my main work unit, because I spend all day in front of it. I also tend to stress the computers. I have a lot of music on the machines and the kids bang on their computers when they play CD-ROMs like Arthur and Putt-Putt.

I like to have one machine that's entirely for downloads if I'm going to be testing software, so that it won't crash my other systems. Quite often when you download and test new software, it's still in beta, and it's not reliable. If you download two or three a day, after a week you've got twenty programs all in beta and they may not work well together, let alone with your existing software. I've had to reformat my hard drive so many times thanks to these kinds of incompatibilities, and it's just too painful to do that.

I'd like to ask you how you market yourself, but I'll take a guess that you're going to say "speaking and writing." Beyond that, do you do any specific marketing efforts?

No, I really don't. I'm lucky in that most of the stuff I do gets fairly high visibility on its own. Simply by being with About.com or Search Engine Watch, people see what I do. I'm fortunate in that respect, because people come to me.

What role does your own Web site play in your various professional activities?

I have one, but it's the classic case of the shoemaker's children having no shoes, or very bad shoes at best. My Searchwise site is very sparse, very minimal. I try to keep it updated with links to presentations and articles I've done, but I find that, frankly, it's the lowest priority on my list compared to everything else I do.

What do you like about being an independent consultant?

The number one thing is I don't have to go to meetings. I don't have to figure out how to achieve consensus with other people. That alone gives me the ability to be objective, whereas I think people working in a team environment may not have that flexibility. I'm not in any way bashing teams. I've worked on teams, I enjoy working in teams, and they can be very useful. But there's also a time when you do want to have an outside perspective, and the objectivity that you get with that. I think my clients value that, because they know I have no reason to BS them. I'm just going to tell it like it is. I did that when I worked with About.com and I'm doing it with Search Engine Watch now. People don't always like to hear that what they're doing isn't the best, but recently I was told by a site development group, "Thank you, nobody in Washington tells the truth. You were the only one that we got a review from that said there were some rough edges. And we knew it, because we were involved in it. So we appreciate that." That's always nice to hear.

The downside is that you don't get the support you get when you're an employee. It's like you're out on an exposed rock face, and if a lightning bolt is going to get you, it's going to get you, and you're toast. You don't have the protection or the backup or the support network that you have as an employee. I frankly prefer the freedom and the independence over a support network, but I can see why a lot of people wouldn't.

Another challenge in working for yourself is that you've got to have your own routines to motivate yourself in the morning. Even if you're having a bad hair day, it doesn't matter, you've got to work, you've got to crank, you've got to get going. The good part is that, if you have interesting and fun work to do, then you can just jump in and go.

Do you struggle with managing your time, and dividing it between work and home?

It's a huge struggle. But I have worked hard to draw very clear lines between work and family. Basically, when I'm home, I try to put work aside and be with the family. That said, I'm not above getting the family together to watch TV, and be reading a technical document at the same time.

I find, too, that I have cycles. I can get as much done in the first couple hours of the day as I can in the later stage, just because that's my focused "on" time. So I tend to guard that time very, very carefully. It's "do not disturb." I don't take client calls, I don't answer email, and I don't look at email. I just tunnel down and head in for those first few hours, and then spend the rest of the day doing everything else. I think everybody has to find their cycle, and if they can tune in to it, it does help with managing their time.

Also, I try to step back occasionally and look at everything I'm doing—all the email lists that I subscribe to, all the newsletters, all the whatever, and purge. Just turn them off. Go no-mail for a while, and then a month or so later, revisit everything and ask myself, "Did I miss this?" No? Then it's gone. And it's surprising how often that happens. You tend not to realize when you sign up for a mailing list, and you say, "This will be interesting," oh, one more, "That will be interesting," oh, one more, "That will be interesting." And pretty soon you have twenty or thirty of these things coming and flooding your mailbox, and you feel bad because you can't give them the attention that you want. It's a neat little trick. Just put yourself on a sort of temporary vacation, and if you didn't miss it, you're not going to miss it in the future, so don't bother starting it up again. And that's good, because you're already starting to add new ones. Of course I only recommend this technique for mailings other than my daily *SearchDay* newsletter!

Kind of like going through your closet and, if you haven't worn it in a year, you're not going to and you should just get rid of it.

That's exactly right.

What is your perspective on future opportunities for independent researchers and consultants? Is the Web going to get so good that one day humans won't be needed to sift through it all?

Five or ten years ago all the pundits were predicting that, with the advance of online information systems and the Web, librarians weren't going to be needed anymore. Well, librarians are in more demand now than ever, because the critical information skills they possess are totally different than the ability to simply find information or stumble across it on the Web.

As the Web expands and grows—the current best estimate I've heard is that by 2003, it will be up to about 13 billion pages—it's going to be vital to have filters. And information professionals are going to provide that filtering process. It's not a question of finding. Anybody can find. But you get so overwhelmed with what's out there, you need somebody to help you filter information, and then organize it, make sense of it, maybe prune it, and take it down to "I just want an answer." People are frustrated with a million results. They want a solution, and information professionals can provide that.

I see almost infinite opportunities for people with research, Web, or online skills under their belts. I actually see it moving beyond the realm of just companies, because individuals are going to start feeling the need. Think about the world of personal finance. You've got financial planners who help you manage your money long term, but what if you're just interested in this one particular stock or mutual fund? You don't really want a broker because they're not set up to give you tailored advice. They're going to tell you what their firm believes; they'll give you the party line. If you go to a financial planner, they're going to charge you a fortune. So right in the middle there is a niche for people to do this kind of research on demand. I see lots of these personal information concierge opportunities, if you will, opening up. There's going to be no end of demand in the corporate environment, either.

Personal information concierge. I like that. How can this message be communicated to the corporate sector?

Corporate America starts to listen when the pain threshold becomes great enough. Real, gut-wrenching change occurs only after companies experience what we're going through now in the economy—layoffs, missed earnings targets, inventory problems. If you open up the lid of a corporation that's going through these sorts of changes, I can guarantee you'll find people looking for solutions and asking, "How are we going to survive? We just lost fifty percent of our staff. We still have the same amount of work to do. How are we going to do this?" If you can find those people and offer your skills to them, those are the ones who will listen, because they're the ones who need your services. Not the information technology group, not the human resources department, but the people within the company who have just been stripped of the resources they need to do what was already an overwhelming task. Then it becomes less an issue of selling the tools or the capabilities, but selling a solution to their needs. Essentially what you're trying to do is take away their pain. You want to help them solve their problem in a broader context, and information is just one component of that.

For the aspiring information consultant, what advice would you have for preparation? Certainly what you do is not found in a typical curriculum anywhere.

I don't think there is any one path. The way I got to where I am is that I tend to be insatiably curious. I mean, I read the back of cereal boxes if there's nothing else to read. I'm constantly hungry for information.

Yes, it's an illness of sorts.

It is, but it's a good illness, fortunately. It doesn't kill you. I think you need to try to learn everything you can about everything you can, and start at the simplest levels. You need to know the basic search tools. All the major search engines and many of the invisible Web sites offer extensive help in the form of tutorials, descriptions, and how to's, yet the search engine folks tell me that very few people—something like one tenth of one percent of all their page usage—come from those help files. They have to maintain those files, because if they don't, the three or four people who rely on the on-site help are going to scream. But with that information right there, you can teach yourself so much just by looking at what's offered.

Beyond that, it's useful to take a look at some of the better directory sites that have been compiled in particular subject areas, and stretch yourself into areas that you're not comfortable with. If you're a language major, go out into a math site. If you're a science major, then go into a poetry site. You need to push yourself in directions where you're not comfortable.

One of the things that I'm doing right now for pleasure that my wife thinks is absolutely nuts is reading information retrieval textbooks. I'm going back to some of the classics. How do these machines work, how do these algorithms work, how do these things get processed? I don't need to do this. I have a reasonably good understanding of how this stuff works anyway. But I'm finding it fascinating and I'm learning so much that it's not only a way of broadening myself, but it also has the side benefit of building confidence. I don't feel like a total pretender when I'm writing about information retrieval on the Internet.

So, if I were to ask you about balance in your life and how you escape work, you'd say you read information retrieval texts?

No, that's what I do for fun. But seriously, one of the reasons we moved to Colorado from Los Angeles was specifically because of the opportunities to do things as a family outdoors. We so enjoy that escape where we can get out with the kids and just be outside, experiencing the environment and doing things as a family. It was a very conscious lifestyle decision on our part to leave LA. It's very, very difficult to do anything in Los Angeles, let alone with a family, because you have to get in a car and drive and wait in line and then the day is gone, and it's like, what did we do all day? Colorado provides a nice balance to the world we otherwise live and work in.

Well, the Internet has changed so much of that world....

It has indeed. And the change is here to stay, regardless of the disruptions we've seen with the bursting of the dot-com bubble. Through all the carnage and chaos, I've seen people and companies continue to invest in the Internet, and to support people who can either add value to it by creating great content, or harvest that value through their searching skills.

It's a great time to be an information professional, and an even greater time to be an *independent* information professional. To mangle Shakespeare's marvelous aphorism, these days the *Web* is our oyster, which with browser we will open.

Super Searcher Power Tips

➤ Searching is something of a psychological game—
trying to figure out how to do it and what works—as
well as the cognitive issues behind finding things on
the Web.

➤ There's a lot more authoritative information out there
on the Web than some information professionals are
willing to give credit for.

➤ Invisible Web resources are much like reference works
in the library. They tend to be very focused, they're on
a particular subject, and they're quite often produced
by extremely authoritative sources.

➤ After a while, you get used to talking to large groups.
Your confidence level improves. It's a great thing for
anybody in business on his or her own to consider
doing, because it pays off multifold. It's one of the most
effective marketing tools you could possibly have.

➤ I don't have to go to meetings, so I don't have to figure out how to achieve consensus with other people.
That alone gives me the ability to be objective, where
people working in a team environment may not have
that flexibility.

➤ One downside of working on your own is that you don't have support. It's like being on an exposed rock face, and if a lightning bolt is going to get you, it's going to get you, and you're toast.

➤ You've got to have your own routines to motivate yourself in the morning. Even if you're having a bad hair day, it doesn't matter, you've got to work, you've got to crank, you've got to get going.

➤ People need somebody to help them filter information, and then organize it, make sense of it, maybe prune it, and take it down to "I just want an answer." They are frustrated with getting a million results. They want a solution, and information professionals can provide that.

Amelia Kassel
Online Information Expert

Amelia Kassel is president and owner of MarketingBASE, which has specialized in market research, competitive intelligence, and worldwide business information since 1984. She has taught online searching at the graduate level for more than fifteen years and is an internationally recognized speaker and author. Based in northern California, Amelia offers an email-based mentoring program for information brokers and corporate searchers.

amelia@marketingbase.com
www. marketingbase.com

Amelia, you have a rich background in the information business. Could you give me a brief overview of where you came from and how you got started?

After college, I attended graduate school in library science at UCLA and earned my MLS in 1971. I spent one additional year as an intern in a special predoctoral program for becoming a biomedical librarian, sponsored by the National Library of Medicine (NLM) [86, see Appendix]. This led to a position at the UCLA Biomedical Library's Pacific Southwest Regional Medical Library Service, where I consulted for small hospital libraries in a four-state region during the next few years. I provided training to hospital library staff who needed additional help by conducting workshops and assisting with grant applications to receive funding from NLM.

I also worked part-time in the interlibrary loan department and verified difficult-to-find citations from all over the four-state region.

Things like incomplete citations?

Right. Verifying citations is a type of detective work. I would find out that the requested item was a paper from a conference proceeding or a chapter in a book rather than a journal article, and then complete the citation. There were all sorts of weird requests. Starting very early on, I liked finding hard-to-find information, and enjoyed the process of training. Over the next thirty years of my career, those are two themes that emerged—answering questions or conducting in-depth research, and providing training related to some kind of information work.

In 1974, I left the Biomedical Library for the northern California wine country. There were no medical libraries to speak of in this area, which at that time was primarily rural and agricultural. After interviewing at a community college and writing a federal grant for an area medical resource specialist, neither of which panned out, I landed a position at a public library. My job as a public librarian was a huge change for me, and what I remember the most about my first tour of the library was that I felt like a kid in a candy store with all the different kinds of books. There were children's books and mystery stories and science fiction and all that fun reading.

How large a staff did the library have?

This was a medium-sized public library system with about one hundred employees. I worked in the central library as one of ten or twelve adult reference librarians. The whole system had a dozen branches. Working in this capacity you answer a lot of different kinds of questions. "How do you cook a turkey?" "What's the definition of honky-tonk?" "How do I find a business located in Japan?" In the ten years I worked there, I became more and more interested in business reference in particular. Around 1981, the director of our library decided that we finally needed to get Dialog [35]. It had been available since 1971, and although I had been exposed to it through some continuing education workshops, I never really used it until they brought a Dialog trainer to our library.

Was it love at first sight?

Yes! In those days the training was two full days, and one of my fellow librarians and I invited the trainer to lunch and wined and dined him to try to learn as much as we could about online services. We returned quite late from that lunch, but had excellent training from him just the same. I went wild, thinking this was the best thing since sliced bread. I was thrilled with the information we could get using online databases!

Did you get to experience the broad topic coverage of Dialog? Or were you just looking at the general *Reader's Guide to Periodical Literature* [105] kind of stuff?

Because I worked at an adult reference desk where patrons ask every imaginable question, I attempted to answer everything I could with an online database from Dialog. I didn't care whether I should use a reference book instead or whether it was appropriate. I just went straight to the computer terminal any time someone came up to me with a reference question—which was all day. We were very busy. Because of that, I used all the databases I could and learned so much.

I was responsible for overseeing the online reference collection and purchased all the Dialog reference guides on standing order. When they came in, I would study them from cover to cover on my breaks, and would take the Bluesheets, which were the documentation for each of the individual databases, home with me and read them in bed. About the fourth month into searching, the library director came by with the county's budget officer while I was online and said, "This is a new service the library offers. Would you like us to do a search for you?" He asked for a search on budgets for the juvenile justice system. I did it, and we didn't hear back for a while. But as it turned out, the library director and the budget officer were very happy with the search I performed, and, as a result, the library was given an online budget of $14,000 for one year, which was very unusual for a public library in 1982.

And so I went merrily on my way, continuing to learn about online databases and pumping up the online database collection, attending advanced and subject-oriented Dialog workshops, and evaluating other online services for our library, like BRS [15] and LexisNexis [69].

You just prompted my question: When did other online providers come onto the scene?

In our public library, based on budget and need, we decided not to add other services. We felt that Dialog had everything we wanted at the time.

As much as I enjoyed the online searching, during that same period I gradually became somewhat dissatisfied with the work I was doing. I loved the people I was working with, and I really liked the patrons who came into the library. But I grew tired of answering the same old questions about recipes and tune-up specs for cars.

And you don't get to go real far in depth.

No. It's very quick reference for the most part. Or showing someone how to use the *Reader's Guide* or helping them find a particular section of books in the library. I felt the need for more challenge and applied for a higher position in the system—the North Bay Cooperative Library System Reference Coordinator.

At the same time, however, in the back of my mind, I was thinking about the possibility of starting my own business. I had been to a California Library Association meeting in San Francisco, and at the exhibits I saw a booth for Information on

Demand, which was Sue Rugge's information brokerage business. She was demonstrating online searching using Dialog. I saw that she provided this as a fee-based service, and I'd never heard of such a thing. The moment I saw that, I said to myself, "Oh, now *that's* what I'm going to do! If she can do it, I can do it." And years later when Sue and I became close friends, I told her that she had been the major inspiration for the development of my next career.

When I applied for the new position, part of me was saying, "If I like this job, I'll stay in the library system. But if it doesn't work out, I have this new, potential career that I'm going to explore." I accepted the position and really worked hard to make it a success, but decided to explore the field of information brokering on my own time. I started researching what type of equipment to use, and found out that Dialog had compiled a list of information brokers that was available for the asking. I made phone calls to seven or eight of them around the country. The response was everything from a friendly, warm reception to "you're nuts if you think I'm going to tell you how I did it." One man in particular stands out, however, because he spent nearly an hour on the phone with me telling me why I must have a computer. I didn't understand a word he was talking about, but took copious notes.

So he was explaining that a PC rather than a dumb terminal was the way to go?

Right. I was trying to decide whether I should just get a teletypewriter terminal or a "real" computer. I started reading trade magazines and computer magazines, and talking to people in the computer retail stores and asking lots of questions. At that time the choice was between Apple and IBM. The Apple displayed only forty characters and the IBM allowed eighty characters, which was the way the online information was sent across a screen, so I chose the IBM. It was a little nerve-wracking for me in those days because whenever I went into a computer store, there were all men there. Once I took a male friend with me, and although I asked the questions, the salesman looked at him the whole time. And then I became angry. The next time I went, I went alone because I wanted the salesman to talk to *me*.

I also did a literature search and found one book on the market called *Information Brokers* [231] by Kelly Warnken, which I still have on my bookshelf today. I also found that somebody had published a very strange collection of articles about information brokering, and I purchased those. I was trying to find everybody and everything I could about the field.

So at the time, you had several key factors coming together: You had learned Dialog, you had seen the future of the PC, and you had seen Sue Rugge's business. And you were methodically adding these things up in your mind. How did you finally take the plunge?

In 1982, I established A. S. K. Information Specialists—A.S.K. are my initials—Amelia Stephanie Kassel. A few months later, I hired a graphic artist whom I'd met at an ad club meeting to design a business card, and started going to breakfast club and chamber of commerce meetings to develop business contacts. I didn't know anybody at all who could use my services at that time, nor would it have been ethical to try to make any contacts through the public library. My networking was completely separate, going to meetings before and after work. I took classes at the junior college on how to write a business plan and how to do sales and marketing, and I attended brown bag lunch lectures on various business topics. Later that year, I officially began moonlighting. In 1984, on my birthday, as a present to myself, I handed in my resignation letter with the thought that I would go into business full-time and sink or swim. As you can see, I managed to keep my head above water.

Tell me about your first client.

My first client was a word-of-mouth referral from another librarian who had been doing some moonlighting as well, but didn't consider herself an information broker. It was just that this man had come to the library one day and wanted someone to do his research for him. He said he would pay her, so she just did it. She decided to move on to a different type of career and knew that I had just started my business. He was a writer for a major national magazine, and from time to time needed some research done. He called me and told me what he needed and I didn't have a clue how to find it. He must have sensed my lack of confidence, and when I didn't have an immediate idea of what to do, he made a suggestion, which turned out to be the best way to do the research he needed. In fact, it was telephone research, not online. All he needed was college football statistics, and he even told me whom to call at each college—the sports information director—and exactly what to ask for. What he wanted was public information that all colleges make available for the asking. This client is still a client to this day and has referred several magazine editors to me, which has led to other projects from many different writers.

I'll bet this opened your eyes to some broader possibilities. It was an unusual request, and yet somebody was willing to pay you to do the work.

Exactly. It was very interesting to me because it was completely different from the work that I imagined would come my way based on the kinds of questions that were asked in the public library. But, with regard to my public library work, what was particularly motivating me to start my own business was the fact that some of the patrons observing me conduct searches at the terminal were inspired to take out their wallets and offer to pay me for my efforts, though I explained that the public library could not accept money.

You really took things slowly and carefully and methodically, and probably avoided a lot of mistakes because of that.

Yes. I never made any major mistakes. I took only calculated risks and a long time to get where I was going. I stayed at the public library ten years, when I probably could have stayed just two or three years before starting a business. The first five years of my business, I primarily did networking. Building on the contacts I made, I worked with a lot of very small businesses, primarily ad agencies and marketing consultants. The size of any given sale was usually very small. In order to make the business profitable, I had to generate a lot of volume. It took me a long time to learn that it's almost as easy to make a $5,000 sale as it is to make a $500 sale. I was slow in learning how to move toward making larger sales. Mine was a very slow evolution. Now I tell people to go straight for the jugular. If you're interested in a niche market, get out there and start working in that niche quickly. You don't need to spend all the years that I spent evolving.

Let's bring the picture up to date. How do you describe MarketingBase today?

One quick sentence: MarketingBase provides competitive intelligence and market and Internet research to businesses worldwide. The other part is that MarketingBase provides Internet training seminars both on-site and online, as well as training for other information brokers.

Do you have corporate clients where you go into a company and teach nonresearchers about Internet research?

Yes, most of the Internet training I do is for organizations or associations where I'm hired to teach one-day seminars. I might also be hired by, say, an advertising agency, where eight to ten people attend a seminar. One example was an agency that specializes in writing medical ad copy. I provided tailored training to help them learn how to use MEDLINE [80] and other health and medical databases, because they work with medical information.

Can you explain your Mentor Program?

The Mentor Program is an email-based one-year program for either new or aspiring information brokers, or for existing information brokers who want to expand into new markets. The Program focuses on two important components. One is business development and marketing. Marketing, which seems to be the most challenging aspect of developing an information brokering business, encompasses communication skills, pricing, negotiation, and closing sales. The other component is helping to evolve the student's online searching capabilities using commercial databases while helping them understand when to use commercial vendors and/or the Internet. Each student has such a different background that every program is essentially tailored to the individual, although I send everyone the same basic readings about information brokering and marketing that I have written myself.

And the mentoring takes place entirely in an electronic dialogue between you and the student.

Most of the time it does. There are some questions and answers that are best asked or discussed on the phone because of gray areas or nuances. The idea of the Mentor Program, however, is to be primarily email based. I've never even heard some students' voices. The reason I use email rather than the telephone is that written responses are more cohesive, with descriptions of alternative methods and pros and cons of one technique or another. I consider the many individually tailored responses I provide to be what I call customized mini-lectures. On the phone, it's very easy to digress from the subject at hand and talk about everything else under the sun. It's not a good use of time nor the best way to provide what I want to be an educational experience.

I noticed on your Web page that you also market the Mentor Program to corporate clients.

Right. At one time I put some ads in a few information-oriented magazines, and some of the responses I got were from individuals in corporations and organizations. This led me to create a separate and different type of program, which I call the Corporate Mentor Program. The focus is on developing in-depth online research capabilities for the student's particular environment or corporation. Here, we are not dealing with the brokering or marketing side of the business but, instead, focusing on research skills.

You also teach at UC Berkeley. Can you talk about that?

I was invited to speak on a panel there in the mid-1980s called "Alternative Careers for Librarians," in which I had a twenty-minute gig talking about my information brokerage business. The coordinator of the program sent me a very nice personal letter thanking me for my presentation and saying that she loved it, and that any time I wanted to teach there, to just let her know. Well, I didn't want to teach at that time. I wanted to do research. Nevertheless, she contacted me six months later and said that they needed someone to take on the online research class for the Library Science Extension Program from a person suddenly bailing out. During her tenure, I developed five different courses over the next few years: Online Research, Advanced Online Research, Business Research Using Online Databases, Information Brokering, and How to Find Clients: Marketing an Information Business. When she left, the entire program came to a complete stop and has not been reinstated.

I had about a year off from teaching at Berkeley when someone else contacted me as a result of one of my yellow-pages ads. It turned out that she was on the Board of the UC Berkeley Extension Business and Management Program and thought I would be perfect for teaching a course about the Internet. I went back under the auspices of the Business and Management Extension, teaching a course called "How to Conduct Internet Research for Competitive and Market Intelligence." I was also invited to teach that course for the UC Berkeley International Diploma Program on E-Commerce in the year 2000.

Interesting. Your experience and credentials got you started teaching in the library science program, and now you teach much of that same information in the business department.

Yes. That was really a good change for me, too, because the people who attend courses in the business department are also potential clients for me in the future. After I began teaching, I realized how much I liked it. It's also become one of my key marketing strategies, since I almost always pick up a couple of excellent client accounts from each course.

When I talk to people about what they do in their business besides research, it all seems to revolve around their marketing. Writing, speaking, teaching, all these kinds of activities create exposure and eventually become revenue sources. So, now we need to hear about your writing.

I started writing many years ago for local publications like the *Santa Rosa Business Journal* [222] or the Santa Rosa Chamber of Commerce newsletter. In 1989, I decided to enter the national scene by submitting an abstract to the National Online Meeting [87]. It was accepted, which meant going to

New York and presenting my paper. My first national magazine article for the information industry was in *Database*, now *EContent* [212], and my wonderful editor, Paula Hane, patiently worked through some four drafts with me before I got it right. Somewhere along the way Barbara Quint asked me to write an article or two for *Searcher* [223], and several articles later I was honored when Barbara invited me to write a regular column that I named *Web Wise Ways*. And of course there was *Super Searchers on Wall Street* [238], which allowed me to branch out into a completely different direction and deepen my knowledge about investment banking and financial services research as well as sharpen my interview, writing, and editing skills.

Okay, let's talk research. Which commercial online services do you subscribe to?

One time I counted up all my subscriptions and I think it was about twenty. But in reality, I use only the big three regularly—Dialog, LexisNexis, and Factiva [45]. I can get most of the information I need from them for most of the work that I'm doing.

When would you use a commercial service as opposed to Internet searching?

The commercial services make it possible for me to be much more productive. I can gather a lot more information more quickly from commercial databases than anyone could possibly ever think of getting on the Internet, at least given the technology at this time. I'm sure that will change. There's no question, however, that for just about every project, both commercial and Internet research is necessary to cover all the bases.

Where do you like to search on the open Web?

For most of my Web research, I use Google [53], Northern Light [89], and AltaVista [8], in that order. If and when I don't find what I'm looking for, I start adding other sources and tools. It's hard for me to say I have a favorite Web site, because most of them are so inadequate for my purposes.

How would you say the rapid growth of the Internet has changed your business? A lot of people are saying that more intelligent questions are coming to information brokers.

I can't say that has been the case for me, exactly, because of the way I do my marketing. Almost all of my clients have always asked intelligent questions and are qualified buyers. I do get a few calls from my yellow-pages ads that would best be served by the public library, and I refer these on.

The Internet has changed my business by helping it grow. Sales are up, as is the size of each sale. Internet research takes more time—time that I can bill back to clients. Not only can the Internet be used as a marketing tool, but it also expands what information brokers can provide. Now I can access obscure information that was much more difficult to get ahold of in the past.

Do you have an example of that?

On a recent competitive intelligence project, one of the sites I found included a transcript from a Federal Communications Commission (FCC) [46] hearing. The transcript contained a speech by the president and CEO of one of my client's competitors. The company is a private company without the usual analysts' reports or Securities and Exchange Commission (SEC) [130] filings available. In that talk the CEO reviewed his company's activities for the past two years, its current status, and projections about where it was headed in the future. There was nothing even close to that kind of information in any commercial database system, nor was it mentioned in press releases or trade press articles or at the Web site.

So he was providing strategic information on the company, probably without even thinking about it.

Yes! This hearing before the FCC, which is publicly available information, would not have been easy to even find out about, let alone get your hands on, before the Internet. Another interesting find involved this same competitor. The company had posted a slide presentation with general company and industry statistics on their Web site about nine months earlier, and my client had found that information herself before hiring me. By the time they hired me for competitor research, the first slide show had been replaced with a different one that described the sales strategies. Together, the two slide shows provided some unique strategic information. That also illustrates why it's important to monitor competitors on a regular basis.

Those are very good examples. Do you try to think really broad at the beginning of a new project?

I do consider myself a "broad"—a broad searcher that is. I start with large search engines and consider what will be necessary for narrowing a search. When using commercial databases, I often scan hundreds of headlines to help me identify the best items based on a client's goals. Interestingly, many aspects of what I do often tie together, from research to writing to teaching. For example, for a market research project, the client wanted background information on financial service professionals. My interviews for *Super Searchers on Wall Street* laid the groundwork. In particular, my client was interested in a day in the life of an investment research analyst. Usually that type of information comes from telephone research rather than online research. However, one site, Vault.com [131], has company and industry profiles, career-oriented discussion groups, bibliographies, and reference books about careers. I had heard about this site from someone in an electronic discussion group I belong to. Right before I began the market research project, I was teaching a course at UC Berkeley and a student wanted to learn more about a company for a job interview. Though I could not remember the Vault.com site right offhand, I searched around and found it for him because I had remembered that some of the company profiles contain information about corporate culture, which is not something you can easily find in the traditional media. With the name of the site on the tip of my tongue when I began my market research project, I checked it and found several books about becoming a financial professional, including a book chapter online, at the site, containing exactly what my client needed—both a day in the life of and three months in the life of research analysts. I purchased the book to study and review, and included the online information of interest to the client in his deliverable. Some of what I found was then used to identify contacts for some in-depth telephone interviews, another component to the project.

Do you ever find yourself back at the library looking through books on behalf of clients?

Never. Wouldn't do it. I started this business because I *love* doing online research. I will not go to a library except for pleasure, but that doesn't mean I won't have someone else go on my behalf.

There you go. I was going to ask if this is where you would use a subcontractor for archival or special collection manual research.

I certainly have hired subcontractors to do manual library research, but I will say that I purposely and deliberately developed a business concept that targets buyers of online information services. People who hire me need information so quickly that there isn't time for manual research, as a rule. I must be able to find what they need online and I do. I may make recommendations for additional research strategies, but they rarely go forward with other methods. That's the nature of my particular business and the clients I serve.

When your secondary research leads you to the need to talk to an expert, do you get on the phone and do that yourself, or do you sub it out?

It depends on the situation. Sometimes I'll make phone calls myself for starters to see what types of challenges there may be. Then I'm in a better position to brief someone. In certain instances, I know so much about a topic that it's best for me to conduct the interview. In some cases, I don't want to be bothered making calls so I subcontract to someone with expertise. I'm fairly demanding about how I want results reported from a sub-contractor and I maintain very high standards.

What works best for you for pricing your services? Do you have an hourly rate or do you quote by the project?

I charge hourly rates or by the project depending on the situation or type of client. Usually the project fees are do-not-exceed budgets. It's preferable to charge hourly since I usually come out ahead compared to project fees, which can lock me into a situation where I don't always earn the quoted hourly fee. When I work with professional service firms such as consulting or law firms, it's easier to charge time and expenses; that's what they do and they understand this type of pricing.

Given the daily grind and mechanics of running a business, do you handle everything yourself? Do you outsource any office tasks?

From the very beginning of my business, I have used the services of family members, friends, or other small businesses for office support, mailing list maintenance, and bookkeeping. I've never done it all myself because there are other things I would rather spend time and energy on, like marketing, research, writing, teaching, or communicating with others electronically. I don't much like clerical work or bookkeeping, especially when I could be doing something else I enjoy. I think it's a bad use of my time to take on these types of responsibilities.

What about professional services?

I've always retained an accountant, but never have needed an attorney, with the exception of one time, when I received a cease-and-desist letter from a company called ASK Computer Systems in Silicon Valley, telling me to stop using the initials ASK. I called an attorney from one of my breakfast clubs and she told me, very informally, what to do, and it all came out fine.

Interesting. So you feel comfortable navigating through your contracts and so on?

In some businesses it makes complete sense to seek legal advice. I would never tell another information broker not to use an attorney for certain situations. I always recommend that people read T.R. Halvorson's book, *How to Avoid Liability: The Information Professional's Guide to Negligence and Warranty Risks* [228], but in my own business, based on my own feelings about what I do and how I do it, I have not felt the need for an attorney.

We're hearing about doing more analysis rather than just providing information. How much of your work on a typical project is actual information retrieval vs. information analysis?

I'm doing more analysis than I used to, but if I look at the whole spectrum, I'm still spending most of my time conducting online research and compiling and delivering it with a fairly quick turnaround. My work is value-added even without analysis. I'm very careful about calling what I do analysis because, to me, the word "analysis" implies making recommendations or suggesting ramifications. Although I know some information brokers do analysis because of their expertise, my background as an information professional does not really qualify me to write analyses for particular industries because I don't have the knowledge base to do that. I like to use terms like "synthesis," or "writing a report" or "preparing an executive summary" in which I describe or highlight major trends or key points based on the research I've conducted. I refer to the research by citing it, and strongly believe in providing all the secondary research results as part of the deliverable. I'm careful about how I describe what I do when talking to clients and when training new information professionals about how to use that terminology.

That speaks to your earlier response about not seeing a need for ongoing attorney services in your business. You're essentially a conduit.

Yes, rather than a consultant providing advice about where to take a business. I feel that consultants subject themselves to potential liability that I don't really want to expose myself to. Though I rarely use formal contracts in my business, most of the work I do involves purchase orders or letters of agreement, which of course are forms of contractual agreements. Usually, when I sign more extensive contracts, they're with large corporations and that's their standard operating procedure. Occasionally, I make changes on the contracts to comply with my terms.

Do you usually send your finished product out electronically now?

Yes. I don't print hard copy very often anymore. In the last few years, just about all my clients have finally caught up with knowing how to use email. Almost all the work I do now goes out by email as Word documents.

As far as marketing goes, we've talked about your speaking, writing, and teaching. Is there anything else you specifically do to get the word out about your services?

I've done just about every type of marketing you could think of, including networking, telephone sales, direct marketing, a subscription newsletter, yellow-pages advertising, industry-specific directory advertising, and display advertising in various media. Contrary to some experiences I've heard about, my direct marketing program was very successful, and I did it for about ten years. Now that I've been in business for a long time, I hardly do any of the kind of proactive marketing I used to do. The majority of my business is from repeat clients and word-of-mouth. A great deal of business comes from my own colleagues in the information industry, and I generate a lot of visibility through my participation in electronic discussion groups. When I started out, very few people were doing this kind of work. There weren't the kinds of alliances that there are today, such as those available through the Association of Independent Information Professionals (AIIP) [172].

As a long-time member of AIIP's electronic discussion list, I've always admired your contributions. You pour considerable time and expertise into answering questions, and always seem willing to help. How has AIIP played a role in your business?

For me, AIIP has been a major source for business companionship and business opportunities. AIIP-L [146], a private electronic discussion group, is how I stay in touch with colleagues and on top of new trends. Often, by the time I start my day, those on the East coast have been up and about and learned of some important piece of breaking news that affects either the business community in general, or the information industry more specifically, and have posted about it to the list.

I enjoy sharing my knowledge and experiences, and the contributions I make don't go unrecognized. Much of the work I do involves referrals or subcontracting relationships with AIIP colleagues. To assist me in my business, I find specialists to subcontract to from AIIP and backup help for when I'm out of town teaching or speaking or on vacation. Since I speak and teach fairly regularly these days, I call on trusted and experienced associates to provide research services to my clients when I'm gone. Where else could I turn to but AIIP? I remember the early days: no AIIP, no backup, and no vacations.

How do you regard your Web page? Does it serve as a marketing piece?

I don't give it as much attention as I could. If somebody calls me on the phone while I'm away, my answering machine message says, "I'm not available just now but will be soon and will call you back. In the meantime, we invite you to visit our Web site at www.marketingbase.com." The Web site is one more marketing tool, and I actually do get some business from it, because there's a section that contains some examples of projects I've done in the past. Search engines pick those up when somebody is looking for information about, say, the ice cream industry or household bleach products—or any of the many examples I've listed. I sometimes get email requests and phone calls because of this part of my site.

What kind of bottom-line results can you deliver for your clients as an independent, that perhaps you could not do as someone's employee?

Information professionals, whether employed or independent, use basically the same tools. When I worked in the public library I used Dialog to answer reference questions. In my work as an independent I use Dialog for in-depth research, and must also package the results into high quality, value-added deliverables. I've been hired by fee-based services in libraries or received referrals from them to do projects that they would never have the time to do. Most librarians I've talked to tell me that they do not spend more than an hour or two on typical research questions, whereas I can spend a day, several days, weeks, or even a year working on a given project as an information broker.

You maintain your office at home. What are the advantages of that?

I get out of bed and fall into my office chair one room away. The major reason I started a business was to work at home. I live in the country and I have several acres, and the only way to stay in the country with my several acres, my chickens, my cats, and that type of lifestyle is to work at home.

How do you handle dividing your time between work and home? How do you manage to feed the chickens when you're on a tight deadline?

Well, that presents a challenge. Of course, I didn't start my business until my kids were grown and off to college. I was a very young mother and waited for them to leave home before taking the risk of starting a business. I never really had to cope with managing a family at the same time as my business. One of the benefits of my personal situation is that my companion is a night person and I'm a day person. When I start working around five A.M., he ends his day. Often, I've put in a full day's work before I see him again. As far as feeding the chickens and the cats is concerned, it's my job in the morning and his at night. One problem in all this is that I do like to work a lot. People who like to work a lot get called names, like workaholic. If you don't want to be called a name, you'd better think of some other things you like to do and let people know.

Well ... what about those other things?

I like to watch old movies, and read mystery novels. But mostly I like to stare at all the green around me. I was raised in a big city with concrete everywhere, and loved cows at an early age. I also have two grandchildren, and have enjoyed caring for them as infants and toddlers. Nowadays, sometimes Grandma is just too tired to handle two kids at once, although I love to spend time with them. I love the flexibility and lifestyle that this business affords me.

Are you one of those people who carry a Palm Pilot and other assorted electronic devices?

No. I like to keep things very simple. I don't run around with any of that stuff. I made a decision a couple of years ago that when I travel to conferences and seminars, I won't even take my laptop anymore because most organizations provide PCs. Why carry extra weight around? When I teach workshops all day long, I put out a lot of energy and I don't want to go back to my hotel room and be faced with email—and more demands! I have all the technology I need at home, and when I go out into the world, I'm there to interact with people.

What about staying current? Part of our business is to help others stay on top of trends, but there's a lot to keep track of in our profession.

For me the best way to stay on top of the most important news and trends has been through electronic discussion groups such as AIIP-L and BUSLIB-L [148]. I'm also on several other lists including the SLA (Special Libraries Association) [201] News Division [159], Business and Finance Division [157], and Law

Librarians Division [158] lists, as well as lists for prospect researchers [156], new business development professionals [153], and the Patent Information Users Group [155]. From time to time, I add or delete those of greater or lesser interest at the moment.

During the past few years, I've subscribed to electronic newsletters and alerts from a wide array of sources, depending on my interests. I receive daily alerts, for example, from the *Wall Street Journal* [136] and *Industry Week* [60]. I subscribe to Individual.com [59], AllNetResearch [7], and several e-commerce and technology newsletters. I use the tracking and monitoring capability of BullsEye [16] to monitor mentions of my own name and my business name on the Web. I subscribe to all the major information industry publications in print. From time to time, I've subscribed to industry-specific periodicals depending on what's of interest to me.

What associations do you belong to?

AIIP, SLA, and the Society of Competitive Intelligence Professionals (SCIP) [199]—that's it. I find it difficult to be active in more than one organization at a time, and three is almost more than I can handle. All provide excellent services, including newsletters, magazines, and conferences that are important for my professional development.

Do you have any thoughts on the future of the independent information profession and where you think it's headed?

It's grown and continues to grow. The Internet has made this business a much more viable environment for independents for several reasons that we've already talked about. Some of the first-generation information brokers are starting to think about retirement, and we need new people with leadership ability to take us to the next level.

People who have information backgrounds have many more options today. When I was exploring alternative careers for librarians many years ago, there weren't many choices. Now, people coming out of both information and other professional backgrounds are becoming information entrepreneurs of many types. With so much opportunity, it's hard to know exactly what direction the profession will take. I think it's important for information professionals—and those who are trained librarians in particular—to broaden their thinking about the diversity in backgrounds among people in the field. Many of us have already done this as we work with colleagues from market research, computer technology, private investigation, healthcare, or business management backgrounds. We're seeing all kinds of success stories and synergy among the many types of information professionals. This is doing much to grow and strengthen the independent information community as a whole.

Super Searcher Power Tips

➤ I took only calculated risks and a long time to get where I was going. The size of the sale was usually very small. In order to make the business profitable I had to generate a lot of volume. It took me a long time to learn that it's almost as easy to make a $5,000 sale as it is to make a $500 sale.

➤ Marketing, which seems to be the most challenging aspect of developing an information brokering business, encompasses communication skills, pricing, negotiation, and closing sales.

➤ There's no question that, for just about every project, both commercial and Internet research is necessary to cover all the bases.

➤ Internet research takes more time—time that I can bill back to clients. Not only can the Internet be used as a marketing tool, but it also expands what information brokers can provide.

➤ I consider myself a broad searcher. I start with large search engines and consider what will be necessary for narrowing a search. When using commercial databases, I often scan hundreds of headlines to help me identify which are the best items based on a client's goals.

➤ A great deal of business comes from my own colleagues in the information industry. I generate a lot of visibility through my participation in electronic discussion groups.

➤ My Web site is one more marketing tool. I actually do get some business from it, because there's a section that contains some examples of projects I've done in the past. Search engines pick those up when somebody is looking for information about, say, the ice cream industry or household bleach products.

➤ Some of the first-generation information brokers are starting to think about retirement, and we need new people with leadership ability to take us to the next level.

Appendix

Referenced Sites and Sources
www.infotoday.com/supersearchers

INTERNET SITES, SEARCH ENGINES, SOFTWARE, AND ONLINE RESOURCES

1. **10K Wizard**
   www.10kwizard.com
   Search tool for information available to the public via the U.S. Securities and Exchange Commission's EDGAR (Electronic Data Gathering, Analysis and Retrieval) system, including keyword searches on up-to-the-minute SEC filings.

2. **80-20 Retriever**
   www.80-20.com
   Software to organize and search files, including email, on personal computers and enterprise-wide systems.

3. **ABI Inform**
   www.silverplatter.com/catalog/umai.htm
   Commercial database consisting of business and management literature covering hundreds of industries around the world.

4. **About.com**
   www.about.com
   A subject-based guide to the Internet, with content selected and written by individual subject experts.

5. **Adobe Acrobat**
   www.adobe.com
   Software that allows users to view, print, and create Adobe Portable Document Format (PDF) files.

6. **Allaire's HomeSite**
   www.allaire.com
   Macromedia's HTML editor that allows users to build and maintain Web sites.

7. **AllNetReseach**
   www.allnetresearch.internet.com
   Part of the internet.com network, a complete marketplace for Internet research reports, newsletters, directories, and databases.

8. **AltaVista**
   www.altavista.com
   A leading search engine among Web users and provider of high-powered search software to intranet, enterprise, and e-commerce clients.

9. **AOL—America Online**
   www.aol.com
   A leading Internet service and content provider.

10. **Arizona State University College of Engineering and Applied Science**
    www.eas.asu.edu
    General information about the university and the college.

11. **Ask Jeeves**
    www.ask.com
    A natural language search engine providing links to relevant Web sites.

12. **Bitpipe**
    www.bitpipe.com
    A leading syndicator of in-depth information technology (IT) content.

13. **BRB Publications, Inc.**
    www.brbpub.com
    Publisher of sourcebooks and news used by public records researchers.

14. **British Medical Journal**
    www.bmj.com
    Journal Web site with full text medical articles and archival searching.

15. **BRS**
    www.opentext.com
    Formerly BRS Online, BRS/Search is now part of Open Text's LiveLink Intranet product.

16. **BullsEye**
    www.intelliseek.com
    A Windows-based application to find, track, and manage relevant information on the Web.

17. **Business.com**
    www.business.com
    A comprehensive Web directory and search engine that focuses exclusively on business.

18. **Calendar Creator**
    www.microsoft.com
    Windows-based software program for creating customized calendars.

19. **Call Notes**
    www.swbell.com
    Voice mail management system offered through Southwestern Bell.

20. **CDB InfoTek**
    www.cdb.com
    Provider of search tools and access to county, state, and federal public records information.

21. **CEO Express**
    www.ceoexpress.com
    A business news and information portal designed by and for company executives.

22. **Chemical Abstracts**
    www.cas.org
    Producer of the world's largest and most comprehensive databases of chemical information.

23. **ChoicePoint**
    www.choicepoint.net
    Provider of decision-making intelligence to businesses and government, including public records information.

24. **Chris Olson and Associates**
    www.chrisolson.com
    A full-service marketing firm that specializes in promoting the services and products of information service professionals.

25. **CompuServe**
    www.compuserve.com
    An early Internet Service Provider, offering a wide range of Internet services today.

26. **Computers, Freedom and Privacy**
    www.cfp.org
    Annual conference exploring the role of computers in society.

27. **Corporate Information**
    www.corporateinformation.com
    Business portal offering company, industry, country, and state searching.

28. **CorpTech**
    www.onesource.com/products/corptech.htm
    The CorpTech database is now being marketed as OneSource CorpTech Profiles. It covers more than 50,000 U.S. high-tech companies.

29. **Cumulative Index to Nursing and Allied Health Literature (CINAHL)**
    www.silverplatter.com/catalog/nurs.htm
    Database serving as an authoritative source of information for the professional literature of nursing, allied health, biomedicine, and health care.

30. **DataStar**
    www.dialog.com
    Europe's leading online database service, providing access to more than 350 databases with worldwide coverage; part of the Dialog Corporation, a Thomson company.

31. **DBT**
    www.dbtonline.com
    See ChoicePoint.

32. **Delphi**
    www.delphi.com/dir
    An early Internet service provider, now focusing on development for forum communities.

33. **Delphion Intellectual Property Network**
    www.delphion.com
    A Web site for searching, exploring, analyzing, and tracking patents and related information.

34. **Derwent**
    www.derwent.com
    Provider of value-added patent and scientific information.

35. **Dialog**
    www.dialog.com
    A Thomson company, offering more than 600 industry databases with specialized indexing software.

36. **Directsearch**
    http://gwis2.circ.gwu.edu/~gprice/direct.htm
    A growing compilation of links to the search interfaces of resources that contain data not easily or entirely searchable/accessible via general search tools.

37. **Disclosure**
    www.primark.com/pfid
    Information on companies publicly traded on U.S. exchanges, including annual reports, SEC filings, stock price data, earnings estimates, and research reports.

38. **Dow Jones Business Directory**
    www.bd.dowjones.com
    Business portal for Internet resources selected by Dow Jones Interactive staff.

39. **Dow Jones Interactive (see also Factiva)**
www.djinteractive.com
A customizable, enterprise-wide business news and research solution, including content from Dow Jones & Reuters newswires, business journals, market research reports, analyst reports, and Web sites.

40. **Dun & Bradstreet**
www.dnb.com
A leading provider of business information for credit, marketing, purchasing, and receivables management decisions worldwide.

41. **eContent Expo**
www.econtent2001.com
Produced by Online Inc., a conference for people, companies, products, and issues in the electronic content industry.

42. **Educational Resources Information Center (ERIC)**
www.accesseric.org
A national information system designed to provide ready access to an extensive body of education-related literature.

43. **Electronic Frontier Foundation (EFF)**
www.eff.org
A donor-supported membership organization founded to protect individual rights regardless of technology.

44. **EudoraPro**
www.Eudora.com/email
Windows-based email management software.

45. **Factiva**
www.factiva.com
Provider of Web-based global business information from more than 8,000 sources; producer of Dow Jones Interactive.

46. **Federal Communications Commission (FCC)**
www.fcc.gov
U.S. government agency charged with regulating interstate and international communications by radio, television, wire, satellite, and cable.

47. **First Call**
www.firstcall.com
A Thomson Financial company, providing real-time, commingled equity and fixed income research, corporate news, quantitative, and shareholdings data.

48. **FirstGov**
www.firstgov.gov
A public-private Internet partnership connecting the world to extensive U.S. government information and services.

49. **FreeEdgar**
   www.FreeEdgar.com
   Offers the individual user easy, basic access to SEC EDGAR filings.

50. **Gale Group**
   www.galegroup.com
   Publisher of reference books, CD-ROMs, and Internet-delivered products to serve the information needs of students, businesspeople, and other researchers.

51. **GDSourcing**
   www.gdsourcing.com
   A reference point for Canadian statistics and an official distributor of Statistics Canada products.

52. **Gnutella**
   www.gnutella.wego.com
   A Web-based file-sharing network.

53. **Google**
   www.google.com
   General search engine with broad Internet coverage.

54. **Google Web Directory**
   www.directory.google.com
   Search directory for the Internet arranged by topic.

55. **Grateful Med**
   http://igm.nlm.nih.gov
   Search tool for MEDLINE using the retrieval engine of the National Library of Medicine's PubMed system.

56. **Hoover's**
   www.hoovers.com
   Company profile and business news portal, offering in-depth reports with subscription.

57. **HotBot**
   www.hotbot.com
   General Internet search engine.

58. **Index Medicus**
   www.nlm.nih.gov/pubs/factsheets/jsel.html
   International indexing system to provide access to the world's biomedical journal literature.

59. **Individual.com**
   www.individual.com
   Personalized general news subscription site.

60. **Industry Week**

    www.industryweek.com

    Daily news and information portal, with specific industry news options.

61. **InformIT**

    www.informit.com

    An information technology portal with customizing options.

62. **InfoUSA**

    www.infousa.com

    Verified business profile information provider, specializing in customized mailing lists.

63. **Intelliscope**

    www.intelligencedata.com

    Customized reports and current business news and expert analysis for subscribers.

64. **International Market Research Mall (IMR Mall)**

    www.imrmall.com

    Specialized access to search, select, buy, and view full-text market research reports online.

65. **Internet Lawyer**

    www.internetlawyer.com

    Research and information portal for the legal profession.

66. **Knowledge Express**

    www.knowledgeexpress.com

    Business development and competitive intelligence for organizations involved with science/technology research and new inventions.

67. **KnowX**

    www.knowx.com

    Web-based public records information provider.

68. **Law Seminars International**

    www.lawseminars.com

    Professional education programs focusing on the risks and opportunities created by current and emerging legal issues for lawyers, executives, and government officials.

69. **LexisNexis**

    www.lexis-nexis.com

    Major online information provider of legal information (Lexis) and specialized business and news databases (Nexis).

70. **Librarians' Index to the Internet**

    www.lii.org

A searchable, annotated subject directory of Internet resources selected and evaluated by librarians.

71. **Library and Information Science Abstracts (LISA)**
www.silverplatter.com/catalog/out/LISA
Scholarly information clearinghouse covering the library and information science field.

72. **LLRX**
www.llrx.com
Web journal dedicated to providing legal professionals with information on a wide range of Internet legal research and technology-related issues.

73. **LookSmart**
www.looksmart.com
A Web-based directory for business listings around the world.

74. **Lycos**
www.lycos.com
General Internet search engine.

75. **Maricopa Community College District**
www.maricopa.edu
General Web page of Maricopa Community College.

76. **MarketResearch**
www.marketresearch.com
Search and information portal for buying market research reports.

77. **MD Express**
www.mdexpress.com
Portal for physicians and health professionals that provides links to medical search engines, professional associations, education resources, health statistics, office tools, business news, and more.

78. **Medical Data International**
www.medicaldata.com
Provider of compliance, coding, reimbursement, and market and technology intelligence for the worldwide healthcare industry.

79. **Medical Subject Headings (MESH)**
www.nlm.nih.gov/mesh/meshhome.html
U.S. National Library of Medicine's (NLM) controlled vocabulary terminology source.

80. **MEDLINE**
www.nlm.nih.gov/databases/medline.html
U.S. National Library of Medicine's (NLM) premier bibliographic database, containing more than 11 million references to journal articles in life sciences with a concentration on biomedicine.

81. **Metacrawler**
    www.metacrawler.com
    Web directory and search engine with capability to search multiple search engines at once.

82. **Mighty Words**
    www.mightywords.com
    Web-based digital document distribution network.

83. **MindBranch**
    www.mindbranch.com
    Market research clearinghouse offering reports and other information from a variety of publishers.

84. **Multex**
    www.multex.com
    A global provider of investment information and technology solutions for the financial services industry.

85. **Napster**
    www.napster.com
    Web-based music file sharing network; no longer available.

86. **National Library of Medicine**
    www.nlm.nih.gov
    Official medical library of the United States.

87. **National Online Meeting**
    www.infotoday.com/nom2000/default.htm
    2000 North America's largest electronic information conference and exhibition sponsored by Information Today; now part of InfoToday 2002.

88. **Neat New Stuff**
    www.marylaine.com/neatnew.html
    Weekly reviews of new sites and developments by "librarian without walls" Marylaine Block.

89. **Northern Light**
    www.northernlight.com
    A research engine covering both free and fee-based Web resources.

90. **Online Public Access Catalogs (OPACs)**
    www.libdex.com
    Searchable library catalogs available through the Internet.

91. **Online World**
    www.onlineinc.com
    Former online industry trade show sponsored by Online, Inc. Last held in September 2000.

92. **Orbit**
    www.questel.orbit.com
    Online database information provider in the areas of intellectual property, scientific research, and international business.

93. **Pacer**
    http://pacer.uspci.uscourts.gov
    Public records information provider offering U.S. party/case indexing.

94. **Paintshop Pro**
    www.jasc.com
    Windows-based program for graphics management and capturing screenshots.

95. **PatentValuePredictor.com**
    See StockPricePredictor.com.

96. **Paul & Sarah Edwards: Working from Home**
    www.paulandsarah.com
    Web site of work-at-home experts Paul and Sarah Edwards.

97. **PowerMarks**
    www.kaylon.com/power.html
    Bookmark manager and personal search engine for the Internet.

98. **PR Newswire**
    www.prnewswire.com
    Newswire service for press releases and company news.

99. **Price's List of Lists**
    http://gwis2.circ.gwu.edu/~gprice/listof.htm
    Clearinghouse for lists of information on the Internet, including rankings of people, organizations, and companies. Compiled by Gary Price.

100. **Profound**
     www.profound.com
     Online business information service for end-users and professional searchers.

101. **Psychiatry-Online**
     www.psychiatry-online.com
     A fee-based consulting service that provides individuals with access to psychiatrists online.

102. **PubMed**
     www.pubmedcentral.nih.gov
     A digital archive of life sciences journal literature managed by the National Center for Biotechnology Information.

103. **Query Server**
     www.queryserver.com

A meta-search tool that broadcasts a single query across a set of Web-enabled search engines.

104. **QuickBooks / QuickBooks Pro**
www.quickbooks.com
Accounting and financial management software for small businesses.

105. **Reader's Guide to Periodical Literature**
www.silverplatter.com/catalog/wipl.htm
An index to general-interest periodicals and magazines.

106. **Reference Manager**
www.refman.com
Software for Internet reference searching, database management, and bibliography development.

107. **Research Bank / Investext**
www.investext.com
A comprehensive collection of market research analyst reports on the Web.

108. **ResearchBuzz**
www.researchbuzz.com
Web site devoted to Internet research news and information.

109. **Robot Wisdom Weblog**
www.robotwisdom.com
Weblog providing links to obscure Web sites.

110. **Salomon Smith Barney**
www.salomonsmithbarney.com
Subscription site for financial services and portfolio management.

111. **The Scout Report**
www.scout.cs.wisc.edu/scout/report
Weekly news of Internet resources; professional librarians and subject matter experts select, research, and annotate each resource.

112. **Search Adobe PDF Online**
www.searchpdf.adobe.com
Search tool for locating Adobe PDF files.

113. **SearchDay**
www.searchenginewatch.com/searchday
Chris Sherman's daily column featuring news and analysis of search engine technologies.

114. **Search Engine Watch**
www.searchenginewatch.com
Danny Sullivan's Web site devoted to trends and developments on the search engine front.

115. **Sears List of Subject Headings**
www.hwwilson.com/print/searslst.htm
Authoritative listing of subject headings for cataloging materials in libraries.

116. **Sherlock**
www.apple.com/sherlock
Specialized search tool for the Apple Macintosh system.

117. **Slashdot**
www.slashdot.org
Offbeat "news for nerds and stuff that matters," featuring articles, interviews, and online discussion forums.

118. **Small Business Administration (SBA)**
www.sba.gov
U.S. government agency charged with small business development and regulation.

119. **Standard & Poor's**
www.standardpoor.com
In-depth opinions and analyses on global equities, fixed-income credit ratings, risk management, and market developments.

120. **Stat-USA**
www.statusa.gov
Offers CD-ROM and Internet access to international trade and business information.

121. **STN**
www.cas.org/stn.html
Online information for a broad range of scientific fields, including chemistry, engineering, life sciences, pharmaceuticals, biotechnology, regulatory compliance, patents, and business.

122. **StockPricePredictor.com**
www.patentvaluepredictor.com
Subscription-based information service to assess values of individual patents and company patent portfolios.

123. **Superior Information Services**
www.superiorinfo.com
Online search service for public records data.

124. **SurfWax**
www.surfwax.com
Innovative meta-search engine featuring real-time page summaries.

125. **Thomson & Thomson**
www.thomson-thomson.com
Online search service specializing in trademark and copyright searches.

126. **Uniform Commercial Code (UCC)**
www.law.cornell.edu/uniform/ucc.html
Federal law designed to simplify, clarify, and modernize the law governing commercial transactions; filings are public record.

127. **Uniform Computer Information Transactions Act (UCITA)**
www.ucita.com
A proposed state contract law designed to standardize the licensing of software and all other forms of digital information.

128. **Usenet**
http://groups.google.com
Wide-ranging Internet-based discussion groups; searchable and browsable.

129. **U.S. Patent and Trademark Office (USPTO)**
www.uspto.gov
U.S. government agency charged with regulation and recording of all patents and patent applications.

130. **U.S. Securities and Exchange Commission (SEC)**
www.edgar.sec.gov
U.S. government agency charged with regulation of publicly traded companies and their stocks and other investment instruments.

131. **Vault.com**
www.vault.com
An employment and career information portal, offering specific industry and company news and profiles.

132. **Venture Source**
www.venturesource.com
Online database of focused research on the venture capital industry.

133. **Verizon**
www.verizon.com
Telecommunications provider; formerly GTE and Bell Atlantic.

134. **Virtual Acquisition Shelf**
http://resourceshelf.blogspot.com
Gary Price's weekly updates of resources and news for information professionals and researchers.

135. **Vivisimo**
www.vivisimo.com
Search engine technology available for licensing for use on the Web, an extranet, or an intranet.

136. **Wall Street Journal**
www.wsj.com
Online version of daily newspaper, available by subscription.

137. **Wall Street Research Net**
     www.wsrn.com
     Up-to-date customized market and company news.

138. **WebCrawler**
     www.webcrawler.com
     General Internet directory and search engine.

139. **Web Search University**
     www.websearchu.com
     Conference launched in 2001 by Online, Inc. Focused on the specifics of the latest news and developments in Web searching.

140. **WIRED**
     www.wired.com
     Technology-oriented news and information for Web users.

141. **World Intellectual Property Organization (WIPO)**
     www.wipo.org
     An international organization dedicated to protecting intellectual property through legislation, regulation, and standardization.

142. **World Wide Web Consortium (W3C)**
     www.w3c.org
     Organization that develops specifications, guidelines, software, and tools to promote the Web as a forum for information, commerce, communication, and collective understanding.

143. **World Wide Web Virtual Library**
     http://vlib.org
     Subject-based, decentralized Internet directory.

144. **WS-FTP**
     www.ipswitch.com/Products/WS_FTP
     Windows application used to transfer files between a local PC and a remote computer on the Internet.

145. **Yahoo!**
     www.yahoo.com
     General Internet search engine and subject directory.

ELECTRONIC DISCUSSION GROUPS, MAILING LISTS, AND NEWSLETTERS

146. **AIIP-L**
     Available to AIIP members only
     www.aiip.org

147. **The Airline List**
 To subscribe, send email to:
 LISTSERV@LISTSERV.CUNY.EDU

148. **BUSLIB-L**
 To subscribe, send email to:
 Listserv@listserv.boisestate.edu
 In message body type:
 Subscribe buslib-l firstname lastname

149. **Chemical Information Listserv (CHMINF-L)**
 listserv.indiana.edu/archives/chminf-l.html

150. **Free Pint**
 To subscribe, send email to:
 subs@freepint.co.uk
 Monthly news and developments in Internet information research.

151. **LIMS (Environmental regulation of laboratories list)**
 To subscribe, send email to:
 Listserv@list.uvm.edu

152. **MEDLIB-L**
 To subscribe, send email to:
 Listserv@listserv.acsu.buffalo.edu
 In message body type:
 SUBSCRIBE MEDLIB-L firstname lastname

153. **New Business Development**
 Groups.yahoo.com/group/NewBizDev/join
 A public discussion list for sharing new business development ideas.

154. **Nua Internet Surveys Newsletter**
 www.nua.ie/surveys/subscribe.html
 Weekly newsletter containing news on Internet trends and statistics.

155. **Patent Information Users Group**
 www.piug.org

156. **PRSPCT-L**
 www.usc.edu/dept/source/research.htm
 Discussion list for Internet fundraising prospect researchers.

157. **SLA Business & Finance Division**
 To subscribe, send email to:
 listserv@lists.psu.edu
 In message body type:
 Subscribe SLABF-L firstname lastname

158. **SLA Law Librarians Division**
    To subscribe, send email to:
    listserv@listserv.uh.edu
    In message body type:
    Subscribe SLA-LAW firstname lastname

159. **SLA News Division**
    To subscribe, send email to:
    Listproc@listserv.oit.unc.edu
    In message body type:
    Subscribe NEWSLIB firstname lastname

160. **SLA Pharmaceutical and Health Technology Division**
    To subscribe, send email to:
    listserv@lists.sla.org
    In message body type:
    Subscribe SLA-DPHM firstname lastname

161. **SLA Solo Librarians Division**
    To subscribe, send email to:
    listserv@silverplatter.com
    In message body type:
    Subscribe SOLOLIB-L firstname lastname

162. **SLA Toronto**
    To subscribe, send email to:
    Lists@lists.sla.org
    In message body type:
    Subscribe SLA-CTOR firstname lastname

163. **Wall Street Journal daily alerts**
    www.wsj.com
    Customized news coverage available to subscribers.

164. **Web Search Newsletter**
    To subscribe, fill out form on Newsletter page at www.websearch.about.com
    Weekly news on Web research and search engines from About.com.

ORGANIZATIONS

165. **Aero Club of Washington**
    www.aeroclub.org

166. **Aircraft Owners and Pilots Association (AOPA)**
    www.aopa.org

167. **American Health Information Management Association (AHIMA)**
    www.ahima.org

168. **Arizona Software and Internet Association (ASIA)**
www.azsoft.net

169. **Arizona State University**
www.asu.edu

170. **Arizona Telecommunications & Information Council (ATIC)**
www.ArizonaTele.com

171. **Association of Consulting Chemists & Chemical Engineers (ACC&CE)**
www.chemconsult.org

172. **Association of Independent Information Professionals (AIIP)**
www.aiip.org

173. **Association of Internet Professionals (AIP)**
www.association.org

174. **Biotechnology Industry Cluster**
www.azbiocluster.org

175. **California Association of Licensed Investigators**
www.cali-pi.org

176. **Canadian Library Association (CLA)**
www.cla.ca

177. **Copyright Clearance Center (CCC)**
www.copyright.com

178. **Dallas Association of Law Librarians**
www.aallnet.org/chapter/dall

179. **Dayton Chamber of Commerce**
www.daytonchamber.org

180. **E-Healthcare World**
www.ehealthcareworld.com

181. **Environmental Technology Industry Cluster**
www.futurewest.com/economy/etic

182. **Experimental Aircraft Association (EAA)**
www.eaa.org

183. **Fast Company**
www.fastcompany.com

184. **Federal Aviation Administration (FAA)**
www.faa.gov

185. **Global Arizona E-Learning**
www.gazel.org

186. **Governor's Strategic Partnership for Economic Development (GSPED)**
www.commerce.state.az.us/gsped.htm

187. **High Tech Industry Cluster**
www.azhitechcluster.org

188. **IHS—Emerging Medical Technologies**
www.ihshealthgroup.com

189. **International Aviation Club of Washington DC**
www.iacwashington.org

190. **Medical Library Association (MLA)**
www.mlanet.org

191. **Medical Marketing Association**
www.mmanet.org

192. **Medtech Insight**
www.medtechinsight.com

193. **National Air Transportation Association (NATA)**
www.nata-online.org

194. **National Association of Women Business Owners (NAWBO)**
www.nawbo.org

195. **National Transportation Safety Board (NTSB)**
www.ntsb.gov

196. **Public Record Retriever Network (PRRN)**
www.brbpub.com/prrn

197. **Service Corps of Retired Executives (SCORE)**
www.score.org

198. **Small Business Development Center (SBDC)**
www.sba.gov/sbdc

199. **Society of Competitive Intelligence Professionals (SCIP)**
www.scip.org

200. **Software & Information Industry Association (SIIA)**
www.siia.net

201. **Special Libraries Association (SLA)**
www.sla.org

202. **Tech Oasis**
www.techoasis.org

203. **United States Department of Transportation (DOT)**
www.dot.gov

PRINT JOURNALS, MAGAZINES, NEWSLETTERS, NEWSPAPERS

204. **African Aviation**
African Aviation Services Limited, UK, monthly
www.africanaviation.com

205. **Airport Business**
Cygnus Business Media, Janesville, WI, 9x/year
www.airportbiz.com

206. **Aviation Week**
McGraw-Hill, New York, NY, weekly
www.aviationnow.com

207. **Business 2.0**
Imagine Media, Brisbane, CA, monthly
www.business2.com

208. **Business & Commercial Aviation**
McGraw-Hill, New York, NY, monthly
www.AviationNow.com/BCA

209. **Business Week**
McGraw-Hill, New York, NY, weekly
www.businessweek.com

210. **CyberSkeptic's Guide to Internet Research**
Bibliodata, Needham Heights, MA, monthly
www.bibliodata.com/skeptic/skepdata.html

211. **The Economist**
Economist, New York, NY, weekly
www.economist.com

212. **EContent**
Online Inc., Wilton, CT, bimonthly
www.ecmag.net
www.onlineinc.com/database (archives)

213. **Financial Times**
Financial Times, New York, NY, daily
www.financialtimes.com

214. **The Globe and Mail**
Bell Globemedia, Inc., Toronto, ON, Canada, daily
www.theglobeandmail.com

215. **Information Advisor**
Find/SVP, New York, NY, monthly
www.findsvp.com

216. **Information Outlook**
Special Libraries Association, Washington DC, monthly
www.sla.org/pubs/serial/io/index.shtml

217. **Information Today**
Information Today, Inc., Medford, NJ, monthly
www.infotoday.com

218. **Library Journal**
American Library Association, Washington DC, monthly
www.libraryjournal.com

219. **New York Times**
The New York Times Company, New York, NY, daily
www.nytimes.com

220. **Online**
Information Today, Inc., Medford, NJ
www.infotoday.com/online

221. **Regional Airline World**
Shephard Press Limited, UK, monthly
www.shephard.co.uk

222. **Santa Rosa Business Journal**
www.busjrnl.com
Regional news for Santa Rosa, California.

223. **Searcher**
Information Today, Inc., Medford, NJ, 10x/year
www.infotoday.com/searcher

224. **Women in Management**
Ivey Publishing, University of Western Ontario, quarterly
www.ivey.uwo.ca/publications/wim

BOOKS

225. **Encyclopedia of Associations**
Gale Research, Detroit, MI, annual
www.galegroup.com

226. **Free Agent Nation: How America's New Independent Workers Are Transforming the Way We Live**
By Daniel H. Pink
Warner Books, New York, NY, 2001

227. **Growing a Business**
By Paul Hawken

Simon and Schuster, New York, NY 1987
www.simonandschuster.com

228. **How to Avoid Liability: The Information Professional's Guide to Negligence and Warranty Risks**
By T.R. Halvorson
Burwell Enterprises, Dallas, TX 1998
www.burwellinc.com

229. **Information Brokering: A How-To-Do-It-Manual**
By Florence Mason and Chris Dobson
Neal-Schuman, New York, NY 1998
www.neal-schuman.com

230. **The Information Broker's Handbook (3rd Edition) and Information Broker's Seminar**
By Sue Rugge and Alfred Glossbrenner
Windcrest/McGraw-Hill, New York, NY 1997
Out of print

231. **Information Brokers: How to Start and Operate Your Own Fee-Based Service**
By Kelly Warnken
Out of print

232. **The Invisible Web: Uncovering Information Sources Search Engines Can't See**
By Chris Sherman and Gary Price
CyberAge Books, Information Today Inc., Medford, NJ, 2001
www.infotoday.com/catalog/books.htm

233. **Mining for Gold on the Internet: How to Find Investment and Financial Information on the Internet**
By Mary Ellen Bates
McGraw-Hill, New York, NY, 2000
www.mcgraw-hill.com

234. **Pan Africa: Across the Sahara in 1941 with Pan Am**
By Thomas M. Culbert
Paladwr Press, McLean, VA, 1998

235. **Researching Online For Dummies (2nd Edition)**
By Reva Basch and Mary Ellen Bates
Hungry Minds Inc., (formerly IDG Books), New York, NY, 2000
www.hungryminds.com

236. **Super Searchers Cover the World: The Online Secrets of International Business Reseachers**
By Mary Ellen Bates

CyberAge Books, Information Today Inc., Medford, NJ, 2001
www.infotoday.com/catalog/books.htm

237. **Super Searchers Do Business: The Online Secrets of Top Business Researchers**
By Mary Ellen Bates
CyberAge Books, Information Today Inc., Medford, NJ, 1999
www.infotoday.com/catalog/books.htm

238. **Super Searchers on Wall Street: Top Investment Professionals Share Their Online Research Secrets**
By Amelia Kassel
CyberAge Books, Information Today Inc., Medford, NJ, 2000
www.infotoday.com/catalog/books.htm

239. **World Aviation Directory**
McGraw-Hill, New York, NY, annual
www.wadaviation.com

About the Author

Suzanne Sabroski is principal of Sabroski & Associates, providing general research and writing support to business professionals since 1995. Prior to going on her own she worked as a corporate librarian, with additional experience in nonprofit administration, tourism, and freelance writing. She obtained her bachelor's degree in political science and mass communications from the University of Wisconsin-Superior, and her master's in Educational Media from the College of St. Scholastica, writing her thesis on company information needs assessment. Suzanne was editor of the Association of Independent Information Professionals' first white paper, *The Independent Information Profession,* and has written for *Searcher* and Washington Researchers. She is a recipient of AIIP's Myra T. Grenier Award, and served on the AIIP Board of Directors as Chair of Public Relations.

Suzanne lives with her husband, Alan; their three children; and their dog in the beautiful wilderness of northern Minnesota, where she is an active volunteer in school and church activities, and Suzuki parent to their three young violinists.

About the Editor

Reva Basch, executive editor of the Super Searchers series, has written four books of her own: *Researching Online For Dummies* (Hungry Minds, 2nd edition with Mary Ellen Bates), *Secrets of the Super Net Searchers* (Information Today, 1996), *Secrets of the Super Searchers* (Information Today, 1993), and *Electronic Information Delivery: Evaluating Quality and Value* (Gower, 1995). She has edited and contributed chapters, introductions, and interviews to several books about the Internet and online information retrieval. She was the subject of a profile in *Wired* magazine, which called her "the ultimate intelligent agent."

Prior to starting her own business in 1986, Reva was Vice President and Director of Research at Information on Demand, a pioneering independent research company. She has designed front-end search software for major online services; written and consulted on technical, marketing, and training issues for both online services and database producers; and published extensively in information industry journals. She has keynoted at international conferences in Australia, Scandinavia, and the United Kingdom, as well as North America.

Reva is a Past-President (1991–1992) of the Association of Independent Information Professionals. She has a degree in English literature, *summa cum laude*, from the University of Pennsylvania, and a master's degree in library science from the University of California, Berkeley. She began her career as a corporate librarian, ran her own independent research business for ten years, and has been online since the mid-1970s.

Reva lives on the remote northern California coast with her husband, cats, and satellite access to the Internet.

Index

I

IBM patent server, 241
Identity theft, 117
IHS-Emerging Medical Technologies, 72
IIPs. *See* Independent information
    professionals
Images in online patent literature, 88
IMR Mall, 143
In-person research in aviation industry,
    41–42
Independent information professionals (IIPs)
    business of, 5–7
    choice of term for industry, 5
    continuing need for, 8
    trend toward becoming more specialized,
        53
    type of people who succeed as, 8–9,
        30–31
    work of, 7–8
Indexing and patent searches, 86
Individual.com, 275
Industry contacts, 45
Industry Week, 275
Infomart, 159, 160–161, 162
InformAction. *See* Sharp, Crystal
Information Advisor, 24
Information audits, 164, 170
*Information Brokering: A How-To-Do-It
    Manual* (Mason & Dobson),
    174–175
Information brokers
    use of term for industry, 5, 134
Information Broker's Handbook, The
    (Rugge), 1, 38, 103, 104
    advice from, 15
Information Brokers (Warnken), 258
Information Consultancy, 207
Information Crossroads, 207
Information on Demand, 256–257
Information Outlook, 175
Information overload, 2, 8, 151, 198, 246
Information professionals. *See* Independent
    information professionals (IIPs)
Information technology (IT) sites on Internet,
    241
Information Today, 175
InformIT, 240
InfoUSA, 142
Intellectual property searching. *See* Patent
    searching

Intelliscope, 64
International Aviation Club, 47
International Research Center. *See* Goldstein,
    Mark
Internet, 42. *See also* Search engines; Web
    sites
    basic information available on, 7
    changes to IIP business due to, 265
    client's direct use of, 8, 17, 32, 42, 52,
        143, 167, 182, 209, 216, 233
    invisible vs. open, 19, 34, 65, 168,
        238–239
    keeping current with developments on,
        235
    patent searching on, 88
    public's perceptions of, 4, 42, 64, 233,
        238–239
    referenced sites and sources, list of,
        279–292
    research projects on, 167–168
    searching open Internet, 64–65, 88, 168,
        264–265
    training by IIP, 260–261
    use of, 191–192, 200, 213
Internet Lawyer, 116
*Internet Resource Guide for Research and
    Exploration* (Goldstein), 140–141
Internet Resource Hot Sheet, 141
Interviews. *See also* Reference interviews
    for preliminary information gathering,
        170
Investext, 167
Invisible Web, 19, 20, 34, 143, 214, 237,
    238–239
Invisible Web, The (Sherman & Price), 214,
    227, 237

J

Journals. *See* Newsletters and journals

K

Kapor, Mitch, 130
Kassel, Amelia, 253–277
    advantages of home office, 273–274
    advice for aspiring independent
        researchers, 260
    association memberships and confer-
        ences, 256, 258, 275
    authorship, 263–264
    background, 253–256

billing and rates, 268, 277
citation verification, 254
clients, 259
competitive intelligence project, 265–266
Corporate Mentor Program developed by, 262
Dialog use, 255–256, 257
future trends in independent researching, 275–277
hard copy vs. electronically delivered reports, 270–271
high-tech devices used by, 274
information brokerage as home business, 256–258
information retrieval vs. information analysis, 269–270
Internet training by, 260–261
Internet use, 265, 277
keeping current in field, 274–275
legal and accounting advice for home business, 269, 270
leisure time, 273–274
library research, 267
market research project, 266–267
marketing by, 261, 263, 265, 271–272, 276
Mentor Program developed by, 261–262
networking, 258, 260
niche market, 260
online services subscribed to, 264
open Web searching, 264–265
outsourcing by, 268–269
Rugge's influence on, 257
searching strategy, 266, 277
secondary research, 268
services offered, 260
startup of business, 258–259
subcontracting, 267, 272
Super Searcher tips, 276–277
teaching by, 262
telephone research, 268
value-added service, 270, 272–273
Web site of, 272, 277
KEDS (Knowledge Express Data Systems), 141
Kiwanis, 217
Knowledge Express, 64
Knowledge Express Data Systems (KEDS), 141
KnowX, 142
Kraver, Ted, 136

L

Laptops, 70, 274
Law Seminars International, 140
Lawson Health Research Institute, 192
Layoffs and independent work opportunities, 247
Learning curve, billing for, 61, 75, 181, 182
Legal and accounting advice for setting up business, 7. *See also under names of interviewees*
Legal research and public records, 105–106
Leisure time. *See under names of interviewees*
Levine, Alan, 147
LexisNexis
  as employer, 55, 56
  evaluation of, 256
  in-house reference service, use of, 208
  patent searching on, 87
  preference for, 17, 64, 141, 167, 264
  public records searching on, 111
  trade literature searching on, 213
Liability of IIPs, 7
Librarians, 6, 145
  continued need for, 246
  placement of, 163, 165
Librarians' Index to the Internet, 20, 191, 235
Library Journal, 175
Library of Congress, 208, 215
Library research
  browsing, 215, 224
  mental health literature, 192–193
  patents, 87
  subcontracting, 22, 65, 169, 267
  use of, 144–146, 157
Library school as training for information business, 12–13, 34
LIMSList, 93
Linux, 235
LISA, 191
LLRX, 116
Local researchers, use of, 113
Lockheed Martin, 211. *See also* Martin Marietta Laboratories
Logo design, 13–14, 34
Long-term relationships between IIPs and clients, 7
LookSmart, 173
Lucent, 83
Lycos, 227

More CyberAge Books from Information Today, Inc.

The Extreme Searcher's Guide to Web Search Engines

A Handbook for the Serious Searcher, 2nd Edition

By Randolph Hock
Foreword by Reva Basch

In this completely revised and expanded version of his award-winning book, the "extreme searcher," Randolph (Ran) Hock, digs even deeper, covering all the most popular Web search tools, plus a half-dozen of the newest and most exciting search engines to come down the pike. This is a practical, user-friendly guide supported by a regularly updated Web site.

2001/250 pp/softbound/ISBN 0-910965-47-1
$24.95

International Business Information on the Web

Searcher Magazine's Guide to Sites and Strategies for Global Business Research

By Sheri R. Lanza
Edited by Barbara Quint

Here is the first ready-reference for effective worldwide business research, written by experienced international business researcher Sheri R. Lanza and edited by *Searcher* magazine's Barbara Quint. This book helps readers identify overseas buyers, find foreign suppliers, investigate potential partners and competitors, uncover international market research and industry analysis, and much more.

2001/380 pp/softbound/ISBN 0-910965-46-3
$29.95

The Quintessential Searcher
The Wit and Wisdom of Barbara Quint

Edited by Marylaine Block

Searcher magazine editor Barbara Quint (bq) is not only one of the world's most famous online searchers, but the most creative and controversial writer, editor, and speaker to emerge from the information industry in the last two decades. bq is a guru of librarians and database professionals the world over, and, as her readers, publishers, and "quarry" know, when it comes to barbed wit she is in a class by herself. Whether she's chastising database providers about unacceptable fees, interfaces, and updates; recounting the ills visited on the world by computer makers; or inspiring her readers to achieve greatness; her voice is consistently original and compelling. In this book, for the first time anywhere, hundreds of bq's most memorable, insightful, and politically incorrect quotations have been gathered for the enjoyment of her many fans.

2001/232 pp/softbound ISBN 1-57387-114-1 $19.95

The Information Professional's Guide to Career Development Online

By Rachel Singer Gordon and Sarah L. Nesbeitt

This is the first book designed to meet the needs of Internet-connected librarians interested in using online tools to advance their careers. Authors Gordon and Nesbeitt provide practical advice on topics ranging from current awareness services and personal Web pages to distance education, electronic resumes, and online job searches. Up-and-coming librarians will learn how to use the Internet to research education opportunities, and experienced information professionals will learn ways to network through online conferences and discussion lists. Supported by the Career Development Online Web Page, featuring updated links to important reader resources.

2002/softbound/ISBN 1-57387-124-9 $29.50

Super Searchers Cover the World
The Online Secrets of International Business Researchers

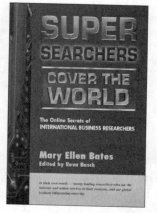

By *Mary Ellen Bates* • *Edited by Reva Basch*
Foreword by Clare Hart

The Internet has made it possible for more businesses to think internationally, and to take advantage of the expanding global economy. Through 15 interviews with leading online searchers, Mary Ellen Bates explores the challenges of reaching outside a researcher's geographic area to do effective international business research. Experts from around the world—librarians and researchers from government organizations, multinational companies, universities, and small businesses—discuss such issues as nonnative language sources, cultural biases, and the reliability of information. Supported by the Super Searchers Web page.

2001/250 pp/softbound/ISBN 0-910965-54-4 $24.95

Super Searchers on Mergers & Acquisitions
The Online Research Secrets of Top Corporate Researchers and M&A Pros

By *Jan Davis Tudor*
Edited by Reva Basch

The sixth title in the "Super Searchers" series is a unique resource for business owners, brokers, appraisers, entrepreneurs, and investors who use the Internet and online services to research Mergers & Acquisitions (M&A) opportunities. Leading business valuation researcher Jan Davis Tudor interviews 13 top M&A researchers, who share their secrets for finding, evaluating, and delivering critical deal-making data on companies and industries. Supported by the Super Searchers Web page.

2001/208 pp/softbound/ISBN 0-910965-48-X $24.95

Super Searchers on Health & Medicine
The Online Secrets of Top Health & Medical Researchers

By Susan M. Detwiler
Edited by Reva Basch

With human lives depending on them, skilled medical researchers rank among the best online searchers in the world. In *Super Searchers on Health & Medicine*, medical librarians, clinical researchers, health information specialists, and physicians explain how they combine traditional sources with the best of the Net to deliver just what the doctor ordered. If you use the Internet and online databases to answer important health and medical questions, these Super Searchers will help guide you around the perils and pitfalls to the best sites, sources, and techniques. Supported by the Super Searchers Web page.

2000/208 pp/softbound/ISBN 0-910965-44-7 $24.95

Super Searchers in the News
The Online Secrets of Journalists and News Researchers

By Paula J. Hane • Edited by Reva Basch

Professional news researchers are a breed apart. The behind-the-scenes heroes of network newsrooms and daily newspapers, they work under intense deadline pressure to meet the insatiable, ever-changing research needs of reporters, editors, and journalists. Here, for the first time, 10 news researchers reveal their strategies for using the Internet and online services to get the scoop, check the facts, and nail the story. If you want to become a more effective online searcher and do fast, accurate research on a wide range of moving-target topics, don't miss *Super Searchers in the News*. Supported by the Super Searchers Web page.

2000/256 pp/softbound/ISBN 0-910965-45-5 $24.95

Super Searchers Go to the Source

The Interviewing and Hands-On Information Strategies of Top Primary Researchers—Online, on the Phone, and in Person

By Risa Sacks • Edited by Reva Basch

For the most focused, current, in-depth information on any subject, nothing beats going directly to the source—to the experts. This is "Primary Research," and it's the focus of the seventh title in the Super Searchers series. From the boardrooms of America's top corporations, to the halls of academia, to the pressroom of the *New York Times*, Risa Sacks interviews 12 of the best primary researchers in the business. These research pros reveal their strategies for integrating online and "off-line" resources, identifying experts, and getting past gatekeepers to obtain information that exists only in someone's head. Supported by the Super Searchers Web page.

2001/420 pp/softbound/ISBN 0-910965-53-6 $24.95

Super Searchers on Wall Street

Top Investment Professionals Share Their Online Research Secrets

By Amelia Kassel • Edited by Reva Basch

Through her probing interviews, Amelia Kassel reveals the online secrets of 10 leading financial industry research experts. You'll learn how information professionals find and analyze market and industry data, as well as how online information is used by brokerages, stock exchanges, investment banks, and individual investors to make critical investment decisions. The Wall Street Super Searchers direct you to important sites and sources, illuminate the trends that are revolutionizing financial research, and help you use online research as a powerful investment strategy. Supported by the Super Searchers Web page.

2000/256 pp/softbound/ISBN 0-910965-42-0 $24.95

The Invisible Web
Uncovering Information Sources
Search Engines Can't See

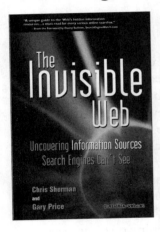

By Chris Sherman and Gary Price

Most of the authoritative information accessible over the Internet is invisible to search engines. This "Invisible Web" is largely comprised of content-rich databases from universities, libraries, associations, businesses, and government agencies. Authors Chris Sherman and Gary Price introduce you to top sites and sources and offer tips, techniques, and analysis that will let you pull needles out of haystacks every time. Supported by a dedicated Web site.

2001/450 pp/softbound/ISBN 0-910965-51-X $29.95

Naked in Cyberspace
How to Find Personal Information Online, 2nd Edition

By Carole A. Lane
Foreword by Beth Givens

In this fully revised and updated second edition of her bestselling guide, author Carole A. Lane surveys the types of personal records that are available on the Internet and online services. Lane explains how researchers find and use personal data, identifies the most useful sources of information about people, and offers advice for readers with privacy concerns. You'll learn how to use online tools and databases to gain competitive intelligence, locate and investigate people, access public records, identify experts, find new customers, recruit employees, search for assets, uncover criminal records, conduct genealogical research, and much more.

2002/586 pp/softbound/ISBN 0-910965-50-1 $29.95